ENTREPRENEURSHIP FOR SCIENTISTS AND ENGINEERS

Kathleen Allen

University of Southern California

Prentice Hall
Upper Saddle River, New Jersey 07458

Library of Congress Cataloging-in-Publication Data

Allen, Kathleen R.
    Entrepreneurship for engineers and scientists/Kathleen Allen.—1st ed.
      p. cm.
    Includes bibliographical references and index.
    ISBN-13: 978-0-13-235727-2 (alk. paper)
    ISBN-10: 0-13-235727-5 (alk. paper)
    1. Engineering firms—Management. 2. Entrepreneurship.
    3. Business planning. 4. Science. I. Title.
TA190.A524 2010
620.0068—dc22

                    2008039106

Dedication

To my son Greg and his wife Melissa, who belong to this exciting new generation of engineers.

Acquisitions Editor: Kim Norbuta
Editorial Director: Sally Yagan
Product Development Manager: Ashley Santora
Editorial Project Manager: Claudia Fernandes
Marketing Manager: Nikki Jones
Permissions Project Manager: Charles Morris
Production Manager: Wanda Rockwell
CreativeDirector: Jayne Conte
Cover Designer: Karen Salzbach
Cover Illustration/Photo: Angelo Cavalli/Digital Vision/Getty Images
Full-Service Project Management: Integra
Printer/Binder: RR Donnelley
Typeface: 10/12, Times Ten Roman

Credits and acknowledgments borrowed from other sources and reproduced, with permission, in this textbook appear on appropriate page within text.

Pearson Education Ltd., London
Pearson Education Singapore, Pte. Ltd
Pearson Education, Canada, Inc.
Pearson Education–Japan
Pearson Education Australia PTY, Limited

Pearson Education North Asia, Ltd., Hong Kong
Pearson Educación de Mexico, S.A. de C.V.
Pearson Education Malaysia, Pte. Ltd
Pearson Education Upper Saddle River,
   New Jersey

Prentice Hall
is an imprint of

www.pearsonhighered.com

10 9 8 7 6 5 4 3 2 1
ISBN-13: 978-0-13-235727-2
ISBN-10:   0-13-235727-5

BRIEF CONTENTS

PREFACE

As a budding scientist or engineer, you have chosen a difficult and rigorous path for your studies. Upon graduation with a bachelors, masters, or even PhD, you will find that your technical skills in demand in the field you have chosen. But increasingly, science and engineering graduates are learning that to enhance their chances of going to the top in their fields they need to understand various aspects of business, such as finance, marketing, management, and operations. Moreover, today understanding how large, established corporations work is not enough. Many graduating scientists and engineers are heading to start-ups and rapidly growing smaller ventures rather than to traditional jobs in their fields. Because these smaller technology companies typically don't have bureaucratic structures and everyone is expected to do multiple tasks, it is important that technical graduates understand and can adapt to the unique environment of the entrepreneurial venture. This means that developing an opportunistic way of looking at the world and some entrepreneurial skills will give you a distinct advantage in the marketplace as compared to the average science or engineering graduate.

OBJECTIVES OF THE BOOK

The objective of *Entrepreneurship for Scientists and Engineers* is simple: to help you understand the potential role of entrepreneurship in your career and learn what it takes to successfully bring a new technology from the laboratory or your garage to the marketplace. This book helps you get into the mind of an entrepreneur to be able to view the world from a very different perspective—one that is opportunistic and based on spotting unmet needs in markets. Unlike research and development in science and engineering, entrepreneurship is not resource dependent but rather comes about despite any resources entrepreneurs may or may not have at their disposal. The book also walks the reader through the process of technology commercialization discussing how the technical and business skills come together to turn a new technology into a product, process, or service that customers will pay for.

DISTINGUISHING FEATURES

Two features of this book help to make the students' journey into the world of technology entrepreneurship interesting and useful.

Four distinct parts address the most important issues in technology entrepreneurship. Part I serves as an introduction to the subject of entrepreneurship for scientists and engineers and it covers the core topics of commercialization, opportunity, starting a company, and building an effective team. The remaining parts delve deeper into specific topics of particular importance to technology entrepreneurship. Part II focuses on the development and protection of intellectual property and considers patents, trademarks, copyrights, trade secrets and licensing of intellectual property as a commercialization strategy. Part III examines critical aspects of strategy, from product development to market entry strategies, technology adoption patterns and their associated marketing strategies. Finally, Part IV focuses on financial strategy by going deeper into business models, funding of technology start-ups, and funding growing technology companies. It concludes with a chapter on technology valuation.

End-of-chapter case studies. Each chapter concludes with a relevant case study that gives the instructor the opportunity to discuss some of the points of the chapter within the context of the experiences of a real technology entrepreneur.

Companion Web site. A useful companion Web site, www.prenhall.com/ entrepreneurship, offers free access to teaching resources for all books in the Prentice Hall Entrepreneurship Series including additional activities, links to latest research, sample entrepreneurship curriculum and syllabi, teaching tips, and Web resource links.

CourseSmart textbooks online is an exciting new choice for students looking to save money. As an alternative to purchasing the print textbook, students can subscribe to the same content online and save up to 50 percent off the suggested list price of the print text. With a CourseSmart e-textbook, students can search the text, make notes online, print out reading assignments that incorporate lecture notes, and bookmark important passages for later review. For more information visit www.coursesmart.com.

THE TRANSITION TO ENTREPRENEURSHIP

An important study of a cohort of academic founders of biotechnology companies and their "risk" of becoming entrepreneurs has given us a clearer window into who decides to transition to entrepreneurship and why.[1] Stuart and Ding's research (2006) found that if scientists worked around other scientists who had started companies, they were more likely to become entrepreneurs themselves, particularly if they worked in medical schools. Part of the reason for this entrepreneurship-by-association phenomenon was the recognition that entrepreneurship was possible; but perhaps more importantly, these academic entrepreneurs, whether students, faculty, or researchers, opened the door for others to make the needed connections that would increase their likelihood of successfully making the transition. Within the work context, this research also found that the more prestigious the university and the more accomplished the scientist, the more likely he or she was to become an entrepreneur. The rationale for this conclusion was that biotechnology companies require significant capital and generally investors are more interested in dealing with prestigious scientists and important discoveries. Another explanation is that the very status that these scientists enjoy makes them safe from threats to their reputation for engaging in business.[2]

Engineering has faced a similar evolution in becoming more entrepreneurial. As an applied science, engineering seems to have a "natural symbiosis" with entrepreneurship in that the term *entrepreneur* comes from the French word *entreprendre,* which means to undertake an action. Entrepreneurs recognize opportunity and gather the resources needed to launch a venture—they take action. Similary, engineers apply mathematics, science, and systems integration to "conceive, design, build, and operate useful objects or processes."[3] Both sets of actions are required for successful entrepreneurship. Engineering entrepreneurship has produced a wealth of new companies. For example, along Route 128 in Boston alone, more than 75 percent of the companies were founded by MIT engineering graduates and Sloan School of Management graduates. Some researchers have argued that engineering education is a logical foundation for understanding entrepreneurial concepts such as return on investment, risk, and opportunity. In their rigorous educational programs, engineers develop robust analytical skills.[4] When they add to their technical creativity by learning business concepts and developing strong communication skills, they are rational candidates for entrepreneurship.

What does not translate well from science and engineering to entrepreneurship is the "tell me what you want and I'll build it" attitude. In other words, the formulaic approach to solving problems, which is inherent in both science and engineering, is the antithesis of what is required for successful entrepreneurship. Entrepreneurs must be comfortable with ambiguity and uncertainty, be flexible in their thinking, and be prepared to change course quickly should the market give them new information that warrants it. Engineers understand the product development process thoroughly, but going from bench to market is not a linear process and it has relatively little to do with the technology itself. It requires crossing the "valley of death," that ambiguous gap between product development and a successful product that customers will pay for (see Figure 1-1). The gap is called the "valley of death" because the skills and focus on the market required to move the technology through the valley are distinctly different from the skills required during product development, so the scientist or engineer who tries to navigate this unknown territory with technical skills often fails. The frame of mind of the technology person has often been "we will build it and they (customers) will come," but that is rarely the case. The gap between technology development and the market must be filled by a business model—a means to create and capture value from customers. Customers don't buy technologies; they buy solutions to real problems they have. There has to be a value that customers recognize and are willing to pay for or no business model will succeed. The greatest technology in the world will fail if customers do not perceive a benefit from it or there is no way to monetize the value offered. The subject of business models is tackled in Chapters 3 and 10.

The transition from the technical disciplines to entrepreneurship also involves a challenging gap of knowledge. The scientist who cannot understand the way entrepreneurs think will find it extremely difficult to employ the business tools required to commercialize his or her technology. Entrepreneurs are not bound by formulas, rules, and linear patterns of thinking. Their thought processes revolve around making unusual connections—much like an inventor does—and thinking "outside the box." Most entrepreneurs have a strong internal locus of control, which means that they believe they are in charge of their destiny; consequently, they tend to take responsibility for both their successes and their failures rather than attributing them to some other source. Entrepreneurs are typically comfortable with ambiguity and uncertainty because they recognize that stable environments do not generally produce breakthrough business concepts. Entrepreneurs enjoy the independence of working for oneself and many entrepreneurs would never consider working for someone else. This mindset of the entrepreneur is, in many respects, different from that of the average technical person, particularly with respect to uncertainty and

FIGURE 1-1   From Bench to Market

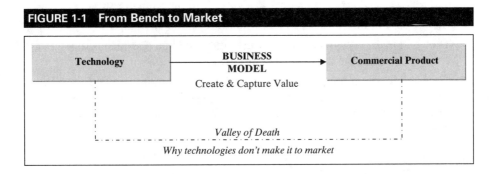

Why technologies don't make it to market

ambiguity. Nevertheless, with so many scientists and engineers becoming more opportunistic, it makes sense for them to understand and perhaps learn some entrepreneurial skills.

WHY STUDY ENTREPRENEURSHIP?

The fact that scientists and engineers are increasingly entering the world of the entrepreneur with skills that will be valuable in the launch of a new venture does not speak to why they should study entrepreneurship in the first place. Why not simply partner with an entrepreneur to launch the venture? While that may be the logical choice, it is rarely the choice that scientists and engineers make. One could argue that some aspect of their education and training led them to believe that they could run a company (business is easy) or, more probably, their belief that it's the technology that determines business success has made it difficult for them to understand why investors will rarely invest in a start-up where the entire management team is comprised solely of technical people.

So why should they study entrepreneurship? A number of reasons become evident.

- The most commonly held expertise by CEOs of S&P 500 companies since 1997 is finance, followed by operations and marketing.[5] CEOs understand that the product is only one component of a very complex enterprise.
- Scientists and engineers who desire to lead the companies for which they work into new areas of opportunity will face intense opposition from upper management unless they can back up their new ideas with hard numbers and solid projections for a positive return on investment to the company. This requires knowledge of finance, marketing, and operations.
- By studying entrepreneurship, scientists and engineers will experience the opportunity to work through the complex business processes involved in launching a new venture, which will help to instill an entrepreneurial mindset—a way of thinking that is opportunistic, embraces uncertainty, is creative, and is capable of taking calculated risks.
- They will learn how to make trade-offs among product features and benefits, price, market segments, and operations to name a few of the many trade-offs that face entrepreneurs when they launch a company.
- They will learn how to adapt to uncertainty and change, which is the constant state of the environment for entrepreneurs.
- They will learn techniques for managing people—employees and customers—and for dealing with all the day-to-day operational issues that seem to drag technical entrepreneurs away from what they're most passionate about: technology.

To understand the value of entrepreneurship, it is important to begin by considering the role of innovation and entrepreneurship in the economy.

THE ROLE OF INNOVATION
AND ENTREPRENEURSHIP

On August 9, 1995, when Netscape Communications went public and its stock more than doubled in less than 24 hours, it signaled the start of the Internet initial public offering (IPO) market. It was the gold rush of the 1990s. Companies that followed— Priceline.com, eBay, and E*Trade—enjoyed successful IPOs despite having no major products, no profits, and virtually no customers. Between November 1998 and November 1999, ten companies exhibited first-day price increases greater than 300 percent, notwithstanding little or no profit.[6] This was certainly not the first time that technology companies had gone public with no sales and no product yet ready for commercialization. In 1980, biotech giant Genentech, in one of the largest stock run-ups ever, went public. Its stock shot from $35 a share to $88 dollars a share in less than an hour.[7] Yet, it was not until 1985 that Genentech finally received approval from the U.S. Food and Drug Administration (FDA) to market its first product, Protropin, a growth hormone for children with human growth hormone deficiency, the first recombinant pharmaceutical product to be manufactured and marketed by a biotechnology company.

Until the 1980s, technological change such as this was nowhere to be found in economic growth models, which relied solely on inputs of capital and labor. In the 1980s, the work of Paul Romer and others identified technological change as a critical component of a growth model that responds to market incentives.[8] Technological change comes about when an entrepreneur identifies new customer segments, new customer needs, existing customer needs that have not been satisfied, and new ways of manufacturing and distributing products and services. Technological change has been behind the record growth that many companies today have achieved. The period from 1998 to 2001 was one of great experimentation and creativity that shook nearly every industry in one way or another and precipitated what is now referred to as the "new economy." The new economy is characterized by three themes: (1) knowledge workers who are employed in professional, technical, and managerial occupations and now comprise the largest category of occupations, (2) globalization, and (3) innovation. In this new economy, time-to-market is one of the key competitive advantages for new technologies. The ability to get new products to market in record time so as to take advantage of increasingly smaller windows of opportunity has never been more critical to success. Speed produces:

- **Competitive advantage.**   The business can gain a foothold in the market before competitors become aware of what they are doing.
- **More profit potential.**   The business can grab market share at premium prices before competitors enter and force prices down.
- **Fewer surprises.**   The business gets the product to market before customers' tastes and preferences change.[9]

The longer it takes to develop a new product and bring it to market, the less likely it will still meet customers' needs when it gets there. Every aspect of the product development environment is changing at such a rapid pace that any lag time in commercializing a new technology can make it obsolete by the time it hits the market. Getting to market quickly can also mean higher profits. It is estimated that a 6-month jump on competitors in a market accustomed to 18- to 24-month design lives can translate into as much as three times the profit over the market life of the design.

DEFINING INNOVATION

Innovation has been defined in a number of different ways:

> Innovation is imaginative activity fashioned so as to produce outcomes that are both original and of commercial value, *Institute for Innovation and Information Productivity.*
>
> Innovation is introducing something new, *Business Week.*[10]
>
> Innovation is concerned with the process of commercializing or extracting value from ideas; this is in contrast with 'invention' which need not be directly associated with commercialization, Rogers, 1998.[11]

In the 1930s, economist Joseph Schumpeter identified five types of innovation:[12] (1) a new product or substantial change in an existing product, (2) a new process; (3) a new market, (4) new sources of supply, and (5) changes in industrial organization. Strictly speaking, mere improvements are not considered innovation even though these incremental improvements may generate economic growth. Furthermore, new products and processes are not judged to be innovations until commercialization takes place, which requires the identification of a market.

Innovations can be grouped into two broad categories: incremental (or sustaining) innovations and disruptive (or radical) innovations. At one end of the spectrum are incremental innovations that build on existing technology but in a substantially new way. The iPod, for example, was a major improvement over MP3 players (although some would argue that the major improvement was branding and marketing). At the other end of the spectrum are disruptive innovations that have no precedent and are game changers, obsoleting previous technology. Two examples are the Internet (the commercial version of the ARPANET commissioned by the U.S. Department of Defense) and the birth control pill, both of which carried huge ramifications for social interaction and business, among other things. The work of Clayton Christiansen has helped us understand the nature of disruptive technologies.[13] Disruptive technologies are not a rational decision on the part of the company that invests in their development because there is no identifiable market in the beginning and when finally introduced to the market, disruptive technologies typically perform poorly, at least initially (sustaining technologies usually improve on performance and are far less risky). Often, the time to mass adoption of a disruptive technology is many years, sometimes decades, or alternatively the technology may come "out of the blue" and surprise everyone, as did the personal computer.

Successful incremental innovation comes only after intense questioning of existing products and patterns, and going beyond the limits of existing capabilities.

Sustaining or incremental innovation is certainly less risky and more predictable. It will meet customer needs for a time, but it must be supplemented by periods of disruptive or radical innovation because eventually incremental innovation produces diminishing returns.[14] This concept is embodied in the theory of S-curves, which is discussed in Chapter 7.

DISPELLING INNOVATION MYTHS

A number of myths have grown up around innovation since the earliest writers attempted to describe the source of an invention. One of the earliest was the myth that Sir Isaac Newton was struck on the head by an apple, which led to his formulation of the theory of universal gravitation. While this myth helped to popularize his theories, it was not true. More recently, it has been said that one of the founders of eBay Corporation started the company so that his fiancée could trade PEZ dispensers, but that story was an invention of the founders because the real reason for starting the company was too mundane. They actually launched eBay simply to create the perfect market economy where users could freely trade with each other.[15] The following are some myths about innovation that should be dispelled before we consider the process of technology commercialization.

THE MYTH OF THE GREAT IDEA

It is often believed that innovators experience an epiphany or eureka moment that results in a great idea. The reality is that no such moment occurs because ideas are always the result of many smaller moments of insight over some period of time, much like the process of putting together a jigsaw puzzle. The epiphany is the moment when the last piece of the puzzle is put in place.[16] The Internet was developed on the work of many previous innovators in diverse fields such as electronics, networking, and packet switching software. The development timeline for the Internet can be found at www.pbs.org/opb/nerds2.0.1/timeline/, and it clearly shows the decades of research and development that led to the inflection point in 1995 when Tim Berners-Lee's World Wide Web reached critical mass and became the service with the greatest traffic on NSFNet, which linked all the super-computing centers and established the high-speed Backbone Network Service.

THE MYTH OF THE REPLICABLE PROCESS

It is surprising that many people still believe that innovation is a defined process that once learned can be replicated to produce more innovation, thus reducing some of the risk. Nothing could be further from the truth, but this myth is symptomatic of the need today to find a quick fix for everything from losing weight to growing old. Innovating is a process of experimentation, and experimentation by its very nature involves the unknown, so each experiment tests a different variable in the process. The bottom line is innovation is the result of hard work, trial and error, and persistence, and it is rarely replicable.

THE MYTH OF DOING WHAT'S EXPECTED

Innovation doesn't typically happen when everything is going smoothly, everyone agrees on everything, and all the feedback is positive. The reality is that innovation occurs at the edge of chaos when concepts that don't normally go together are juxtaposed, when innovators are willing to take a chance on something no one believes they can do. In recent years, much innovation has come from the intersection of technology and entrepreneurship where the technology itself was not radically new or exciting but the way it was brought to the market created an interesting opportunity. An example is Google, the number one search engine on the Internet, which defied all the odds in a field of major competitors such as Yahoo and AltaVista. Ignoring the naysayers, Google began building a big company that didn't act like a big company. It created a radically new approach to Internet search, redefined viral marketing, and almost as an afterthought did one of the most successful and creative IPOs that Wall Street has ever witnessed.[17] Much of the innovation that has the greatest impact on society lies completely outside the realm of the expected. The greatest technological breakthroughs were just that—breakthroughs that only revealed themselves after countless hours of tinkering and testing.[18] Nothing about innovation is clear, straightforward, and predictable. Innovation, like entrepreneurship, is messy.

THE MYTH OF THE SOLO INVENTOR

For years the press has decided who gets the credit for a particular invention or accomplishment. It is much easier to build a mythical story around a superhuman character than to acknowledge that this inventor or innovator may have had some help along the way. Bill Gates is Microsoft's superhero, but he received a lot of help, advice, and ideas from Paul Allen and Steve Ballmer. Einstein's famous $E = mc^2$ was the integration of individual concepts developed by Faraday, Lavoisier, Newton, and Galileo. Every invention has connections to ideas from the past and the ability of inventors to set aside egos and take advantage of collaborations and historical precedent can enhance the probability of achieving an innovation that has real value.

THE MYTH OF THE FIRST MOVER

First-mover advantage is often considered a measure of success in the commercialization process. First movers derive their advantage by securing intellectual property (IP) protection (specifically patents) on a particular technology, or by preempting others from gaining access to resources by recognizing and controlling a scarce resource—retail shelf space, key location, limited raw materials, or skilled labor—before others see its value.[19] However, pioneering has its disadvantages as well. Second and third movers often benefit from the pioneer's work and are able to develop around the protected technology without incurring the heavy costs of basic research. Subsequent movers are also free from the costs and delays associated with compatibility issues with complementary products.[20] One study actually found a negative correlation between R&D intensity and success; that is, the greater the investment in R&D, the lesser the chance of success.[21] Therefore, it appears that the uniqueness of a technology in and of itself does not determine success but rather the ability to successfully commercialize that technology in the market.

A more recent study has confirmed, however, that even though first-mover advantage does not indicate success in the long term, it does give the firm an advantage in seeking funding and also provides an initial quiet period or temporary monopoly during which to establish a foothold in the market and build brand loyalty before having to deal with direct competitors, which is particularly important with disruptive technologies.[22]

One of the key determinants of success with new technological innovations is the ability to effectively navigate the commercialization process. This issue will be taken up in the next section.

THE COMMERCIALIZATION PROCESS

The commercialization process is not linear. In fact, it moves more like the balls in a pinball machine—taking off in one direction until it hits a snag, then bouncing off in another direction. This chaotic process continues until the technology either goes to market or fails. Technology innovation and commercialization is inherently an iterative process where the inventor-entrepreneur learns from his mistakes and builds on that learning. Figure 1-2 depicts the commercialization process as categories of activities. Within each category are many nonlinear, often chaotic activities. In the next sections, we examine this process in more detail.

1 DISCOVERY

The invention and innovation process generally consists of four broad categories of activities: connection, discovery, invention, and application or innovation. Briefly, connection involves recognizing a relationship that might lead to a discovery, which is the "ah ha" or "eureka!" phenomenon that occurs when something new is discovered. Generally, the connection that is made is unusual, such as the spiny burr plant in nature that led to the development of the sticky fabric Velcro®. From discovery comes an invention—a new device, process, or composition of matter—that has the potential to produce useful market applications (innovations) in a variety of different contexts. The invention and innovation portion of the commercialization process is discussed in more depth in Chapter 2.

2 OPPORTUNITY RECOGNITION

Inventing a new device or process or innovating on an existing one is important, but that process alone will not produce an opportunity. An opportunity is the intersection of an idea and a market need or unserved space that can be exploited. Once an opportunity is identified, the value proposition must be developed. The value proposition is often described in the form of a business concept statement that defines the technology and its application, the customer/end user for the technology, the benefits and applications of the technology, and the distribution strategy or how those benefits will be delivered to the customer. This concept statement provides a basis for testing the feasibility of the opportunity in the market. Normally an inventor will disclose an invention to the patent office, or university technology transfer office if the inventor works at a university, at the point at which the inventor recognizes a potential opportunity in the market. The

FIGURE 1-2 The Commercialization Process

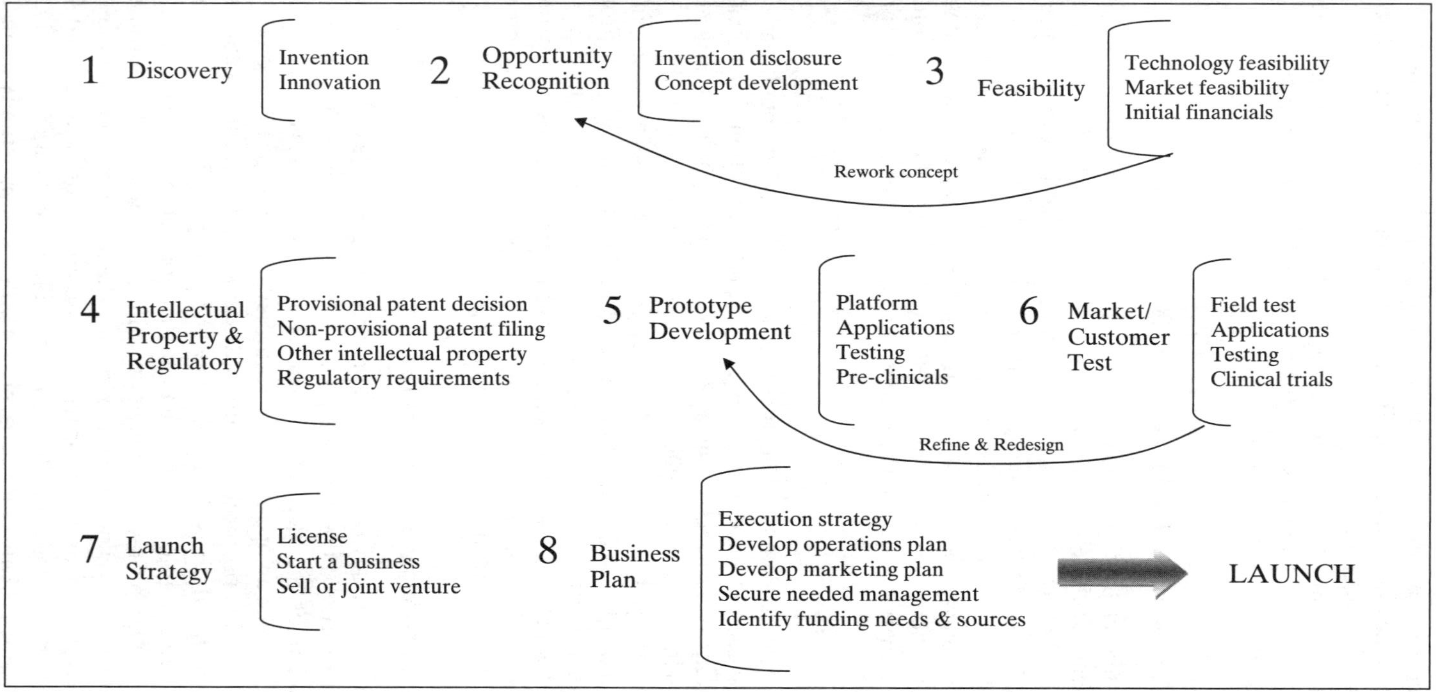

1 Discovery
- Invention
- Innovation

2 Opportunity Recognition
- Invention disclosure
- Concept development

3 Feasibility
- Technology feasibility
- Market feasibility
- Initial financials

Rework concept

4 Intellectual Property & Regulatory
- Provisional patent decision
- Non-provisional patent filing
- Other intellectual property
- Regulatory requirements

5 Prototype Development
- Platform
- Applications
- Testing
- Pre-clinicals

6 Market/ Customer Test
- Field test
- Applications
- Testing
- Clinical trials

Refine & Redesign

7 Launch Strategy
- License
- Start a business
- Sell or joint venture

8 Business Plan
- Execution strategy
- Develop operations plan
- Develop marketing plan
- Secure needed management
- Identify funding needs & sources

LAUNCH

purpose for the disclosure is to document a date of invention. Chapter 2 discusses opportunity recognition and concept development in more detail.

3 TESTING TECHNOLOGY AND MARKET FEASIBILITY

Determining if the invention or innovation is commercially feasible requires a thorough analysis of the industry and market, the capabilities and shortcomings of the founding team, and the resources required to start the venture. This stage highlights the relationship between innovation and the market. Research has found that the chances for commercial success are greater when technology and market factors are considered together.[23] In fact, boundary spanning, as Kanter refers to it,[24] (bringing together diverse functions in the business such as manufacturing, marketing, and finance to provide input to the process) is necessary to build a competitive advantage because the information required to judge feasibility will need to come from a variety of sources both internal and external to the founding team. Feasibility analysis is the subject of Chapter 3.

4 PROTECTING IP ASSETS

Early in the invention and innovation process, the inventor will need to find ways to protect the IP assets that are being created. Many inventors fail to realize how important it is to legally protect their work so that they have the option to apply for a patent or other form of IP at the appropriate time. The protection of innovative ideas and inventions is frequently critical to successful commercialization. However, determining which type of protection to choose and which strategy will best meet commercialization goals is also vital. Three questions must be answered at this juncture.

- Does the technology appear to be a feasible design?
- Is a patent necessary to the successful commercialization of the technology?
- Does the technology meet the U.S. Patent and Trademark Office requirements?

For some products, getting a patent will take longer than the window of opportunity will allow. For others, a patent will provide a brief quiet period to enter the market without competitors. Part II of this book addresses IP issues. Many technologies are regulated so it is important to identify early in the process the requirements that must be met because they will significantly affect the timeline for commercialization.

5 PROTOTYPING

Every new product goes through a design, development, and prototyping phase during which the feasibility of the technology is tested. Today, designing right the first time, shortening the time to market, prototyping early, and outsourcing noncore capabilities are critical components of an effective product development process in a dynamic environment. Field testing with potential users at various stages in the process will reduce the chance of error in the final product. Product development is the subject of Chapter 7.

6 TESTING THE MARKET AND FIRST CUSTOMER

Ideally, the first customer was identified during the feasibility analysis in Step 3 and that customer participated in the design and development of the technology product. At Stage 6, it is time to field test the product, which is simply putting the beta in the hands of customers to use as they see fit. For biotechnology innovations, this stage might signal the start of human trials. Stage 6 is a critical juncture in the commercialization process because the feedback from customers may result in refining or redesigning the prototype to better meet customer needs. The subject of testing the customer is taken up in Chapters 3 and 9.

7 DECIDING ON A LAUNCH STRATEGY

Inventors and innovators have three basic choices of launch strategy. They can license the right to manufacture and market their inventions to an existing company and collect royalties on sales; they can sell the technology outright to another company; or they can build a company to manufacture and sell their invention. This is a particularly difficult decision for researchers and inventors who work in university environments, research institutes, government laboratories, or for large corporations. Deciding to start a company probably means having to leave their current position and seek resources to support the start-up—a culture shock at best—whereas licensing or selling outright may offer more flexibility. These issues are discussed in Chapter 8.

8 DEVELOPING THE BUSINESS PLAN

Once a business concept is judged to be feasible and the decision has been made to create a company, it is necessary to develop the infrastructure for the business. This is typically accomplished by preparing a comprehensive business plan that documents the operations of the business, policies, a marketing and growth plan, and a complete set of financial statements, as well as updated industry, market, and team analyses from the feasibility study. Business development also entails setting up the legal structure of the business and the distribution of equity to the shareholders. If the inventor/entrepreneur is seeking outside capital, negotiations with investors will also take place. The inventor/entrepreneur will need to negotiate with strategic partners to implement certain areas of the business plan.

LAUNCHING THE BUSINESS

The actual start-up of the business includes such activities as finding and negotiating for facilities, hiring personnel, stocking inventories of raw materials and components, and organizing the operations of the business. The transition from research to operations is often jarring for engineers and scientists who would much prefer to remain in their laboratories working on new products. For this reason, it is vitally important that any decision to launch a business include the decision to bring on management expertise to run the operations.

Technology commercialization in today's global marketplace presents new challenges and opportunities for entrepreneurs. Understanding what is required to effectively move research from the lab to the market means that fewer mistakes will be made and the chances of success wil increase.

Summary

The process of taking an invention from idea to business concept to market—technology commercialization—faces a unique set of challenges and opportunities in a fast-paced market. Products must be developed more rapidly, prototyped earlier, and brought to market in record time. Small entrepreneurial companies are in a good position to do that as they tend to be more flexible and fast to respond to environmental changes. In contrast, established companies find that they must break away from traditional strategic thinking and the inertia they tend to experience from having achieved a measure of success with their core products. Creativity and innovation are essential to the development of disruptive technologies, which can result in many new companies and thousands of new jobs. First movers with disruptive technologies can achieve a market advantage but often are overtaken by second and third movers with improved versions of the technology. The technology commercialization process is an iterative one made up of invention and innovation, opportunity recognition and concept development, IP protection, product development and testing, feasibility analysis, and development of the business.

CASE STUDY

Innovation in the Palm of His Hand

How many new products can claim a cultlike status with more than 150 Web sites devoted to extolling its virtues? The PalmPilot did. In 1996, Jeff Hawkins and his long-time partner Donna Dubinsky introduced the PalmPilot and blew the other PDAs out of the water.

Where did the idea for this breakthrough product come from? It was Hawkins' fascination with cognition and neurobiology—the physical basis of human intelligence—that put him on the path to inventing the PalmPilot. So passionate was he about the brain that in 1986, he left his career in business to enroll in a graduate-level biophysics program to begin to understand how the brain works. His research resulted in two insights that influenced his work at Palm Computing. His first insight was that the brain is not like a computer because it has no processor, no software, and no random-access memory. Instead, the brain uses auto-associative memory, which has the ability to generalize, fill in missing information, and work with incomplete or inaccurate data. Hawkins went on to develop a way to apply auto-associative memory to data that varies over time. That insight resulted in the handwriting recognition software, Graffiti, for which the PalmPilot is known.

(continued)

(*continued*)

Hawkins' second insight involved "understanding—that is, how we know something. Intelligent systems don't just act; they anticipate. They make predictions about their environment."[25] Auto-associative memory assists the brain in making predictions. Hawkins' ultimate goal was to develop products that incorporate auto-associative memories and intelligence in a way that lets them understand the world. However, he was a long way from that goal back in the 1980s.

Hawkins graduated from Cornell University in 1979 with a degree in electrical engineering and began work for Intel. He left Intel after 3 years to seek an opportunity that would give him more responsibility, which he found for a time at GRID Systems, a small Silicon Valley company that was doing work in portable computing. After a "sabbatical" from GRID to earn his degree in biophysics at UC Berkeley, he went back to GRID, which had by then been acquired by Tandy Corporation, under an agreement whereby he licensed to the company his patented PalmPrint software and became the vice president of research. His job was to develop pen-based hardware and software. In 1992, he introduced the first real pen-based computer, the GRIDPad. Although it was slow, too large, and lacked aesthetics, it initiated a revolution and foretold the future of handheld computing. Huge companies like IBM, NEC, and Samsung also announced their forays into the handheld, or PDA market as it was dubbed by John Sculley, then CEO of Apple Computers.

Never happy in large organizations, Hawkins finally left Tandy to form Palm Computing in January 1992. Needing funding, he sought out Bruce Dunlevie, a venture capitalist who happened to sit on the board of directors at Geoworks, a company that writes operating systems for portable computers. Between Dunlevie's firm, Sutter Hill Ventures, and Tandy, Hawkins was able to raise $1.3 million to fund his new venture.

Hawkins was wise enough to realize that his strength was as the idea person, so to make sure that the business was run properly, he hired Donna Dubinsky, a Yale graduate who ran Apple Computer's distribution network. The success of PalmPilot can be attributed in large part to the success of the partnership between Jeff Hawkins and Donna Dubinsky. They had compatible strengths and usually agreed, but they were not free from mistakes.

In the early days, they took on several big partners: Casio to manufacture the handheld device, Geoworks to provide the operating system, Intuit to provide personal financial software, and America Online as the Internet service provider. The problem came when they discovered that a committee of all the partners was making every decision, both major and minor. Consequently, it is no surprise that their first product, Zoomer PDA, bombed. It was big, expensive, and terribly slow. The only fortunate outcome of their first failure was that it was not the first PDA in the market. Apple had released its Newton MessagePad 2 months before, and the hype over it and the subsequent ridicule over its ineffectiveness overshadowed Zoomer's faults.

Rather than try to improve on the Zoomer, Hawkins and Dubinsky decided to conduct in-depth interviews with Zoomer users. What they learned changed the entire direction of the company. They learned that people were not purchasing a PDA as a replacement for the computer, but to replace paper, the daily paper record keeper they toted around. They also learned that users appreciated the ability to transfer files from their PC to their PDA. Hawkins decided that it was time for a radical shift in how they viewed the PDA. At the time, PDA developers had been focusing on handwriting recognition software as the basis for communication, which was an impossible feat because

(*continued*)

(*continued*)

it meant that the software had to recognize millions of different combinations and permutations of handwriting. Hawkins believed that they should reverse their thinking and ask the customer to learn a few easy characters that would enable the software to better understand their handwriting. As a result, Graffiti was born. Hawkins also believed that the device should be small enough to fit in a shirt pocket.

This time they were not going to make the same mistakes. Hawkins and Dubinsky formed a virtual company and outsourced hardware design and manufacturing. However, funding for marketing was a problem. Dubinsky figured they would need $5 million to properly launch this product, which they were calling "Touchdown." Raising that amount was difficult, and the young company soon found itself in dire straits financially. Dubinsky frantically looked for a potential strategic partner with enough synergy to make the deal worthwhile. She finally found that partner in U.S. Robotics, the fast-growing modem manufacturer. U.S. Robotics was trying to make its way into Silicon Valley, and Palm offered a solution. Hawkins and Dubinsky wanted $5 million in cash, but U.S. Robotics surprised them with an offer to buy Palm. After much debate, the partners agreed to become a division of U.S. Robotics for $44 million in stock, and Touchdown became the Pilot. The first PalmPilots shipped in April 1996 and by midsummer, it was impossible to keep up with demand. What Hawkins and Dubinsky learned from their experience with Palm would translate into faster development times and more efficient operations when they started their next company, Handspring; but it would not shelter them from mistakes. Hawkins is first and foremost an inventor and his most recent companies, Redwood Neuroscience Institute and Numenta, reflect that passion.

Sources: Numenta, www.numenta.org, accessed May 26, 2008; Redwood Neuroscience Institute, www.rni.org, accessed May 26, 2008; Adapted from Pat Dillon (June 1998). "The Next Small Thing," *Fast Company* 15: 97; Pat Dillon (June 1998). "This Is Jeff Hawkins on Brains," *Fast Company* 15: 104; Pat Dillon (August 1998). "Exit Interview: Jeff Hawkins, Inventor of the PalmPilot," *PalmPower* (www.palmpower.com); www.handspring.com; Stephanie Miles (October 20, 1999). "Palm Cofounder Shares Design Philosophy," *Cnet News* (www.cnet.com/news/); www.palm.com.

Discussion Questions

1. Why is continual innovation critical to business success today?
2. How has the new economy affected entrepreneurial decision making?
3. When it is time to commercialize an invention, what options are available to an inventor to navigate the business side of commercialization, and what are the advantages and disadvantages of each?
4. How are disruptive technologies different from sustaining or incremental technologies?
5. Why might engineering and science students, despite their inventive ideas, resist becoming entrepreneurs?

Endnotes

1. Stuart, T.E., & Ding, W.W. (2006). "When Do Scientists Become Entrepreneurs? The Social Structural Antecedents of Commercial Activity in the Academic Life Sciences," *American Journal of Sociology* 112(1): 97–144.

2. Phillips, D.J., & Zuckerman, E.W. (2001). "Middle-Status Conformity: Theoretical Restatement and Empirical Demonstration in Two Markets," *American Journal of Sociology* 107: 379–429.

3. Tan, L.L. (2008). "Can a University Turn an Engineer into an Entrepreneur?" *Innovation* 5(3), www.innovationmagazine.com.

4. Arnold, M.J. (September 2002). "Engineer to Entrepreneur: Making the Career Enhancing Transition," *Today's Engineer Online*, www.todaysengineer.org.

5. Spencer, S. (2004). *CEO Study: A Statistical Snapshot of Leading CEOs.* In Mitchell, G.R. (November–December 2007). "Instill the Entrepreneurial Mindset," *Industrial Research Institute*, 0895–6308/07, pp. 11–13.

6. NASDAQ, November 1998–November 1999.

7. www.gene.com/gene/about/corporate/history/timeline/1980.jsp.

8. Romer, P. (1986). "Increasing Returns and Long-Run Growth," *Journal of Political Economy* 94: 1002–1037.

9. Cooper, R.G. (2001). *Winning at New Products* (Cambridge, MA: Perseus), p. 3.

10. Sylver, B. (January 31, 2006). "What Does 'Innovation' Really Mean?" *Businessweek,* www.businessweek.com.

11. Rogers, M. (May 1998). "The Definition and Measurement of Innovation," *Melbourne Institute of Applied Economic and Social Research, The University of Melbourne,* Working Paper No. 10/98.

12. OECD (1997). *The Oslo Manual: Proposed Guidelines for Collecting and Interpreting Technological Innovation Data* (OECD: Paris), p. 28.

13. Christensen, C. (1997). *The Innovator's Dilemma* (Boston, MA: Harvard Business School Press).

14. Leifer, R., McDermott, C.M., O'Connor, G.C., Peters, L.S., Rice, M.P., & Veryzer, R.W. (2000). *Radical Innovation* (Boston MA: Harvard Business School Press), pp. 1–4.

15. Cohen, A. (2003). *The Perfect Store: Inside ebay* (New York: Little, Brown and Company).

16. Berkun, S. (2007). *The Myths of Innovation* (Sebastopol, CA: O'Reilly Media, Inc.), p. 9.

17. Batelle, J. (2005). *The Search* (New York: Penguin Group).

18. Taleb, N.N. (2007). *The Black Swan: The Impact of the Highly Improbable* (New York: Random House).

19. Lieberman, M., & Montgomery, D. (1988). "First-Mover Advantage," *Strategic Management Journal* 9: 41–58.

20. Slaybaugh, R. (2000). "Investigation into the Effects of an Inventive Idea on the Success of a Firm," Unpublished Paper Prepared For BAEP 551, Marshall School of Business, University of Southern California.

21. Stuart, R., & Abetti, P. (1987). "Start-up Ventures: Towards the Prediction of Initial Success," *Journal of Business Venturing* 2(3): 215–230.

22. Lieberman, M., & Montgomery, D. (1998). "First-Mover Disadvantages: Retrospective and Link with the Resource-Based View," *Strategic Management Journal* 19: 1111–1125.

23. Noori, H. (1990). *Managing the Dynamics of New Technology* (Upper Saddle River, NJ: Prentice Hall).

24. Kanter, R. (1985). "Supporting Innovation and Venture Development in Established Companies," *Journal Of Business Venturing* 1: 47–60.

25. Dillon, P. (June 1998). "This Is Jeff Hawkins on Brains," *Fast Company* 15: 104.

RECOGNIZING AND SCREENING TECHNOLOGY OPPORTUNITIES

Opportunity is the lifeblood of an entrepreneur. The ability to recognize or create an opportunity and bring the resources to bear to commercialize that opportunity is the essence of what it means to be an entrepreneur. A good way to begin this chapter is by distinguishing between an idea and an opportunity. Idea has been defined as "what exists in the mind as a representation or as a formulation of something seen or known or imagined."[1] Ideas are plentiful; they come to everyone throughout the day, but they're typically dismissed or are not assigned any value or potential. An opportunity, on the other hand, is an idea that has commercial potential. So, imagining what an Internet business that serves senior citizens might look like constitutes an idea. Figuring out what kinds of products and services might be offered to those customers also falls into the realm of idea. Opportunity, by contrast, is defined as "a favorable juncture of circumstances."[2] So, an entrepreneur may have an idea for products and services that serve senior citizens, but the appropriate circumstances must be in place before that idea can become a business opportunity—a pain or need in the market, a way to address that need, a way to make money from the idea, and funding to support a business, for example. A technology may be a great idea for technology's sake, but unless there is an application for that technology—a need in the marketplace and a way to make money—in other words, a favorable juncture of circumstances, it remains merely an idea.

This chapter explores how opportunity comes about and how businesses and inventors screen initial ideas and opportunities so they can focus on those that have the greatest potential for success.

OPPORTUNITY RECOGNITION AND CREATION

Opportunity recognition happens when three activities are in place: (1) when entrepreneurs are involved in an active search for opportunities, (2) when they have the skills to spot an opportunity in the market, and (3) when they have experience in an industry or field of endeavor.[3] For example, biotech scientists saw a way to apply genetics to the world of agriculture to increase crop yields and rid farmers of the problems associated with using pesticides. Most new products are the result of incremental or evolutionary innovation, which is recognizing a need in the market that can be served by the incremental improvement of an existing technology. Disruptive or radical innovation, by contrast, creates an opportunity that never existed previously by making the preceding technology obsolete. Opportunity creation often comes about when the technology is emergent, that is, radical or disruptive, with no precedent and no readily identifiable market. In this case, the entrepreneur must create the opportunity—the right conditions in the market—over time because in the early stages of this type of technology, there is generally no "pain" in the market. In other words, customers don't yet have a problem that can't be solved by currently existing technology or work-arounds.

A growing body of research is providing an understanding of how entrepreneurs recognize opportunities. One thing is certain: The vast majority of people who identify business opportunities encounter them in industries with which they are familiar or in a business for which they have worked.[4] Moreover, entrepreneurs who network in a variety of social circles tend to recognize more opportunities. In fact, the number of weak ties—connections outside immediate family and friends in the entrepreneur's network—is positively correlated to the number of opportunities recognized.[5] Creativity also plays an important role in entrepreneurs' preparedness for opportunity; and not surprisingly, entrepreneurs have been found to be more creative than the average person.[6]

The literature is unclear, however, as to whether opportunity recognition is a planned process. Although some early research claimed that planning is not involved in opportunity recognition,[7] more recent research associates opportunity recognition with active, well-planned searches for opportunities.[8] The reality is that both active searches and serendipity play significant roles in the ability of entrepreneurs to discover new opportunities.[9]

EMPLOYING CREATIVE PROBLEM-SOLVING SKILLS FOR OPPORTUNITY RECOGNITION AND CREATION

Effective problem-solving skills are an important asset in the entrepreneur's arsenal of opportunity recognition and creation tools. No matter how complex or dynamic a problem is, only a few major factors actually affect the ultimate solution. Nevertheless, most people have difficulty identifying the major factors in a problem. More often than not, they tend to identify those factors that easily come to mind or are most important to them.[10] The problem-solving process typically involves both divergent and convergent thinking. Divergent thinking pulls a person away from a central point to explore different directions and ideas. It is a technique used to generate many different ideas quickly by deconstructing a topic or idea into its various parts to reveal potential opportunities. Questions such as the following help to uncover the aspects of the topic that might lead to an opportunity. Suppose the topic is senior citizens as customers for computer technology.

- How does one describe the problem that seniors face with computer technology?
- What are the effects of this problem?
- What is important about seniors and computers?
- What are the various aspects of the problem?
- What do we know and not know about this problem?

Many additional questions could be asked, but the important outcome is that in asking these questions, the entrepreneur is not converging too quickly on a solution before the problem has been correctly identified. Divergent thinking can be encouraged through brainstorming, mind mapping, and journaling ideas, to name a few techniques.

Convergent thinking, by contrast, brings a person back from divergent thinking to more focused thought. The entrepreneur begins to weed out ideas that don't describe the real problem or are less important in an effort to reach a conclusion on what the problem really is and to combine various ideas in an organized and meaningful way. Both divergent and convergent thinking are needed to effectively devise solutions to problems.

In general, there are four basic types of problems:

1. **Simplistic.**   When there is only one answer to the problem.
2. **Deterministic.**   A formula produces one answer.
3. **Random.**   Different answers are possible and can be identified.
4. **Indeterminate.**   Many different answers are possible, but getting to the correct one requires all of the information or the right formula.

Developing radical or disruptive innovations typically involves solving complex problems that are random or indeterminate. Solving these types of problems consists of scanning for ideas and information, integrating and processing the ideas and information, and then evaluating and selecting solutions.[11] Pattern recognition, or linking diverse events into a connected and comprehensible whole, has also been found to be effective in solving complex problems.[12] Entrepreneurs normally use their knowledge and experience to "connect the dots" during an active search for opportunity. They do this through mental or physical models, called "prototypes," or through the comparison of something new with something known, called "exemplar models."[13]

A number of techniques have been used effectively to undertake problem solving. A few of the more common are discussed here.

RESTATING THE PROBLEM

The more information there is, the easier the problem is to solve, whereas the less information there is, the more difficult it is to solve and the longer it takes to pull all the pieces of the opportunity together. In the latter situation, limited information must be expanded upon. One good technique for doing this is to state a problem and then restate it in different ways. For example:

Initial problem statement: We don't have enough lab space.
Restatement: There are too many people for the space we have.
Restatement: How can we reduce the number of people we have?
Restatement: How can we use the space we have more effectively?

There are many more possible restatements of this problem, but what this exercise points out is that any problem can and should be viewed from a number of different perspectives because each perspective will lead potentially to a different opportunity.

Table 2-1 displays an example of restating problems using the original problem statement.[14] It is clear that by the time the question has been asked and restated four times, the problem is not really how to get more lab space, but how to finish the project on time. Without going through this process, however, a wrong assumption about the source of the problem would have been a likely outcome. Had that outcome been followed as an opportunity, the result might have been less than optimal.

AN ENGINEERING APPROACH TO CREATIVE PROBLEM SOLVING

Engineers and scientists are well trained in structured problem-solving skills, but they sometimes stumble when asked to apply creative, out-of-the-box thinking to those skills. Recognizing that, Clegg and Birch came up with a four-step problem-solving approach that is analogous to an engineering process but allows for more creativity in approaching problems.[15]

1. Surveying: In this first stage of the process, information needed to solve the problem is gathered and a goal is set for the end of the process. Too many people skip over this initial stage and do not spend enough time understanding and defining the problem; then they wonder why the solution they arrived at did not work. This is particularly true when working with potential customers on problem solving. Too often scientists and engineers (and entrepreneurs as well) expect the customer to provide the solution—in other words, what they want in terms of a product or service. This approach is hazardous at best because customers are not solution providers; they are problem identifiers. Therefore, a preferred approach is to find out what is troubling the customer—the problem—and then go back and brainstorm possible solutions.

TABLE 2-1 Restating the Problem	
Original problem statement.	*We don't have enough lab space.*
The opposite of the original statement.	*We have too much lab space.*
Broaden or narrow the focus. Put the statement into a larger or narrower context.	*What would we do with more lab space?*
Ask "why at least five times to get to the root of the problem?"	Original: We need more lab space.
	Why? Because we don't have room for all our researchers.
	Restatement: How can we accommodate all the researchers we need?
	Why? Because we have had to hire more to complete our work on time.
	Restatement: How can we get more researchers without having to provide lab space?
	Why? Because we don't have the funding to add more lab space right now.
	Restatement: Can we outsource some of the research to another lab?
	Why? Because we need to finish the project on time.
	Restatement: How can we finish the project on time?

This brainstorming involves the use of both divergent and convergent thinking. Some of the critical tasks that should be accomplished at this stage include repeatedly asking "why" until the root problem is identified, recognizing roadblocks to achieving the solution (the goal), looking at the problem from new angles, drawing a map of the problem so all the relationships that affect it can be seen, and reconfirming the goal of the problem-solving task.

2. Building: Based on the information about the problem gathered in the first stage, a method for getting from the destination to the goal is devised that also identifies potential obstacles along the way and uses creativity to overcome them. Clegg and Birch suggest a variety of tools to employ in this stage, including getting past obstacles by making them invisible, challenging long-held assumptions, building "what if" scenarios, and questioning the original destination chosen, since there is generally no one right answer to any problem.

3. Waymaking: This stage takes what has been built in stage 2 and turns it into a fully operational "transportation system" or solution. Waymaking is an iterative process that may require revising something that was done earlier. Here, the views of the stakeholders are considered, the ideas that will continue are chosen, and the advantages and disadvantages of the approach are examined.

4. Navigating: Using the path that was built, the solution can be planned and implemented, resources required for the journey determined, and a way to track progress and mark the arrival at the goal selected.

TRIZ APPROACH TO INNOVATION

TRIZ is a Russian acronym that translates to "the theory of inventive problem solving." It is one of a number of problem-solving tools that enables engineers to quickly design breakthrough products by applying innovative thinking. The natural creativity of engineers has often been stifled by several factors, including rigid company hierarchies that limit interaction, the fear of failure, and overdependence on formulas and computers.[16]

The TRIZ approach focuses on the problem itself in the belief that the problem posed is rarely the actual problem that has to be solved. Most technology problems are a complex mix of useful functions and dysfunctional or harmful functions, so the first task for the engineer is to determine where to begin. Problems suitable for the TRIZ approach include the following:[17]

- **Technical conflict and physical contradiction.** Many technical conflicts occur when an attempt to solve one problem creates another. For example, if an engineer creates a beverage can with very thin walls, it may no longer be able to support the weight of cans stacked on top of it.

- **Inventive problem.** Many engineering problems involve a trade-off in a situation concerning a conflict and a contradiction where the engineer is put in the position of inventing a solution to resolve the conflict. In other words, before the original problem can be solved, the discovered conflict must be resolved. For example, suppose the problem involves the development of a device for applying labels to envelopes that go through the mail system at the post office in a manner that is much faster than what is currently being done. So, speed is the critical factor. A device is created that does an excellent job of applying labels within the required parameters for speed, but the reality is that envelopes going through the system are of varying sizes and thicknesses, which causes the speed at which labels can be applied to vary as well. The engineer must solve the conflict with varying sizes of envelopes before the goal of speed can be achieved.

- **Ideal machine.** Once a device or invention has been conceptualized, the engineer now tries to find the simplest way to make the invention work; that is, how can the device be simplified, what features or components can be taken out, and what can be replaced with something simpler without sacrificing quality or performance.

TRIZ also provides a way to resolve conflicts in technical designs. The traditional way that these conflicts have been resolved is through compromise, but compromise does not produce the optimal solution, as an improvement in one area could result in problems in another. TRIZ is also useful for technology forecasting and concept development[18] and has been very successful in reducing cycle times and generating new ideas. For example, the TRIZ process produced 60 patentable ideas in 1 day for improving an auto component that had been operating poorly for 5 years. Of course, once a problem solution has been identified, the work of identifying how that solution might become a business opportunity begins.

SOURCES OF OPPORTUNITY

Today, technology opportunities can come from many sources. This section looks at how to identify opportunity outside the realm of basic research, including capitalizing on the research of others.

STUDY AN INDUSTRY

Learning an industry is one of the most important first steps in finding opportunity, because most inventor-entrepreneurs discover their best opportunities in industries in which they have had experience. Industry trends, changes, and emerging needs present gaps or white spaces that can be turned into opportunities. Peter Drucker identified seven sources for innovation that can all be found within an industry: (1) unexpected failures or successes, (2) discrepancies between what is assumed and what actually exists, (3) missing links in processes, (4) changes in industry or market structure, (5) changes in industry or market demographics, (6) changes in assumptions and beliefs, and (7) new knowledge or advances in scientific theory.[19]

A good place to start the search for opportunity is by mapping the value chain in the industry to learn not only how the industry works, but also who the major players are. The value chain consists of all the participants in an industry from producers of raw materials to manufacturers, distributors, and retailers. Once the industry has been mapped, consider the following questions:

- How are needs changing in this industry?
- What opportunities could arise from these changes?
- What are the industry drivers?
- How do businesses become profitable in this industry?
- What are some alternative scenarios to what is currently believed about the industry or seen occurring in the industry?

A good example of what not to do is what AT&T did in the late 1980s. The National Science Foundation (NSF) asked AT&T to take control of the Internet because NSF no longer wanted to administer it.[20] However, AT&T's view of the future was that its centrally switched telephony technology was going to dominate for the foreseeable future, and the Internet had no place in that future. Of course, had AT&T considered any alternative scenarios to that future—both best and worse cases—it might have been in a better position to recognize changes occurring in the industry brought about by the Internet and position itself to respond quickly. For more information on how to analyze an industry, see Chapter 3.

SEARCH THE PATENT LITERATURE

The U.S. Patent and Trademark Office's (USPTO) database contains millions of U.S. and foreign patents. Searching their archives is an excellent way to spark an idea. In fact, searching the archives of patents now in the public domain could lead to an invention that was never commercialized. Most patents were never brought to market because they either had no inherent economic value or their owners did not understand how to commercialize the invention they had developed. Nonprofit organizations such as the National Institute for Technology Acquisition and Commercialization (NISTAC) hold hundreds of patents donated by Fortune 50 companies that are available for licensing.

TALK TO CUSTOMERS

More new product ideas have come from customers than probably any other source. Customers experience the pain of not having something they need, and they readily communicate that pain if someone is listening. The best way to understand customer needs is to use an anthropological approach to market research. What did Jane Goodall do when she wanted to understand the habits of chimpanzees? She moved in with them and lived with them for months on end. No one expects entrepreneurs to move in with their customers and devote months to understanding their needs, but they can spend a day in the life of their customer, shadowing what the customer does and listening carefully to detect that customer's pain. The cardiac device division of Hewlett-Packard needed to ensure that its measurement devices were thoroughly tested and worked the way their customers, the hospital staff, needed them to work, as it was literally a matter of life and death. The team spent weeks at the hospital observing and listening in order to create the best product.[21] Focus groups and structured interviews are excellent ways to gather information, but nothing beats camping out with the customer.

LOOK INTO UNIVERSITY OPPORTUNITIES

For years the pharmaceutical industry has relied on university research laboratories for basic research leading to new drugs. The Human Genome Project is one example of how government, universities, and public/private partners can work together to create new products and knowledge. In combinatory chemistry, companies such as Millennium Pharmaceuticals, Inc., a leading producer of cancer therapeutics, have developed software models to build and analyze virtual chemicals that demonstrate biological effects. They can use these models to search for molecules that display similar effects and, using the capabilities of outside partners, test thousands of potential effects per day. With yet other partners, they can conduct animal and human testing.[22]

The basic research performed by university professors and researchers may result in the next major breakthrough in science and engineering. However, most researchers conduct their research without any thought of commercializing their discovery. In fact, fewer than 20 percent of the faculty and researchers at a university disclose patentable research, which is an opportunity for entrepreneurs.[23] A university's technology transfer office is a good place to look for ways to collaborate with university researchers to commercialize their technology.

INVESTIGATE GOVERNMENT SOURCES

Many government agencies regularly publish requests for proposals (RFPs) for technology that they would like to see researched and turned into inventions that can be commercialized. Agencies such as the National Aeronautics and Space Administration (NASA) own technology developed under government contracts that they will license to companies. Other federal agencies and laboratories that deal in technology transfer include the Department of Commerce, the Department of Defense, and the Department of Energy.

FIND NEW VALUE IN EXISTING TECHNOLOGY

Increasingly, companies are finding that some of their greatest opportunities lie with technologies whose patents have lain dormant because, for whatever reason, the inventing company did not move forward with the transfer or commercialization of the technology. Intellectual property (IP) in the form of patents and trademarks is the new opportunity frontier. More and more companies are building growth strategies around finding new value in existing and oftentimes archived technologies. IBM was perhaps one of the earliest companies to reap the financial rewards of new royalty streams by licensing existing IP. Through a judicious effort to mine its patent archives for new applications, it was able to boast its annual royalty stream from $30 million in 1990 to over $1 billion today. This revenue stream represents approximately one-ninth of its annual pretax profits, and it goes directly to its net profit. To achieve that same level of profit, IBM would have to sell about $20 billion in additional products each year, one-fourth of its worldwide sales.[24]

OTHER SOURCES

In addition to the sources already discussed, trade associations are a good source of technology-related information as well as trade publications, suppliers, and distributors. The Internet can also play a role in finding opportunity. Patent exchange sites such as Yet2.com have sprung up that allow inventors to post their issued patents for licensing or sale. Finally, some entrepreneurs have identified opportunities through direct mail solicitations to universities, corporations, government agencies, or trade associations.

SCREENING TECHNOLOGY OPPORTUNITIES

Idea generation, opportunity recognition, and opportunity creation are the starting points for technology commercialization. However, not all opportunities possess equal merit, so it makes sense to have a process for screening opportunities early on so as not to waste precious time and resources on suboptimal opportunities. For the small entrepreneurial company or start-up venture, choosing correctly among many opportunities may make the difference between a business that flourishes and one that barely survives. By contrast, a larger company with a wide variety of products and processes requires a more complex decision-making process because the impact of a new opportunity may be more critical.

The phrase Fuzzy Front End (FFE) first began appearing in the product development literature in 1985. It refers to the portion of the product development cycle between when a new product project should start and when it actually does start, in other words, all the activities leading to the ultimate decision to proceed with a project into product development—in short, the opportunity phase.[25] Today, this concept has taken on a more critical meaning as the window of opportunity for new products continues to shrink and anything that slows a company's ability to recognize or create an opportunity and act on it quickly can mean the difference between supernormal profits and no profits. The skill of quickly screening new product ideas becomes a vital organizational aptitude. Reinertsen has modeled the FFE in economic terms. Simply stated, the amount a person is willing to bet on a new product is a function of the probability of its success, the value of that success, and the cost of failure. Altering any one of these values will change the economics of the bet.[26]

Figure 2-1 depicts the typical process for initially screening technology opportunities to enable a choice of the best opportunity to pursue. This process assumes that (1) a discovery has been made that can be turned into an invention for which an opportunity can be created, (2) the entrepreneur has identified a problem for which a solution can be developed, or (3) the entrepreneur has identified a technology that she wishes to acquire through licensing. Each of the steps in the process is discussed in more detail in the next sections.

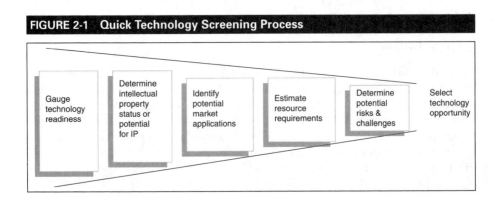

FIGURE 2-1 Quick Technology Screening Process

GAUGE TECHNOLOGY READINESS

Technology readiness is a measure of the status of the technology on a spectrum that starts with idea and moves through laboratory testing to prototype to commercial product. The stages along the path to commercial product vary according to the type of technology being developed. For example, a software product in its earliest stage may be simply a concept that will subsequently go through application formulation, proof of concept, system validation in the laboratory, validation in the relevant environment of use, test, and demonstration, and proof through successful operations. By contrast, a biomedical technology will also need to go through preclinical research and benchmark testing, animal testing, and clinical trials.

DETERMINE IP STATUS

Whether the technology under consideration is new to the inventor or invented by someone else, it is important to consider its IP status. In the case of a new idea, a preliminary search of the USPTO patent files or an in-depth understanding of research being undertaken in the field of use is critical to determining if the idea has the potential to be patented. There is no point spending time on a technology for which there are already patents in place. It's also wise to determine who might have claims on the IP, whether that be a university, a PhD researcher who worked on the invention, or a company that holds that may overlap the new research.

IDENTIFY POTENTIAL MARKET APPLICATIONS

For a new technology to have any chance of success, potential market applications must be identified. The question to ask is, Where is the pain? If there is no need in the market for the invention, it will be a difficult proposition at best to commercialize it. It is important to identify a first customer or early adopter who is willing to pay for the application, recognizing that early adopters are typically a miniscule portion of any market and rarely do they provide clues to a mass market. It is also wise to identify similar technologies that may solve the same problem and serve as substitutes for the customer and complementary applications that may make it easy to educate the customer about the technology. The issue of technology adoption is the subject of Chapter 10.

ESTIMATE RESOURCE REQUIREMENTS

The next step is to estimate the potential resources required to ready the technology for commercial applications. These resources will generally fall into three categories: human, equipment, and capital. In some cases, the resources required are prohibitive and without a strategic partner in the form of a company in the industry in which the technology will reside, commercialization will not be possible. Certainly for many biotech products, access to a large pharmaceutical company to take the technology through clinical trials will be essential. But even non biomedical type products can require enormous resources. For example, Contour Crafting, a disruptive automated fabrication technology developed by Dr. Behrokh Khoshnevis at the University of Southern California, will require $2 million in funding to build a full-scale prototype to take the technology beyond proof of concept (see http://www.contourcrafting.org/).

Technology opportunities come about when entrepreneurs recognize problems in the market that can be solved through a technology product, process, or service or when they team with inventors of radical technology to develop or create opportunities that didn't previously exist. Both processes—opportunity recognition and creation—can produce positive economic impact on the companies that undertake them and on society as well in the form of new products and services that meet critical societal needs.

Summary

Creativity is the source of opportunity recognition, that is, an idea that has commercial potential. The ability to recognize opportunity can be enhanced by increasing knowledge and experience in an industry, building a diverse network of strong and weak ties, and developing an opportunistic mindset. Sources of opportunity include the patent literature, the industry of interest, customers, universities, government sources, online patent exchanges, and existing technologies in a company's archives. Technology opportunities need to be screened to determine whether they will result in a stand-alone product, a derivative opportunity based on core technology that the company already has, or a noncompetitive product with no commercial potential.

Discussion Questions

1. Provide two examples that illustrate the difference between an idea and an opportunity.
2. What two challenges do you face in becoming more creative? How will you deal with those challenges?
3. Why is studying an industry one of the most important things you can do to find an opportunity?
4. How are new technology ideas screened?

CASE STUDY

The Art of Invention—Yoshiro Nakamatsu and Claude Elwood Shannon

Opportunity recognition is a personal journey. Although there are guidelines and suggestions to help bring out latent creativity and teach creative skills, each person creates opportunity in his own unique way. If one were to give an award to a great master of creativity and innovation, it would very likely go to Dr. Yoshiro Nakamatsu, the holder of more than 2,300 patents, more than double the 1,093 of Thomas Edison. Many of

(continued)

(continued)

Dr. Nakamatsu's inventions are part of our daily lives, such as the compact disc player and the digital watch, while others serve niche markets, such as a golf putter and a water-powered engine. Not all inventors are as prolific as Nakamatsu; others such as Dr. Claude Elwood Shannon make discoveries that become the foundation on which others invent. If one were to give an award to one of the people most responsible for the digital age as we know it, that award would go to Dr. Shannon, who gave us the modern concept of digital information and paved the way for the computer and information revolution. Although these two men are from different parts of the world, they share many similarities in how they approach the creative process.

Yoshiro Nakamatsu's parents, recognizing his natural curiosity as a child, encouraged his early interest in invention. In Japan, creativity was not part of a child's academic education; on the contrary, children were under extreme pressure to compete and succeed in a standardized educational system. However, the skills that were engrained in Nakamatsu throughout his childhood contributed to his intellectual ability. For example, Japanese children are taught to memorize until the age of 20 because the Japanese believe that the brain requires this kind of discipline to prepare a person for free associating at a later age. It is the combination of regimentation and freedom that brings about superior levels of creativity.

Regimentation and freedom are critical components of the three-step process to which Nakamatsu subscribes for generating new ideas. Furthermore, each of the steps requires a different location. He begins the creative process in his "static" room, which contains items only found in nature: a rock garden, running water, plants, and wood. The walls of that room are painted white. He uses this room to free associate or brainstorm, generating lots of ideas without judging them to be good or bad. Next, he moves to his "dynamic" room, which has black-and-white-striped walls, leather furniture, and audio/video equipment. He begins his session in this room by listening to jazz, then transitions to easy listening, and finally ends with Beethoven's Fifth Symphony, which helps him draw conclusions from his idea generation phase. The third step entails a trip to his swimming pool where he employs a special method for holding his breath and swimming underwater. He calls it "creative swimming." He has even developed a Plexiglas writing pad so that he can remain underwater while recording his thoughts.

In addition to his unique process, Nakamatsu believes that what you feed your body affects your creative abilities. He eats only the best foods and abstains from alcohol. In addition, he has developed his own "brain food," called Yummy Nutri Brain Food, which consists of dried shrimp, seaweed, cheese, yogurt, eel, eggs, beef, and chicken livers!

In the United States, another inventor, equally eccentric, preceded Nakamatsu, but their inventions would eventually overlap in some industries. In 1948, when Claude Shannon was a 32-year-old researcher at Bell Laboratories, he wrote a theoretical treatise, *A Mathematical Theory of Communication,* demonstrating how information could be defined and quantified with precision, unifying all the previous technologies in communication. He further proposed that all types of information media could be encoded in binary digits, or *bits* (the first time that term was used in print). Once the information was digitized, he believed that it could be transmitted without error. At the time, this was an enormous conceptual leap that would later lead to the development of today's error-correcting codes and data compression algorithms, as well as to compact discs and Nakamatsu's floppy disks. His theorem explains how computer modems are able to

(continued)

(*continued*)

transmit compressed data at tens of thousands of bits per second over ordinary telephone lines without error. Shannon's theory gave engineers the mathematical tools they needed to calculate channel capacity—how much information could go from point A to point B without errors.

As amazing as his foresight was in that paper, it was almost overshadowed by the dissertation he wrote years earlier in 1940 that outlined a blueprint for the computer age. Until that time, it was thought that communication required electromagnetic waves to be sent down a wire. In his dissertation, Shannon proposed that the logical values "true" and "false" could be denoted by the numeric symbols 1 and 0, which meant you could transmit pictures, words, and sounds by sending a stream of 1s and 0s down a wire. The most compelling outcome of his proposition was that circuits could make decisions, which was the basis for the work in artificial intelligence that we know today.

After completing his doctoral degree in mathematics in 1940 at MIT, Shannon went to work for Bell Labs, where he would spend the next 31 years, and he also became a professor at MIT. In 1948, with coauthor Warren Weaver, he published *A Mathematical Theory of Communication,* which formed the basis for what is known today as information theory. By the early 1950s, his theory had become a buzzword. Shannon was hounded by the press and received request after request for lectures and new research papers. Shannon, who disliked celebrity, eventually retreated from the research world, stopped teaching, and in 1978 retired to his home in Winchester, Massachusetts.

Shannon was famous for his creative problem solving. He loved attacking problems from angles that no one had ever thought of. Like Nakamatsu, he had his eccentricities, such as riding a unicycle in the Bell Labs' hallways at night while juggling. He was constantly inventing, particularly things that had funny motions. A classic was his "Ultimate Machine," a box that contained a very large switch on the side. When you pressed the switch, the top of the box would rise, and a large hand would pop out and shut off the switch, returning the lid to its original position. That was its sole purpose!

The mind of the inventor is unlike any other. It is always in motion, constantly playing with new ideas. Even at play, both Shannon and Nakamatsu continued to invent offbeat items and concepts that reflected their childlike wonder at the world and all of its possibilities.

Sources: Adapted from Charles A. Gimon, "Heroes of Cyberspace: Claude Shannon," *Info Nation* (www.skypoint.com/~gimonca/shannon.html); M. Mitchell Waldrop (July–August, 2001) "Reluctant Father of the Digital Age: Claude Shannon," *MIT Technology Review* 64–71.

Endnotes

1. Merriam-Webster Online, www.m-w.com/dictionary/idea, accessed January 27, 2008.
2. Ibid. http://www.m-w.com/dictionary/opportunity.
3. Baron, R. A. (February, 2006). "Opportunity Recognition as Pattern Recognition: How Entrepreneurs 'Connect the Dots' to Identify New Business Opportunities," *Academy of Management Perspectives*, 20(1)104.
4. Zietsma, C. (1999). "Opportunity Knocks—or Does It Hide? An Examination of the Role of Opportunity Recognition in Entrepreneurship," In *Frontiers of Entrepreneurship Research* (Wellesley, MA: Babson College), www.babson.edu/entrep/fer/papers99/X/X_C/X_C.html; Gerald E. Hills, Rodney G. Shrader, & Lumpkin, G.T. (1999).

"Opportunity Recognition as a Creative Process." In *Frontiers of Entrepreneurship Research* (Wellesley, MA: Babson College), www.babson.edu/entrep/fer/papers99/X/X_C/X_C.html.

5. Robert P. Singh, Hills, G.E., Hybels, R.C., & Lumpkin, G.T. (1999). "Opportunity Recognition Through Social Network Characteristics of Entrepreneurs." *Frontiers of Entrepreneurship Research* (Wellesley, MA: Babson College), http://www.babson.edu/entrep/fer/papers99/X/X_B/X_B.html.

6. Vesalainen, J., & Pihkala, T. (1999). "Motivation Structure and Entrepreneurial Intentions," In P. Reynolds, W. Bygrave, S. Manigart, C. Mason, G. Meyer, H. Sapienza, & K. Shaver (Eds.), *Frontiers of Entrepreneurship Research* (Babson park, MA: Babson College), pp. 73–87.

7. Kirzner, I. (1973). *Competition and Entrepreneurship* (Chicago: University of Chicago Press).

8. Herron, C., & Sapienza, H.J. (1992). "The Entrepreneur and the Initiation of New Venture Launch Activities," *Entrepreneurship: Theory & Practice* 17(1): 49.

9. Zietsma, C. (1999). "Opportunity Knocks—or Does It Hide? An Examination of the Role of Opportunity Recognition in Entrepreneurship," *Frontiers of Entrepreneurship Research,* http://www.babson.edu/entrep/fer/papers99/X/X_C/X_C.html

10. Jones, M.D. (1998). *The Thinker's Toolkit* (New York: Three Rivers Press).

11. Mintzberg, H., & Raisinghani, D. (1976). "The Structure of Unstructured Decision Processes," *Administrative Science Quarterly* 21: 246–275.

12. Matlin, M.W. (2002). *Cognition,* 5th ed. (Fort Worth, TX: Harcourt College Publishers); Matlin, M.W., & Foley, H.J. (1997). *Sensation and Perception* (Needham Heights, MA: Allyn & Bacon).

13. Hahn, U., & Chater, N. (1997). "Concepts And Similarity," In K. Lamberts, & D. Shanks (Eds.), *Knowledge Concepts and Categories* (Cambridge, MA: MIT Press), pp. 43–92.

14. Jones, (1998). *The Thinker's Toolkit,* p. 65.

15. Clegg, B., & Birch, P. (2000). *Imagination Engineering* (New York: Pearson Education Limited).

16. Greek, D. (1999). "Beginners' Guide to Genius," *Professional Engineering* 12(7): 44.

17. Syiem, P.R. (January 1996). "An Introduction to TRIZ: A Revolutionary New Product Development Tool," *Visions.*

18. Ibid.

19. Drucker, P. (1993). *Innovation and Entrepreneurship* (New York: Collins).

20. Schwartz, P. (May 2, 2000). "The Official Future, Self Delusion, and Value of Scenarios," *Financial Times,* 6–7.

21. Cooper, R.G. (2001). *Winning at New Products,* 3rd ed. (Cambridge, MA: Perseus Publishing), pp. 162–163.

22. Rivette, K.G., & Kline, D. (January–February 2000). "Discovering New Value in Intellectual Property," *Harvard Business Review* 78(1): 54.

23. Thursby, J.G., & Thursby, M.C. (2005). "Gender Patterns of Research and Licensing Activity of Science and Engineering Faculty." *The Journal of Technology Transfer* 30(4):343–353.

24. Ibid.

25. Reinertsen, D.G. (November/December 1999). "Taking the Fuzziness Out of the Fuzzy Front End," *Industrial Research Institute, Inc.,* 25–31.

26. Ibid., 25.

CHAPTER 3

DESIGNING AND DEVELOPING A TECHNOLOGY START-UP

Developing an exciting technology and launching a technology company are completely dissimilar activities requiring very different skills and experience. Unfortunately, many scientists and engineers without business experience assume that if they successfully bring an idea from design to prototype, they can just as successfully start a company to launch the product. Nothing could be further from the truth. Starting a technology company entails hiring the right personnel, putting in place systems and processes to support the manufacture, marketing and distribution of the technology product, developing an effective business model (the company must have a way to make money), and managing cash flow, to name just a few of the critical activities. But before any of these activities can be addressed, there is the equally important task of designing a feasible business, which means the entrepreneur must develop a business concept, test it, and prove it in the marketplace. Why? Because technology start-ups are generally very costly and time consuming and, like any other venture, vulnerable to the existing environment in which they will operate. Therefore, knowing in advance what to expect can help an entrepreneur prepare to handle the unexpected.

Technology start-ups are unique in many respects. Their innovativeness, which is the intellectual portion of their technologies, if it can be protected, enables the possibility of licensing or selling the technology without ever converting it to a product[1] (see Chapter 6). The time from concept to market-ready product is typically longer than for other types of ventures so there is considerable pre-founding effort. Moreover, if the technology is novel, the entrepreneur will want to protect it with intellectual property vehicles such as patents, an expensive and time-consuming process with no guarantees (see Chapter 5).

Another distinction of technology start-ups is that often the venture does not offer simply a single product but rather a platform technology that serves as the basis for multiple derivative products, usually requiring strategic partnerships with other companies. In the most disruptive of cases, the technology entrepreneur must be able to develop a new industry infrastructure or significantly modify an existing industry to create the value chain support that is needed to commercialize the technology.[2] Due to costly product development, technology ventures often require angel or venture capital financing and sometimes strategic alliances with established firms that can provide manufacturing and distribution capability.

This chapter will help the reader learn how to take a technology opportunity and test it through a process called *feasibility analysis*. Feasibility analysis is an analytical tool and a process by which an entrepreneur can examine a business concept and establish the conditions under which she is willing to go forward with the concept. The results of feasibility analysis determine:

- Whether there are customers who have a need for the product?
- Whether there is a market sufficiently large enough to grow and sustain a business.
- Whether customers will buy the product from the entrepreneur over a competitor.
- The conditions required for the entrepreneur to feel confident to move into the business planning stage (e.g., an appropriate founding team, a way to deliver the product, required start-up resources, and so on).

Feasibility analysis is an important part of the design process for a new technology business. It makes no sense to start a company without knowing that the company is actually feasible. To determine feasibility first requires the development of a business concept.

DEVELOPING A BUSINESS CONCEPT

Ideas, in and of themselves, have very little value. Value is only created when entrepreneurs take a business idea from idea to opportunity to business concept to feasible business model. A business concept is a formal description of an opportunity that incorporates four elements: the product or service being offered, the customer definition, the value proposition (the benefits to the customer in terms of a solution to a real problem), and the means by which the benefits will be delivered to the customer—the distribution channel. Todd Greene was sold on his invention, a patented razor fashioned like a miniature yellow Jet Ski designed to make it easy to shave the head. He tried to sell his product to the Schick division of Warner-Lambert Co., but they rejected it. Determined to bring his invention to market, Green decided to start his business on the Internet.[3] What would a business concept for this product look like?

Product: A 2.25-inch-long razor called the HeadBlade.

Customers: Men who like to shave their heads.

Benefits: The user gains more control of the blade, solving the problem of nicks and cuts.

Distribution: Direct to the consumer via the Internet (www.headblade.com).

A clear and concise concept statement incorporating these four elements might look like this:

> HeadBlade Co. LLC provides a state-of-the-art way for men to easily and safely shave their heads. Customers control the blade with their own hands, preventing unwanted cuts. HeadBlade is delivered direct to the consumer through the company's Internet site.

The exercise of forcing the concept into a couple of well-constructed sentences is important. Too many entrepreneurs, particularly inventor-entrepreneurs, when asked about their new businesses, begin a long drawn-out discussion of the technology and never get to the business proposition. That's fine if the audience is another scientist or engineer, but if the listener is a potential investor or other interested party, that person will quickly deduce that the entrepreneur hasn't considered the market and business potential of the invention. By devising a concise, two-sentence concept statement, the entrepreneur is prepared, no matter what the situation, to present the business in a way that demonstrates to the listener that the entrepreneur knows what she is talking about. Of course, the concept statement presented here is not yet complete. As it is, it is certainly clear and concise, but it lacks a compelling story, something that grabs people's attention: How is the product going to change the world? How is it going to take away the customer's pain? What is the magnitude of the problem being solved? Without a compelling story, it is unlikely that the listener's attention will be held long enough to become interested in the business.

FEATURES VERSUS BENEFITS

Identifying the features a product offers is easy; identifying the benefits customers are looking for is a far more difficult proposition, but it is one of the most important things to do in preparing an invention for market introduction. Entrepreneurs can understand the concept of customer benefit if they put themselves in the customer's shoes and ask, "What's in it for me?" How is this product solving a real pain that the customer is experiencing? Customers want to know why they should purchase the entrepreneur's product over someone else's and why they should buy it from the entrepreneur as opposed to someone else. If these questions cannot be answered, chances are the customer will not make the purchase.

The easiest way to begin is to look at the benefits associated with the product's features. To use the HeadBlade example, suppose one of the features of the product is the ergonomics of the handle. The tendency is to say that the benefit the product is providing customers is a better handle for shaving heads. Actually, the ergonomically superior handle is really a feature of the product, not a benefit to the customer. The benefit is what's in it for the customer, and that is normally something intangible like convenience, better health, saving time, or reliability (saving time and money). In this case, the benefit is comfort and safety (better control of the blade).

A well-defined business concept will now serve as the focus for the feasibility analysis.

CONDUCTING A FEASIBILITY ANALYSIS

It is not an understatement to say that conducting a feasibility analysis is one of the most important things to do prior to starting a technology business. It forces an entrepreneur to undertake some due diligence on the concept and to think critically about whether the most important questions have been answered before starting the business. In general, the feasibility analysis will answer three broad questions about the potential business:

1. **Are there enough customers to make the business work?** The business may have a great technology and a business concept that seems to solve a real problem, but if the market is too small, there may not be enough profit to make the effort worthwhile. Learning that in advance of starting the business will put an entrepreneur in a better position to make adjustments to the concept to broaden its niche. Or, the entrepreneur may decide that this concept is simply not worth pursuing.

2. **Do the capital requirements to start the business make sense?** The amount of capital and other resources required to start the business must be in line with other businesses in the same industry and must be within the reach of the entrepreneur. Start-ups in the life sciences industries typically have long development cycles due to extensive regulatory requirements. In some cases, it may be several years before any revenues can be generated from a first sale. Understanding how the business will survive until there are sales will be an important finding of an effective feasibility study.

3. **Does the entrepreneur have the right team put together to execute the concept?** Most investors look at the team first and the concept/market second because they know that it takes a superior team to make a business work. The entrepreneur must identify people or businesses that can fill any gaps in the founding team.

Conducting a feasibility analysis is a bit like digging at an archeological site. As the layers of sand and rock are pulled away, more and more about the era that is being studied is learned until the researcher finally discovers a particular bone or skeleton that answers all his questions. The next sections discuss these layers in more detail.

ANALYZING THE INDUSTRY

The industry is a group of businesses that lie within the same value chain and are concerned with the production of goods and services. The industry is the context in which the entrepreneur's business will operate. Whether it is accomplished before the opportunity is recognized or after the development of a business concept, the industry analysis provides enormous insight into how similar businesses work and interact. Moreover, understanding an industry makes it easier to find appropriate strategic partners, customers, money sources, and effective distribution channels. Industries are not static; they are dynamic, living organisms that move through stages much like a person progresses from birth to death. In general, the stages are as follows and are depicted in Figure 3-1:

1. **Birth.**   A new industry emerges, often the result of a disruptive technology, like the semiconductor or the Internet.

2. **Growth and adaptation.**   In the early stages of a new industry, there is a lot of volatility as companies maneuver for the strongest position and strive to be the one to establish the standards for everyone else. At this point, there is a lot of uncertainty and the risk is high. Intellectual property rights give the firms that hold them an advantage—a temporary monopoly in which to introduce their technologies.

3. **Differentiation and competition.**   As more and more firms enter the industry, competition becomes fierce, prices come down, and standards are established.

4. **Shakeout.**   At some point, the competition reaches such a high level of intensity that those firms that can no longer compete exit the industry, leaving only a few major players.

5. **Maturity and decline.**   Every industry eventually reaches a mature state with a few dominant firms. Over time, if these firms do not continue to invest in R & D or if new firms do not find a way to enter the industry and shake it up, the industry will decline.

Every industry's life cycle is a little different. Some industries reach maturity sooner or later than others or go through each stage at different rates.

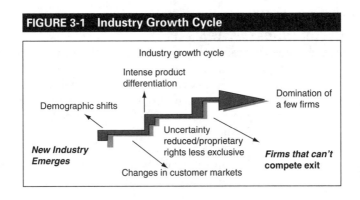

FIGURE 3-1   Industry Growth Cycle

Industry growth cycle

Intense product differentiation

Demographic shifts

Domination of a few firms

New Industry Emerges

Uncertainty reduced/proprietary rights less exclusive

Changes in customer markets

Firms that can't compete exit

Emerging industries are those just coming into being, such as genetic therapy and nanotechnology. In an emerging industry, technological uncertainty exists for a relatively long period of time until the major technology developers enter the industry and determine the technology that will become the standard. Therefore, at the outset, products or processes are not standardized, so production costs are very high. Moreover, companies in an emerging industry may have difficulty obtaining raw materials because supply chains are not well established, which also raises costs. Furthermore, buyers in an emerging industry are generally few in number and are considered early adopters who are willing to pay a premium to experience state-of-the-art technology. Understanding where the industry is in its life cycle is important to the overall business strategy, and, in particular, the new venture's entry strategy.

KEY INDUSTRY INFORMATION

Understanding the life cycle of the industry will help to explain many of the other industry characteristics that could affect the new venture. Some of the critical industry intelligence that should be collected includes:

- Industry demographics: size, life cycle stage, growth rate, opinion leaders, competitive rivalry, supplier power, regulatory requirements.

- Trends and patterns that predict change: What are some of the changes occurring in the industry and what are industry watchers predicting for the future of the industry?

- R&D expenditures: the amount of money spent on R&D speaks to how rapidly new product development is occurring.

- Regulatory requirements: the impact of government regulation on certain types of businesses is critical to designing a product development and launch strategy that is well funded and can survive until the product is approved for sale.

- Intellectual property acquisition: the rate at which companies in the industry file for patents and other intellectual property vehicles speaks to competitive rivalry and also to the percentage of a company's budget that must be devoted to R&D.

Additional industry questions are found in Table 3-1.

A PLAN FOR INDUSTRY ANALYSIS

An effective industry analysis will rely on data from both secondary and primary sources. Secondary sources are those studies and statistics compiled by others, whereas primary sources are the many ways that the entrepreneur collects data, such as interviews, surveys, observation, and so forth. A good way to begin is by identifying an industry's NAICS code. NAICS is the North American Industry Classification System, which permits common standards and statistics across North America and it replaced the Standard Industrial Classification System (SIC). Information about NAICS can be found at the NTIS (U.S. Department of Commerce National Technical Information Service)

TABLE 3-1 Critical Industry Questions	
Is the industry experiencing growth?	Growth can be measured in a number of ways: sales volume, number of employees, units produced, and number of new industry entrants. An industry that is growing provides more opportunities for new entrants.
Where are the opportunities in this industry?	Are there opportunities to innovate in marketing, distribution, or manufacturing? Is the industry ripe for a consolidation play?
How does the industry respond to new technology? How much is spent on R&D?	How quickly does the industry adopt new technology? Does technology play an important role in the competitive strategies of companies in this industry? The amount of R&D investment will also have an impact on the start-up capital needed and determine the product development cycle.
Who are the opinion leaders?	Which firms dominate the industry and what impact do they have on start-ups?
Are young firms surviving in the industry?	If there are no young firms in the industry, it is usually an indication that entry barriers are high and an industry shakeout has already occurred. Many young firms suggest that the industry is still in the early stages of development and growth.
Where is the industry headed?	What will the industry look like in 5 years? What are the trends and patterns of change?
What are the threats to the industry?	Threats from emerging technology that could obsolete current technology should be investigated.
What are the typical gross margins?	The gross margin determines how much room an entrepreneur has to make mistakes and how much of every dollar the company takes in is available to pay overhead and make a profit. An industry that has margins of 3 percent provides very little room for error; therefore, a company must sell in huge volumes to make a reasonable profit.

Web site at www.fedworld.gov. The big improvement with this system is that it now covers 350 new industries, including high-tech areas such as fiber optic cable manufacturing, satellite communications, and computer software reproduction. Also, instead of the familiar four-digit SIC code, it uses a six-digit code that accommodates a larger number of industry sectors. Like the SIC code, the NAICS code can be used to find statistics about size of the industry, sales, number of employees, and so forth.

An effective industry analysis will enable an entrepreneur to determine if the industry will support the entry strategy for the business and provide a healthy environment for its growth and sustainability.

MARKET ANALYSIS

Analyzing the market for a product is arguably the most important task to undertake during feasibility analysis. Identifying the product's primary market, those customers that are most likely to purchase first, is critical to determining an entry strategy. Key questions that should be answered by the research are:

- Who is most likely to be the first customer for this product? In other words, who is in the most pain?
- What does this customer typically buy, how do they buy it, and how do they become aware of it?
- How often does this customer buy, and what is their buying pattern?
- How loyal is the customer to the current solution?
- What are the switching costs to the customer of moving to the new technology?
- How can this company meet the customer's needs?

It is very important to point out that effective market analysis can only be conducted on technology products for which there is an actual market. Analyzing a technology that is too early on the readiness scale—generally a radical or disruptive technology—will not produce satisfactory results because the need for the technology does not yet exist and may need to be created through a long process that is described in the technology adoption-diffusion model in Chapter 10.

Market research can be done very systematically through a four-step process of evaluating information needs, researching secondary sources, talking with customers, and forecasting demand for the product.

EVALUATING INFORMATION NEEDS

Prior to collecting market information, it's important to decide how the data will be used to assess the feasibility of the new venture. This decision will better ensure that the data collected will assist in preparing a profile of the customer and forecasting demand. Additionally, the type of data collected determines the kinds of analyses that can be performed. It is important to do secondary research on the market first to gain a good understanding of its demographics before a plan to test the customer with primary research techniques is developed. This will save the entrepreneur from having to go back to sources for items missed the first time around.

CONDUCTING THE CUSTOMER TEST

An effective customer test will produce several items of value: (1) a realistic definition of the target market, (2) an identification of the first customer (typically the one in the most pain), (3) an estimate of demand, and (4) a sense of how willing the customer is to purchase from the company. To secure this information, a variety of different research techniques can be employed depending on the nature of the business—observation, phone interviews, mail surveys, Internet surveys, structured interviews, and focus groups, among others. Each has advantages and disadvantages, and the choice of technique typically will be based on the entrepreneur's time frame and budget.

Most of the techniques require a representative sample of the population of customers the entrepreneur is interested in. Choosing the sample is a critical part of the process because it determines the validity of the results achieved. For most circumstances, a random sample is appropriate, that is, one where the entrepreneur does not control who is chosen to participate; therefore, the responses are not biased. Because of time and budget constraints, however, most entrepreneurs end up choosing a convenience sample, which simply means that not everyone in the target market has a chance of being selected. Even with a convenience sample, a degree of randomness can be ensured by setting up a system for random selection, for example, choosing every fourth person or using a random number generator to determine which respondents will be selected. What should not be done is to choose a sample consisting only of people known to the entrepreneur. One of the principal reasons for doing a feasibility analysis in the first place is to determine whether a product or service has market potential. Friends and relatives are not always the best source of unbiased information. Moreover, while the surveys and interviews are being conducted, respondents are forming impressions about the product and the entrepreneur's company based on how the entrepreneur deals with them, how she uses the information, and how well she protects their privacy.[4] Table 3-2 displays a comparison of various methods for collecting market research.

CREATING THE CUSTOMER PROFILE

One of the most important outcomes of primary research is an in-depth customer profile that describes the first customer, whether it is a consumer or another business, in great detail. This profile will form the basis for future marketing efforts, as well as identify specific customers who should review the product in the final assessment of technology feasibility. The customer profile typically contains the following information: age, income level, education, buying habits (when, where, how much), where customers find products like the entrepreneur's, and in what manner they would like to purchase the product. Of course, this information will vary depending on whether the customer is a consumer or a business. For a business customer, characteristics such as the type of business and its size, primary customers, location, revenues, and so forth are appropriate.

FORECASTING DEMAND

If one of the most important tasks is testing the customer to ascertain demand for the product, one of the most difficult tasks is actually forecasting how much product will be sold over time. This task is particularly challenging if the product is a breakthrough technology that has not existed in the market previously. In that case, there are no real benchmarks to go by and the entrepreneur will have to extrapolate data from a similar technology. For example, the adoption rate for compact discs was extrapolated from the adoption patterns for cassette tapes. Most entrepreneurs do

TABLE 3-2 A Comparison of Market Research Techniques		
Research Technique	*Advantages*	*Disadvantages*
Structured Interviews: • One-on-one interviews • Common questions asked across several interviewees	• Opportunity for discussion and clarification • Ability to observe nonverbal communication • Highest response rate	• Time consuming and more expensive
Focus Groups: • Several people interviewed simultaneously • Can also be done through Internet user groups	• Opportunity for discussion and clarification • Ability to observe nonverbal communication • High response rate	• Requires an experienced facilitator • More expensive
Mail and Phone Surveys: • Structured questionnaire	• Can reach broad market relatively efficiently	• Low response rate • Can be expensive • Phone surveys are time consuming and prone to surveyor bias • Mail surveys do not provide opportunity for clarification • No nonverbal feedback
Internet Surveys: • Designed and implemented on sites such as surveymonkey.com • Geared toward customers who are Internet users	• Reach a global market of people or can be targeted by pushing respondents to the site • Higher response rate than mail or phone surveys • Less costly than mail or phone	• Same problems as mail and phone surveys

their own research to come up with numbers from which to derive a forecast. This is at once advantageous and disadvantageous—disadvantageous because the entrepreneur may not have the skills required to do the job effectively, and advantageous because the process will provide a better understanding of the target market and its needs.

Perhaps the best way to arrive at a demand figure is to triangulate from three different points of view: (1) the entrepreneur's own knowledge and customer test information, (2) analogous products, and (3) industry experts. By conducting the customer test, the entrepreneur gains a vital piece of the triangle—the customer's point of view. In addition, looking at the sales of a similar product can provide clues as to what results the product might achieve. Studying adoption rates of technology in a particular industry is an excellent way to refine the demand estimate and also develop a realistic timeline so that forecasts are as close to what will actually happen as possible.

Interviewing people who work in the industry in which the new business will reside is another great way to zero in on demand. The numbers derived from distributors, manufacturers, retailers, suppliers, and the like will be some of the most realistic numbers available as they will likely be based on broad-based experience as opposed to the more anecdotal demand estimates secured from customers.

Sometimes, the only way to get really accurate estimates of demand is to actually go into limited production in a test market where it is easier to control production volume, marketing, and distribution. If it is a representative test market, it will be an excellent gauge of what numbers might be achieved in a broader market. Many companies use a benchmark figure of 50 percent. If customer preference for the product over substitutes is less than 50 percent, the product may be in trouble. Of course, this assumes that customers have been correctly targeted.

ANALYZING THE COMPETITION

One of the most important aspects of feasibility analysis is to study the competition. Learning their strategies and goals, how they have positioned themselves in the market, and what motivates them will put the entrepreneur in a better position to find gaps that can be leveraged. Unfortunately, entrepreneurs routinely underestimate the impact of competition on their businesses and they also underestimate the length of time and resources they will need to establish a foothold in their market niche. Entrepreneurs should understand that they face two types of competition: good and bad. As simplistic as that sounds, it is true. Good competition is companies that serve their customers poorly and therefore tend to have many complaints filed at the Better Business Bureau where they do business. By contrast, bad competition is companies that are doing everything right so it becomes more difficult to differentiate from them. Bad competition typically has deep resources and skills that enable these companies to potentially move into the entrepreneur's competitive space whether or not they are currently there.

Finding competitive intelligence on a company is no easy task. An Internet search of the competitors' Web sites, examples of their advertising, and a look at their facilities is a good place to start because it will reveal something about who their customers are and what their stated goals are. If any competitors are public companies, financial information such as revenues, operating expenses, and the like can be found in the companies' annual reports and quarterly Securities and Exchange Commission (SEC) filings. In addition, data on competitors' current market strategies, management style and culture, pricing strategy, customer mix, and promotional mix is important information.

Here are some suggestions for gathering competitive information:

- If possible, visit competitors' physical sites to talk to employees and customers and to observe what goes on.
- Purchase competitors' products to understand their features and benefits. The purchase transaction will also provide valuable information about how they treat their customers.

- Study public companies that serve as benchmarks of excellence in the industry. Three valuable sources are Hoover's Online (www.hoovers.com), the U.S. Securities and Exchange Commission (www.sec.gov), and One-Source (www.onesource.com).

- Find trade associations dedicated to the industry. They are the industry watchers and can provide a wealth of valuable information, as can trade shows.

ANALYZING PRODUCT/SERVICE FEASIBILITY

During the process of determining market feasibility, it is important to also figure out if the technology being proposed or in development is feasible from a technical standpoint. Two of the biggest problems that product developers face are incorrect product definitions and market changes.[5] Often, a product that met customers' needs in the early stages of design was not correctly translated into a final product so its features and benefits fall short of customer desires. Moreover, the market does not stand still while the developer is in the product development phase; therefore, the developer must continually scan the market for potential shifts in needs and preferences, as well as for competitors that may have entered the market.

During this phase of feasibility analysis, it is important to identify product development milestones and requirements to move from concept design to primitive prototype to production quality product. Product development is the subject of Chapter 8. It is also vital to consider the role of intellectual property protections. These are discussed in Chapter 5.

ANALYZING THE MANAGEMENT TEAM

More often than not, the founding teams of technology ventures consist of scientists and engineers. This is fine during the early stages of product development, but as the team gets closer to commercialization, it is important to fill in the gaps in business knowledge. Investors look first at the management team and then at the technology, because it is the founding team that will execute the business concept. If the team cannot execute, the business will never get off the ground. One of the reasons that so many dot-com companies failed is that their teams had no expertise or experience in what they were doing. All they had was a compelling idea with no realistic execution plan. As part of the feasibility analysis, the entrepreneur will determine the knowledge gaps in the start-up team and develop a plan to fill those gaps. For more details about team building in high-tech ventures, see Chapter 4.

BUILDING AN EFFECTIVE BUSINESS MODEL AND ASSESSING CAPITAL REQUIREMENTS

High-tech ventures have several commercialization alternatives for their technologies, and the business model created will be a function of the alternative chosen. To complete the overview of feasibility analysis, the business model alternatives will be discussed in brief here and in more detail in the chapters in Part IV of this book.

In general, a business model is a plan for how the business will create and capture value from the customer — in simple terms, how the business will make money. For most incremental innovations, business models are fairly well established by the relevant industry. Radical innovations present a more difficult case because typically no established business model exists that will fit the product. For example, in the 1990s, Monsanto engineered a tomato that was resistant to insect strains that were threatening tomato crops. Monsanto had been in the textiles and specialty chemicals business since the 1970s and, therefore, did not know how to generate income from this breakthrough technology. It was also faced with the reality that this new genetically engineered tomato might damage its successful pesticide business. Monsanto finally decided to modify its new tomato seed so that it would only reproduce once; as a result, farmers would need to repurchase seeds every two years, essentially creating a consumable product and a much longer revenue stream.[6] This is an example of how a business model can dictate the direction of technology development. By its very nature, a radical innovation disrupts current ways of doing things and requires that the innovators create new value chains and business models to capture this new value.

Depending on the type of technology developed, an entrepreneur has four basic alternatives for commercialization:

- Licensing the technology to third parties.
- Selling the technology outright to a third party.
- Partnering with a larger company and sharing the technology.
- Starting a new venture.

These alternatives are considered in depth in Chapter 9. After deciding on a business model, it is time to consider the capital needs that will be required to execute this model and test it in the market. No matter how many financial analyses the entrepreneur conducts, it all comes down to cash. Income statements and balance sheets can make a company look successful on paper, but cash pays the bills and funds the growth of the business. The first three commercialization alternatives require financing to get through product development and marketing of the technology to a licensee, a buyer, or a strategic partner. Deciding to start a business to launch a product requires additional start-up and operating capital to take the business to a positive cash flow. The entrepreneur will need to identify the key revenue and cost drivers for the business, understand margins, determine the impact of purchase patterns on cash flow, and develop a strategy to keep capital expenditures low at launch. For the feasibility analysis, a sales forecast based on the business model will be calculated as well as a timeline for the projected launch of the product. A resource needs assessment that looks at total capital requirements will also be needed. This topic will be taken up in depth in Chapter 8.

IS THIS BUSINESS FEASIBLE?

At each stage of the analysis, it is important that the entrepreneur draw conclusions about feasibility to that point. For example, upon completion of the industry analysis, it is possible to say whether the industry has an environment that would enable the new venture to be successful and grow. Market research will tell the entrepreneur whether there is a market of sufficient size and in enough pain that the new venture can enter and capture a market niche to establish itself and begin to grow. The analysis of the management team should provide a conclusion as to whether this team has the expertise and experience to launch this type of venture. Finally, the financial analysis will determine whether funding can be raised to support the venture and whether revenues can be generated within a reasonable period of time for this type of business. By the completion of the feasibility analysis, it should be clear to the entrepreneur whether this business has potential or not.

For these reasons, the feasibility analysis is usually considered to be an internal document that helps to reduce some of the risk of commercialization and gives the founding team the confidence they need to proceed. If there is a fatal flaw or deal killer in the concept, generally the entrepreneur will find it very early in the feasibility process if enough time is spent in the industry and market talking to as many people as possible. Inventor-entrepreneurs who get surprised by fatal flaws at the point of launch are generally those who held their concepts too close to their vests, were afraid to talk to people about them, and who did not do their market research. That is why it is so important to begin the feasibility analysis prior to product development, to find those major challenges to the concept before a lot of time and money has been invested in a product for which there is no market or not a big enough market to make the effort worthwhile. Furthermore, a well-conceived feasibility study can be the basis for securing first-round funding. Table 3-3 presents an outline for a feasibility document that can be prepared for investors and other interested parties.

TABLE 3-3 Feasibility Analysis Outline

EXECUTIVE SUMMARY

Include the most important points from all sections of the feasibility study in two pages.

TITLE PAGE

Name of company, feasibility study title, founding team members' names.

TABLE OF CONTENTS

THE BUSINESS CONCEPT

What is the business? Who is the customer? What is the value proposition or benefit(s) being delivered to the customer? How will the benefit be delivered (distribution)? Spin-offs and potential for growth.

TABLE 3-3 *Continued*

INDUSTRY/MARKET ANALYSIS

Industry and market demographics, customer profile, demand analysis, competitor analysis and competitive advantages, entry strategy.

PRODUCT/SERVICE DEVELOPMENT PLAN

Detailed description and unique features of product/service, current status of product development, milestones and time line for product development, intellectual property protection.

FOUNDING TEAM

Qualifications, how critical tasks will be covered, and gap analysis.

FINANCIAL PLAN

Cash needs assessment, cash flow statement, income statement, break-even analysis, assumptions.

TIME LINE TO LAUNCH

Tasks that will need to be accomplished up to the date of launch in the order of their completion.

ENDNOTES

APPENDICES (A, B, C, ETC.)

Questionnaires, maps, forms, resumes, and so on.

Summary

Discovering an opportunity is an exciting process; developing a feasible concept for a business is a much more difficult task. How effectively an entrepreneur defines the customer, the value of the benefits that will be delivered to that customer, and the distribution channel that will be used to reach the customer will determine the success of the commercialization effort. To effectively judge the feasibility of a business concept, the entrepreneur will undertake a variety of analyses, beginning in the broadest sense with the industry. Using both primary and secondary research techniques, the entrepreneur will study the nature of the industry, its place in the industry life cycle, the competitive landscape, trends, and the direction in which the industry is moving. From there, the entrepreneur will move to looking at the market in which the primary customer for the technology will be found. It is the customer who will provide the vital information as to whether there is a market for the product, how big that market is, and whether customers will buy from the entrepreneur's company. It is also from customer information that the entrepreneur can begin to look in depth at the applications of the technology and the features and benefits most valued by customers. The founding team is arguably the most important thing to investors. If the new venture does not have an experienced and talented founding team, it will not be able to successfully execute the business concept. Finding creative ways to fill the gaps in expertise will be one of the important analyses to do in preparing to commercialize the technology. Finally, an appropriate business model should be developed and the start-up costs for this venture calculated. When the results of all the analyses are in, the entrepreneur will have a clear picture of the conditions necessary to make this venture a success and will be able to go forward confident that he has reduced a significant portion of the risk of commercialization.

Discussion Questions

1. Why is it important to focus the business concept?
2. You have developed a new software product that more effectively performs natural language searches through databases using voice recognition technology. What would your plan be for testing this product with customers?
3. Based on the product in question 2, what would you want to know about the industry to feel confident that you could enter it with a new venture? Be specific.
4. What are some ways that you can fill in the gaps in expertise and experience in a founding team?
5. Suppose you determine that there are not enough customers for a new product you're considering. What could you do, short of abandoning the product?

CASE STUDY

Start-ups Begin with a Vision—and This Is a Big One

Elon Musk knows something about starting a technology company. By the age of 27, he had founded and sold the legendary PayPal, an online payment processor, for $1.5 billion to eBay (an equally legendary entrepreneurial company) and Zip2, an Internet media company, for $307 million. Although he certainly didn't have to work again, that would not be like this physicist-turned entrepreneur who went on to found electric carmaker Tesla Motors, solar panel company SolarCity, and SpaceX, an aerospace company that plans to take astronauts to the International Space Station by 2011 and put satelites into orbit for about 25 percent of current cost, with the ultimate goal of ferrying people to colonize Mars.

Unlike most technology companies that simply improve on what already exists, Musk has chosen to change the world with his companies, and although he has a long way to go to achieve that lofty goal, his companies have made significant progress in the right direction. In December 2007, Tesla Motors was set to introduce its first vehicle to the market, having sold 600 of them at $98,000 each before they were market ready. SolarCity in its first year became one of the largest installers of solar panels for homes, with a business model similar to Dell Computers. And in March 2007, his unmanned rocket flew 180 miles above the Earth, farther than any privately built rocket had gone.

(continued)

(continued)

With customers such as NASA and the Malaysian government, SpaceX was on track to become profitable at the end of 2007.

A vision to ferry people to Mars is serious business for Musk, who believes that colonizing other planets is right up there with the evolution of life from the oceans to land. What differentiates Musk from other legendary entrepreneurs, such as Google founders Sergey Brin and Larry Page and Netscape founder Marc Andreesson, is that the latter's ventures were based on concepts that were essentially incremental improvements within growing trends. Musk, on the other hand, goes for the disruptive concept that has the potential to change the world.

Musk's first big venture, Zip2, was born from a realization in 1995 that the Internet was the next disruptive technology that would change society in significant ways. Partnering with Navteq, a digital-mapping company, he purchased a business directory and by writing some software code, he was able to create what was essentially the first "yellow pages" on the Internet. Musk and his partners pitched their concept to Silicon Valley venture capital firm Mohr Davidow Ventures, and managed to secure $3 million in funding. Later funding of about $38 million came from newspaper conglomerates Knight Ridder, Hearst, and the New York Times Company, all of which eventually dominated the board of directors seats. By 1998, Musk's share of the company had been diluted to 7 percent and he was frustrated with the direction of the company.

When the company was sold that year to Compaq, Musk took home $22 million, but believed that the company had not fulfilled his vision. He immediately began working on a new concept in the financial services area fueled by a $25 million investment from Sequoia Capital. His goal was to enable the ability to make payments using e-mail. In 1999, he merged his company, X com, with Confinity, a competitor. That company had developed a product called PayPal. At the merger, Musk became the CEO and the company retained the X com name. The first several months were rocky at best due to the clash of egos that so often occurs with companies that merge. In the fall of 2000, while Musk was traveling in search of investment capital, his two partners convinced the board to replace Musk as CEO with Confinity cofounder Peter Thiel and to name the company PayPal. Although the company went on to a highly successful IPO that gave Musk the capital to start his current ventures, he was yet again discouraged that PayPal never went beyond a trendy feature.

Managing multiple start-ups means that Musk must be involved on a daily basis with all his companies, issuing directives and making sure that they're on track to achieve the vision he holds for each of them. The common trait across these latest companies is disruption, changing the game. They are highly risky ventures in three different industries and many challenges lie ahead before Musk can claim victory, but he is finally going beyond incremental innovation. He knows how to think big.

Sources: Chafkin, M. (December 2007). "Entrepreneur of the Year: Elon Musk," *Inc Magazine;* Hoffman, C. (May 22, 2007). "Elon Musk Is Betting His Fortune on a Mission Beyond Earth's Orbit," *Wired Magazine* 15(6); "Rocket Man," (March 22, 2007). *The Economist.com,* http://www.economist.com/people/displaystory.cfm?story_id=8885970.

Endnotes

1. Hellman, T., & Puri, M. (2000). "The Interaction Between Product Market and Financing Strategy: The Role of Venture Capital," *The Review of Financial Studies* 13(4): 959–984.
2. Utterback, J.M., & Suarez, F.F. (1993). "Innovation, Competition and Industry Structure," *Research Policy* 22: 1–21.
3. Hofman, M. (March 1, 2000). "The Razor's Edge," *Inc.*, www.inc.com.
4. Pruden, P.R., & Vavra, T.G. (Summer 2000). "Customer Research, Not Marketing Research," *Marketing Research* 12(2): 14–19..
5. Cooper, R.G. (2001). *Winning at New Products,* 3rd Ed. (Cambridge, MA: Perseus Publishing), pp. 50–53.
6. Leifer, R., Mcdermott, C.M., O'Connor, G.C., Peters, L.S., Rice, M., & Veryzer, R.W. (2000). *Radical Innovation* (Boston: Harvard Business School Press), pp. 94–95.

CHAPTER 4

BUILDING AN EFFECTIVE TEAM

The days of the lone entrepreneur starting a company with nothing but his or her own resources and experience are, in many respects, a thing of the past—at least for technology start-ups. It is rare today that a single person possesses the breadth and depth of expertise and experience required to launch a successful technology venture in a complex global economy. A collective effort at start-up with a team displaying diverse expertise and experience will tend to be more innovative and better able to create a niche in the market in which to successfully enter.[1] In fact, research has found that companies founded by heterogeneous teams perform at a higher level than those founded by individuals.[2] These teams can consist of the founders, employees, and strategic partners. The reason for higher performance is that teams provide a number of important advantages to a start-up.

- When the team possesses expertise in the major functional processes of the business—marketing, finance, and operations—it can move farther along the growth path before it needs to add people.

- With a team, all the activities, risks, and decisions of a start-up can be shared, making it less likely that the new venture will be abandoned when it faces challenges.

- A founding team with the appropriate skills and experience will be more credible in the eyes of investors, bankers, strategic partners, and others.

- The decision-making ability of the team will be enhanced by a diversity of opinions as long as the team shares a common vision for the company.[3] Furthermore, a heterogeneous team will tend to make better decisions with regard to innovation strategies and tactics.[4]

Despite the importance of the teams, however, a significant body of research also suggests that there is a need and role for a lead entrepreneur. It has been argued that most teams have a lead entrepreneur who holds the vision and can foresee the strategy that will take the company to its highest possibilities.[5] Recent research also supports the finding that lead entrepreneurs typically score higher on entrepreneurial vision and self-efficacy than do other members of the founding team but that they are not necessarily more skilled in recognizing opportunity or carrying out other functions of the organization.[6]

Entrepreneurs are leaders, and one of the unique characteristics of many leaders is that they have the ability to consider opposing ideas simultaneously and then creatively find a way to develop a new idea that represents the best of both and is, in fact, a superior solution.[7] This process is known as integrative thinking and, unfortunately, it is often ignored in favor of quickly attempting to eliminate solutions until the right one is achieved. Integrative thinking is effectively exemplified by entrepreneur Bob Young, founder of Red Hat, the open-source software company that became a huge success, taking market share from software giants like Microsoft. Young looked at the two standard business models employed at the time for operating systems—(1) nearly free software where customers bought the application and the source code and (2) the traditional proprietary software model used by companies such as Oracle and Microsoft where only the operating software was sold—and decided to do something very different. He essentially combined the low price of the free software model with the service associated with proprietary software by allowing free downloads of the software from the Internet and helping customers manage their upgrades and improvements through an open source platform. With this integrative solution, he was able to sell the Linux operating system to corporations.[8] In 1999, Red Hat went public and by 2000, it had captured 50 percent of the global market for servers, a real testament to not settling for an either/or choice. Entrepreneurial teams that employ integrative thinking have a higher likelihood of producing these types of innovative solutions. This chapter explores the founding management team as a critical resource for a start-up technology firm.

FORMING AN EFFECTIVE FOUNDING TEAM

Apart from the fact that investors look to the founding team as perhaps the most critical factor in their decision to fund a venture, the founding team and its capabilities with respect to the market and the technology, or lack of them, will have an important impact on the new venture's success over time.[9] Managerial capabilities are those related to skills, knowledge, and experience needed to solve the very complex and ambiguous problems facing a start-up.[10] Technical competencies refer to the team's "ability to apply scientific and technical knowledge to develop and improve products and processes."[11] In general, teams with the highest levels of technical competence produce radical or disruptive technologies that obsolete existing technologies and take the field on a new path. That was the case for Elon Musk and his partners (see Chapter 3). In addition to technical competency, managerial resources at start-up have been found to be critical not only to performance but to the strategy that a technology firm chooses to employ.

THE PERILS OF TECHNOLOGY FOUNDING TEAMS

Management guru Peter Drucker put engineers, scientists, financial analysts, accountants, and lawyers into a category he called "knowledge workers," which he defined as 'people who get paid for putting to work what one learns in school rather than for their physical strength or manual skill."[12] Knowledge workers are the result of years of belief that linear thinking and logic are the only critical skills required for commercializing technology. However, in a global world where business is more complex and operates at faster speeds and where uncertainty is as certain as death and taxes, researchers are now finding that the right-brain skills—creativity, being able to view the big picture, developing strategic relationships, and looking beyond the obvious—are equally required for success, in fact, perhaps more so than even logic. The ability to take an enormous amount of information and make sense out of it so that it can inform new venture strategy is a talent that requires accessing the right hemisphere of the brain, which controls activities that do not as easily lend themselves to a defined process. Left hemisphere activities—sequence, acquiring facts, and analysis—by contrast, involve more defined processes that can be learned and replicated, and these activities have traditionally been the domain of scientists and engineers. Consequently, when technology entrepreneurs seek business partners, there is often an initial clash of cultures. The mindset of scientists and engineers versus the mindset of business people is discussed more fully in Chapter 1.

Stories abound of scientist-entrepreneurs whose linear thinking, strong ego, and belief in their inventions or discoveries makes them impossibly hard to work with. Frequently with no real experience with markets, they exist in a "field of dreams" mentality or type of cognitive bias, believing that the world will appreciate their discovery and flock to purchase it because its benefits are so obvious. They often lack complementary resources such as manufacturing and connections with potential customers and strategic partners to commercialize their inventions. So strong is their sense of destiny that they often resist taking needed advice from business people. Their need for control (a common trait among entrepreneurs of all types) often leads to an inability to collaborate or share control. For these reasons, among many others, venture capitalists frequently choose not to invest in the biosciences because working effectively with the management team is critical to their success, and research has shown that in new ventures where a scientist-inventor holds the position of CEO, the failure rate can be high.[13]

Another characteristic of technology entrepreneurs is that they tend to cling to their technologies longer despite any declining prospects for commercial success. It appears that as long as the marginal benefit of continuing development exceeds the marginal cost, these entrepreneurs can justify a longer time frame to bring a technology to market.[14] In fact, technology entrepreneurs, who frequently receive their early development funding from governmental sources such as Small Business Innovative Research (SBIR) are more likely to continue with development despite eventual failure because the marginal cost is so low.

As with any type of new venture, a diverse team that captures knowledge, expertise, and experience from the technical and the market sides will increase the chances for a successful launch.

CHARACTERISTICS OF EFFECTIVE TEAMS

Figure 4-1 depicts an example of some of the founding and extended teams that entrepreneurs use to launch new companies. In general, effective start-up teams for technology ventures have the following characteristics:

- Team members share a common vision for the company and are all passionate about creating a successful business.

- Teams that have successfully worked together previously, whether that was in a large company or in another start-up venture, often have an advantage

FIGURE 4-1   The Entrepreneur's Network

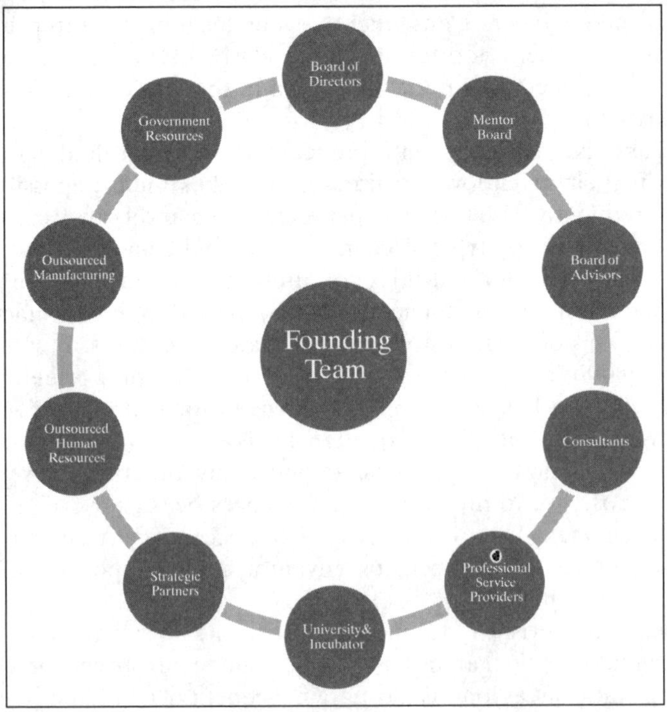

because they have already overcome any collaboration problems common with new teams.

- At least one member of the team has experience in the industry in which the new venture will operate.
- The team has a network of industry contacts it can call upon to help the business grow.
- The team has expertise in the basic functional areas of the business: technology, finance, marketing, and operations.
- The team is dedicated to the start-up and is in a position to endure any financial constraints.

These characteristics reflect an ideal team, but often with technology ventures the founding team is heavy on technical expertise and weak on the business side. If the entrepreneur needs outside capital to launch, investors will likely insist on bringing in professional management to round out the team's capabilities and insure that the company functions effectively.

Many ventures today begin with global customers, so in that case, another important skill needed by the founding team is international experience or an international partner.[15] Research has found that success in international venturing is directly related to the extent to which the founding team has traveled or worked abroad and whether they speak any foreign languages.[16]

As a vital characteristic of a successful team, the ability to leverage social networks to tap expertise and resources to fill any gaps in the team is essential and is considered in the next section.

EXTENDING THE FOUNDING TEAM

Entrepreneurs are never really alone during start-up; rather they are "embedded in a social context, channeled and facilitated, or constrained and inhibited, by their positions in social networks."[17] Entrepreneurs' social networks enable them to identify customers, acquire resources, fill gaps in the management team, grow their companies, and sell them.[18] These extended networks form a web of hubs and spokes with the start-up firm linking to gateway people and firms who open doors to new communities of customers and business partners.

Science and engineering-based firms in particular require the connection to other firms, resources, and knowledge to be able to operate their businesses.[19] The presence of technology incubators, industrial and research parks, and regional or industry clustering all speak to this need of technology firms to associate with other like firms. Recent research has validated the importance of the connections that technology entrepreneurs make, finding that those with a high density of technology connectivity (a high number of technological relationships) were more inventive and ultimately performed better.[20] For companies that have spun out of large organizations, a strong link to the parent company is also an indicator of higher performance. In addition, new ventures that form strong relationships with established companies to access market-based resources also tend to fare better with respect to performance.

PROFESSIONAL ADVISORS

New ventures rarely have all the resources they need to be effective, so the ability to tap into various professional advisors as needed is essential and they become a critical part of the team. Professional advisors include attorneys, accountants, bankers, investors, consultants, and insurance experts, to name a few. If they serve on an advisory board for the company, the entrepreneur can often take advantage of their expertise without having to pay for it. In other cases, they can negotiate to keep payments low until the company is generating revenues. Many professionals are willing to work under such terms if the potential upside is high—securing a new client with a very successful business. A critical factor in selecting advisors is their experience working with start-up technology companies. Therefore, the best way to find appropriate professional advisors is through referrals from other entrepreneurs who have worked with them.

At start-up entrepreneurs often ask others with entrepreneurial experience to serve on the advisory board to provide guidance in the early stages, particularly if the board of directors consists only of the founding team. Examples of these types of advisors include university faculty, consultants, industry people, and entrepreneurs. The board of advisors is critical in providing independent, objective views to the entrepreneurial team that is too close to the business to see everything they should see.

BOARDS OF DIRECTORS

A board of directors is a group of 7–10 members who serve a very valuable service to a technology company. In addition to filling gaps in the founding team's expertise, the board assists in establishing corporate strategy and philosophy. Although they don't have the power to act on behalf of the company in terms of signing contracts and the like, they do elect the officers of the corporation who are responsible for the daily activities of the company. The size of the board is typically determined by the complexity of the company, but research has found that a very large board does not encourage active participation by all the members.[21] Moreover, large boards are more vulnerable to developing factions that could undermine the entrepreneur's efforts. In one case, an entrepreneur actually ended up selling her private company because a majority of the board had decided to take the company in a direction that she didn't want to go. Since many of these board members held equity positions in the company, the only solution was to sell.

The legal form of the business determines the need for a board of directors. In general, the corporate form requires a board of directors, but in the early stages of a new company, that board can (and usually does) consist only of the founders. This is because today boards of directors incur increasing risk from lawsuits, whether warranted or not, so they usually require that the company carry directors and officers insurance to indemnify them. This insurance, in addition to fees paid to directors for meetings and reimbursement of expenses, can mount up to more than a start-up can comfortably afford to spend. That is why so many start-ups have inside boards of directors and an outside advisory board that is not subject to the same level of risk.[22]

However, as a company grows and takes on investment capital, having a board of directors with outsider representation is critical. In fact, investors will often demand a seat on the board of directors from the very beginning so they can help guide the direction of the company. Private company boards are distinguished from public company boards in that their members serve at the pleasure of the entrepreneur, who very often owns the majority of the company stock. By contrast, public board members have legitimate power to oversee the activities of the company on behalf of its many shareholders. Figure 4-2 depicts the various stages of a technology company's growth and the roles that its board members can fill at each stage.

AVOIDING TRAPS WHEN FORMING BOARDS AND MANAGEMENT TEAMS

More than perhaps anything else, entrepreneurs must appoint people to their boards who bring something valuable to the table. Friends and family may gladly offer their services, but they may not be the most objective or qualified source of opinion for an entrepreneur to rely on. When investors look at the founding team

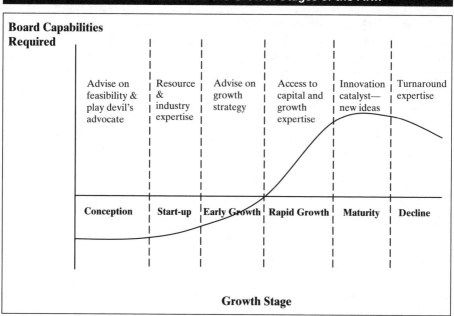

FIGURE 4-2 Boards of Directors and the Growth Stages of the Firm

Board Capabilities Required

Conception	Start-up	Early Growth	Rapid Growth	Maturity	Decline
Advise on feasibility & play devil's advocate	Resource & industry expertise	Advise on growth strategy	Access to capital and growth expertise	Innovation catalyst— new ideas	Turnaround expertise

Growth Stage

and the board of directors, they don't want to see a lot of friends and family that make the business appear less professional than it might be.

Another mistake that entrepreneurs frequently make when forming their founding team stems from the need to conserve capital resources. It involves giving team members stock in lieu of salary or in lieu of fees in the case of independent contractors, such as consultants. Once a person holds stock in the company, it is often difficult to let that time so that the individual receiving it has a chance to prove herself. In any case, one way for entrepreneurs to protect themselves and their companies is through the use of a—buy-sell agreement, which prevents the shareholder from selling her interests in the company to an outsider without the consent of the other equity stakeholders. The—buy-sell agreement also spells out how the departing owner's interest is to be valued. Cross-purchase and stock redemption are the two basic types of—buy-sell agreements. With a cross-purchase agreement, each owner buys an insurance policy on the other owners and is named as a beneficiary. Then if an owner leaves the company or dies, the interest is sold back to the remaining owners. With a stock redemption agreement, the corporation purchases the insurance policies on all the owners and upon their death or departure from the company, it purchases the owner's interest with the proceeds of the insurance policy.

USING INDEPENDENT CONTRACTORS

With limited resources, new technology ventures typically avoid hiring permanent employees as long as possible because employees are generally the largest expense of any business. Consequently, most start-ups outsource at least some of their functions to independent contractors. Independent contractors are businesses that are hired to perform a specific task for the entrepreneur and are responsible to the entrepreneur for the results of their work but not the methods they use to accomplish the task. Typical business functions that are outsourced include IT services, payroll and human resources, and manufacturing and logistics. Some entrepreneurs have gone so far as to use employee leasing firms so they don't have to deal with human resources issues such as healthcare and other benefits.

Although it is widely believed that it costs less to use independent contractors than to have employees, there are actually hidden costs to using them that should be taken into account.

- The cost of finding the appropriate independent contractor.
- Bringing the independent contractor up to speed on the company.
- Managing the relationship with the independent contractor.
- The cost of eventually bringing the activity in-house.

Typically, entrepreneurs will retain core activities or activities that are ideosyncratic to the business in-house. The most frequent exception is manufacturing, which is a very costly undertaking for a new business in terms of plant, equipment, and labor.

The IRS rules regarding independent contractors are very strict, so entrepreneurs should do the following:

- Become familiar with the IRS 20-point test for classifying workers (http://www.fedexaminer.com/FedEx/view-436.html).
- Seek the advice of a qualified attorney.
- Draw up a contract with each independent contractor spelling out all the particulars of the agreement.
- Verify that the independent contractor carries workers' compensation insurance and possesses the appropriate licenses.

OTHER RESOURCES TO EXTEND THE TEAM

Entrepreneurs tap into a number of resources to find the talent and capabilities they lack as depicted in Figure 4-1. Today more than ever before companies have sprung up to provide services to entrepreneurs that enable them to focus on what they do best and not spend time learning new capabilities in the start-up phase. Some examples include employee leasing and human resources services companies; manufacturing, distribution, and logistics companies; and sales agencies.

Resources are also available through governmental and nonprofit agencies such as the Small Business Administration, the Service Core of Retired Executives (SCORE), and the SBIR programs. Many of these programs offer advice and other resources free of charge.

THE MOVE FROM START-UP TO RAPID GROWTH

Rapid growth, the goal that most technology entrepreneurs are seeking, is at once exciting and terrifying because growth is not a simple matter of doing more of what is currently being done. Growth brings on a level of complexity that the company has not heretofore been accustomed to.[23] The entrepreneur and the founding team, who brought the company to this felicitous moment, are often at a loss to understand how to deal with the newfound complexity. Moreover, they cannot find the time to learn the skills required to successfully navigate the challenges brought on by sudden growth. Until rapid growth, entrepreneurs typically develop systems and procedures as needed. During rapid growth there is no time for anything but meeting demand.

The decision about when to bring in professional management to take over for the founding team is a difficult one. If an entrepreneur brings in high-priced management too soon, resources will be wasted. Too late and opportunities could be lost. Entrepreneurs often believe that the skills that successfully launched the venture will certainly hold them in good stead during rapid growth, but usually that is not the case. The skills required to conceptualize and launch a new venture are very different from skills required to manage a venture through rapid growth.

Research has found that corporate governance affects performance and the ability of a young venture to survive over time.[24] Technology start-ups that move from a limited resource base to an initial public offering experience a seismic shift from a team-based entrepreneurial firm to a professionally managed firm where financial investment resides more in people and systems than in products. This is because rapid growth requires systems, controls, and logistics that enable the firm to meet an increasing level of demand from customers. So in the life cycle of the technology firm, at the earliest stages of the venture, management is focused on survival, innovation, and resource acquisition. At the rapid growth stage, by contrast, management shifts its focus to "internal efficiencies."[25] And that is where professional management plays a role, freeing up the entrepreneur to concentrate on the future of the company, designing strategies to realize the vision. This is important because too often entrepreneurs who stay in the CEO position in their companies are so busy solving problems that they have no time to prepare their company to move to the next level of growth. Assuming the task of developing a strategic orientation for the company is, without a doubt, one of the most critical activities an entrepreneur takes on at this stage. Without the unique view to the future that entrepreneurs have, a company can stagnate. Entrepreneurs are opportunity seekers and their ability to discover emerging opportunities that can take the company into new growth areas is vital for sustainability.

Nevertheless, the shift to professional management and systems and controls is never a smooth one because the entrepreneur, who was used to dealing with all the issues that arose in the company, is now asked to step aside in favor of someone with more management or operations experience. Entrepreneurs often dislike details and procedures because they tend to prefer more informal and flexible environments. At the same time, as the business grows under professional management, layers of management develop so that people who normally went direct to the entrepreneur now must go through channels. Furthermore, professional management may also experience culture shock if they came from large, established organizations where plans, organization, and hierarchies were the norm. They typically are not the ones who will direct resources toward new opportunities. It is the entrepreneur who will do that. Some entrepreneurs have succeeded in instilling an entrepreneurial spirit throughout their organizations to help foster continuing innovation. For example, early in the development of his company Dr. Fred Sancilio, founder of AAIPharma Inc., "a global provider of product development and support services to the pharmceutical, biotech, and medical device industries," (http://www.aaipharma.com/aaiportal/) set up an incubator to encourage a constant stream of new ideas and to create an entrepreneurial culture in his company.[26]

Building a team that can execute an entrepreneur's vision is one of the most vital tasks that an entrepreneur undertakes. If the founder is a scientist or an engineer, bringing on business expertise will insure that the company can operationalize the founder's vision and support the strategic direction of the company.

Summary

One of the most important tasks that entrepreneurs must undertake is building an effective founding team that includes the entrepreneur's key strategic partners, board of directors, and advisors. The team should reflect the diversity of education, expertise, and experience required to launch the new venture and take it through its early growth. Technology teams present unique challenges because often the founders have only technical expertise and therefore need to find partners with the appropriate business expertise to insure that the new venture gets an optimal start. With limited resources, new ventures will typically need to outsource some of their requirements to independent contractors. Once the business begins to grow significantly, the entrepreneur will need to consider bringing on professional management to insure that systems and controls are in place and the company is prepared for rapid growth.

Discussion Questions

1. Why is it advantageous for a technology start-up to be launched with a founding team over a solo entrepreneur?
2. What are some of the challenges of technology teams?
3. What would an ideal founding team look like?
4. What is the role and importance of social networking for entrepreneurs?
5. Why is the original founding entrepreneur not always the right person to grow the company to the next level?

CASE STUDY

Turning a Scientist into an Entrepreneur

When Dr. H. Kirk Hammond invented a revolutionary gene therapy technique to treat angina, he never envisioned himself becoming an entrepreneur and he certainly did not expect to reap a lot of wealth. A cardiologist at the University of California San Diego campus, Hammond quickly learned that to insure that his discovery would benefit society, he would need to divide his time between academics and the business world. He filed for a patent on his invention in 1995, but the university was unable to secure a licensing agreement with industry. As a result, Hammond and his partner Christopher Reinhard successfully pitched Hammond's technology to venture capitalists, and later that year the two co-founded Collateral Therapeutics to commercialize the invention. The team now included Reinhard, Hammond, and the venture capitalists. Hammond became the company's chief scientist owning 15 percent of the stock, while retaining his position at the university, where he trained doctors and worked in his gene therapy lab. To avoid any conflicts of interest that could hurt the university's ability to secure grants, he agreed to not treat any patients who were involved in clinical trials with his company.

(continued)

(*continued*)

Collateral licensed the patent rights from the university and in 1998 added a strategic partner to the team, Schering A.G., a German pharmaceutical company to initiate clinical trials on humans in May of that year. To maintain his position at the university, Hammond took unpaid leave when he needed to travel on company business, and his company provided research money to further the research he was conducting in his university lab with no exclusive rights to any of his discoveries. In July 1998, Collateral successfully completed an initial public offering on the NASDAQ.

In 2002, Schering A.G. acquired Collateral Therapeutics for $140 million in stock to expand its cardiovascular and gene therapy products and Hammond sold his stock for approximately $18 million. Then, in 2006 Schering made the decision to move away from cardiovascular research and development and sold Collateral to Cardium Therapeutics, which merged the company into its operations. Hammond, now a wealthy man, remained in his position at the university doing the work to which his life had been devoted. And the university, which has benefited from the royalties off his research discoveries that it had licensed, is now encouraging entrepreneurship by developing programs to assist researchers in starting their own companies and finding ways to overcome the challenges associated the the funding of their clinical trials.

Sources: Collateral Therapeutics, Inc. Hoovers, http://premium.hoovers.com/subscribe/co/boneyard/factsheet.xhtml?ID=56944, accessed December 18, 2007; "Company News: Schering to Buy Rest of Collateral Therapeutics, *The New York Times,* March 21, 2002; Yang, E. (October 26, 2003). "Professors Find a Market for Tech Ideas," *Sign On San Diego.com.*

Endnotes

1. Ruef, M. (2002). "Strong Ties, Weak Ties, and Islands: Structural and Cultural Predictors of Organizational Innovation." *Industrial and Corporate Change* 11: 427–429.
2. Bird, B.J. (1989). *Entrepreneurial Behavior* (Glenview, IL: Scott, Foresman); and Kamm, J.B., Shuman, J.C., Seeger, J.A., & Nurick, A.J. (1990). "Entrepreneurial Teams in New Venture Creation: A Research Agenda," *Entrepreneurship Theory and Practice* 14(4): 7–17.
3. Roure, J.B., & Madique, M.A. (1986). "Linking Prefunding Factors and High Technology Venture Success: An Exploratory Study," *Journal of Business Venturing* 1(3): 295–306.
4. Lyon, D.W., & Ferrier, W.J. (Winter 2002). "Enhancing Performance with Product-Market Innovation: The Influence of the Top Management Team," *Journal of Managerial Issues* 14(4): 452–469.
5. Timmons, J.A. (1994). *New Venture Creation: Entrepreneurship for the 21st Century,* 4th ed. (Burr Ridge, IL.: Richard D. Irwin).
6. Ensley, M.D., Carland, J.W., & Carland, J.C. (October 2000). "Investigating the Existence of the Lead Entrepreneur," *Journal of Small Business Management* 38(4): 59–77.
7. Martin, R. (May 31, 2007). "How Successful Leaders Think," *Harvard Business Review,* http://harvardbusinessonline.hbsp.harvard.edu/hbsp/hbr/articles/article.jsp?articleID=R070.
8. Ibid.

9. Wiklund, J., & Shepherd, D. (2003). "Knowledge-Based Resources, Entrepreneurial Orientation, and the Performance of Small and Medium-Sized Businesses," *Strategic Management Journal* 24: 1307–1314.

10. Choi, Y.R., & Shepherd, D.A. (2004). "Entrepreneurs' Decisions to Exploit Opportunities," *Journal of Management* 30(3): 377–395.

11. McEvily, S.K., Eisenhardt, K.M., & Prescott, J.E. (2004). "The Global Acquisition, Leverage, and Protection of Technological Competencies," *Strategic Management Journal* 25(8/9): 713–722.

12. Pink, D.H. (February 2005). "Revenge of the Right Brain," *Wired Magazine.*

13. Yim, J.W., & Weston, R. (2007). "The Characteristics of Bioentrepreneurs in the Australian Biotechnology Industry: A Pilot Study," Journal of Management & Organization 13: 383–406.

14. Lowe, R.A. & Ziedonis, A.A. (2006). "Overoptimism and the Performance of Entrepreneurial Firms," *Management Science* 52: 173–186.

15. McDougall, P., Shane, S., & Oviatt, B. (November 1994). "Explaining the Formation of International New Ventures: The Limits of Theories from International Business Research," *Journal of Business Venturing* 9: 469–487.

16. Miesenbock, K.J. (1988). "Small Business and Exporting: A Literature Review," *International Small Business Journal* 6(2): 42–61.

17. Aldrich, H., & Zimmer, C. (1986). "Entrepreneurship through Social Networks." In D.L. Sexton, & R.W. Smilor (Eds.), *The Art and Science of Entrepreneurship* (Cambridge, MA: Ballinger), pp. 3–23.

18. Dubini, P., & Aldrich, H. (1991). "Personal and Extended Networks Are Central to the Entrepreneurial Process." *Journal of Business Venturing* 6(5): 305–313.

19. Baptista, R., & Swann, P. (1998). "Do Firms in Clusters Innovate More?" *Research Policy* 27(5): 525–540.

20. Rickne, A. (2006). "Connectivity and Performance of Science-Based Firms," *Small Business Economics* 26: 393–407.

21. Kidwell, R.E., & Bennett, N. (1993). "Employee Propensity to Withhold Effort: A Conceptual Model to Intersect Three Avenues of Research." *Academy of Management Review* 18(3): 429–456.

22. Fiegner, M., Brown, B., Dreux, D., & Dennis, W. (2000). "CEO Stakes and Board Composition in Small Private Firms," *Entrepreneurship Theory and Practice* 24: 5.

23. Harper, S.C. (2001). "Entrepreneurs Beware: Use Caution in 'Professionalizing' Your Firm," *Business Forum* 25(3/4): 29.

24. Filatotchev, I., Toms, St., & Wright, M. (2006). "The Firm's Strategic Dynamics and Corporate Governance Life-Cycle," *International Journal of Managerial Finance* 2(45): 256–279.

25 Kazanjian, R.K. (1988), "Relation of Dominant Problems to Stages of Growth in Technology-Based New Ventures," *Academy of Management Journal* 31:257–279.

26. Harper, *op. cit.*, p. 35.

CHAPTER 5

THE CONCEPT OF INTELLECTUAL PROPERTY

Never before has the concept of intellectual property (IP) captured the imagination and interest of companies, large and small, with such intensity as it does today. Intellectual property refers to that group of legal rights associated with patents, trademarks, copyrights, and trade secrets. These rights grant their holder the right to exclude others from making, selling, using, or distributing the protected asset. Today, many companies are scrambling to secure as much IP as possible to gain a competitive advantage, use it as a bargaining chip in negotiations with competitors, enhance of value of their company, and to develop new revenue streams from licensing those rights to others. Large companies with huge patent portfolios are now mining those portfolios for any IP with value that was overlooked or that could be used offensively to go after a company that is inadvertently or intentionally infringing on the company's IP rights. Those patent portfolios are now available to entrepreneurs to license, develop applications, and commercialize those applications without having to go through the enormous expense of research and initial development.

Before going further, it is important to make a distinction among three concepts that come into play when one talks about protecting and exploiting innovations: intellectual capital, intellectual assets, and intellectual property. *Intellectual capital* is fundamentally knowledge—the tacit knowledge held within an organization by its employees, its management, and its organizational culture. Simply put, it's the knowledge gained from having worked on a project that is not typically written down. However, when that knowledge is codified, that is, written down to preserve it in some explicit form, it becomes an *intellectual asset* of the organization. Now it can be used by others and retained as part of the organization's culture. Some forms of

FIGURE 5-1 · Intangible Assets Pyramid

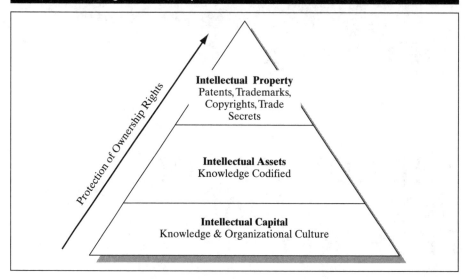

intellectual assets qualify for protections under the law and are known as *intellectual property.* Figure 5-1 depicts the relationship among these categories of assets.

This chapter covers the fundamentals of IP rights, how to determine which rights can be acquired, under what circumstances, and in what manner.

THE THEORY BEHIND IP PROTECTIONS

A number of economic theories form the basis for the rationale behind IP protections and the limited monopoly they create for the inventor.[1] In general, these economic theories speak to the activities that IP protection encourages, which include incentives to invent, disclose, and commercialize.[2]

INCENTIVES TO INVENT

The incentive-to-invent theory asserts that in the absence of a temporary monopoly created by IP protections, an invention can easily be stolen and produced, often at a lower price, before the original inventor is able to recoup the costs of research and development. In this situation, the commercial advantage logically goes to the second mover who does not incur the high cost of product development and, therefore, can introduce the product at a lower cost, effectively putting the original inventor out of business. With IP protections, however, inventors have an incentive to invest money and time in new inventions with the realization that they will enjoy a "quiet" period in which to sell the product at a high enough price to recoup their R&D costs before competitors enter the market. Although research conducted in the 1970s and 1980s found that patents were not necessarily an incentive to innovate, more current research suggests that IP rights play a significant role in the innovation process, particularly in volatile industries such as pharmaceutical, software, and telecommunications where research and development costs are significant.[3]

INCENTIVES TO DISCLOSE

With formal and legal IP protections, inventors are able to disclose their inventions publicly without fear of losing legal rights or risking loss of value. Furthermore, disclosure adds to the knowledge base in the field of invention, preventing the duplication of research efforts and encouraging complementary innovations. Without legal protections, inventors would likely keep their inventions as trade secrets to maintain their value. Unfortunately, trade secrets are difficult to sell or license because once the secret is disclosed, it loses its proprietary value. Trade secrets will be discussed more fully later in the chapter.

In a global environment, issues of geography play into decisions about disclosure. Companies typically determine whether to conduct R&D in a particular country based on how IP is respected or treated, among other factors.[4] In countries where IP laws are not respected, many companies will choose not to disclose their inventions or simply do all of the research and development in their own country.

A great deal of innovation is occurring today in industries that historically have not had strong patent protections and have suffered from almost immediate imitation: computers, software, semiconductors, and the Internet. In these industries, innovation tends to be sequential and complementary, with each new innovation building on previous innovations. In fact, the work of Bessen and Maskin at MIT suggests that strong, broad patents may actually inhibit innovation in these types of industries, particular from competitors with valuable complementary innovations.[5] For the inventor, imitation certainly reduces profits, but it also increases the potential for complementary innovation, which is important when an entrepreneur is attempting to establish his or her technology as the industry standard.

INCENTIVES TO COMMERCIALIZE

Research and development is an economically risky endeavor for the inventing entrepreneurial firm, but there are also commercial risks for strategic partners, such as manufacturers, who must incur the expense of additional design and development to get the technology commercially ready, and the expense of setting up for manufacture, seeking resources, and producing the product. Manufacturers, however, benefit from the inventor's temporary monopoly provided by patent rights. They enjoy a quiet period to produce and distribute the product at a fair price, given their higher initial costs of manufacture, before they must find a way to lower costs to compete with other manufacturers who have entered the market.

In the following sections, the various forms of IP are addressed, moving from the weakest to the strongest protections.

TRADE SECRETS

The Uniform Trade Secrets Act defines trade secrets as:

> . . . information including a formula, pattern, compilation, program, device, method, technique or process that derives independent economic value, actual or potential, from not being generally known to, and not being readily ascertainable by proper means by, other persons. . . .[6]

Trade secrets include novel and useful inventions for which the company chooses not to seek patent protection, such as computer source code, manufacturing processes, designs and drawings, technical know-how, and business information such as customer lists, vendors, supply sources, marketing plans, and in-house talent. However, any information that is commonly known or in common use or any information that is easily reproduced from known data cannot be treated as a trade secret. Thus, commonly used industry manufacturing processes cannot be protected as trade secrets. Unlike patents and trademarks, trade secrets are not public, they do not need to be registered with any governmental agency, and they are easy to obtain. The only requirement for a trade secret is that there must be documentation that establishes the existence of the protected information and proves that the company produced it and made a strong effort to protect it. Consequently, although trade secrets are easy to obtain, they are difficult to value. The true ownership and value of trade secrets can often only be determined through litigation.

Trade secrets convey some rights to their holders. For example, the holder of a trade secret can prevent specific groups of people, such as employees and strategic partners, from copying, using, and benefiting from the trade secret or disclosing it without permission.[7] However, anyone who uncovers a trade secret independently without using illegal means (such as reverse engineering a competitor's product) is not barred from using the information. For example, if a competitor has developed a new formula for cleaning oil from concrete and another company purchases the product and uncovers its composition in its own lab, that company can legally use this information to develop its own version of the formula and market it.

NONDISCLOSURE AGREEMENTS

Nondisclosure agreements (NDAs) are a common way to protect trade secrets, and they have become an important document in the information age. An NDA is a contract between the inventor or information source and another party that prohibits that party from disclosing information provided in confidence. Today, if an idea is shared without proof that it was shared in confidence, the trade secret holder will likely have inadvertently given up trade secret rights. Not only that, if the idea involved a potentially patentable invention, the disclosure may have started the clock on the one-year requirement for filing a patent application after publication and rights to file for foreign patents may have been lost. In addition to serving as documentation of the existence of the trade secrets, the NDA makes it possible to defend trade secrets in a court of law.

To be legally binding, an NDA must contain the following:

- It must provide for consideration, which is what is exchanged for the promise to do something or refrain from doing something.
- It must define what is confidential by specifying what is being protected so that the other party cannot claim they did not know what was confidential.
- It must identify how the other party will be using the information, for example, to secure a manufacturer, seek start-up capital, or find a new member of the management team.
- It must designate what is to be done with any materials exchanged, for example, destroying documents or returning them to the owner.

Entrepreneurs should be aware that investors and others who see a lot of business plans in their daily work, such as entrepreneur professors, will generally not sign NDAs because it places them in a difficult legal position. It is likely that they have heard a similar idea along the way, and they don't want to risk being sued. Companies such as Mattel, for example, don't sign NDAs from toy inventors because they have a staff of inventors who are always working on new ideas. This fact should not discourage entrepreneurs from talking to investors and potential strategic partners because in the development of a new technology, there is a lot of tacit knowledge to which others will not be privy. Furthermore, unless an entrepreneur is willing to talk about the business, he or she can't expect to get the critical help needed.

COPYRIGHTS

Copyrights protect the original works of authors, composers, screenwriters, computer programmers, and other developers of creative works. In a very real sense, even the technical manuals that entrepreneurs might write to explain their products are copyrighted. Contrary to common belief, copyrights do not protect ideas, but simply the form in which those ideas appear. For example, an author can write about business communications, but that author cannot copyright the idea of business communications. This is why several authors can write about the same topic without violating another's copyright. The First Sale Doctrine (Section 106 of the 1976 Copyright Act) grants six rights to a copyright holder: reproduction, preparation of derivative works, distribution, public performance, public display, and digital transmission performance.[8] The owner can distribute or dispose of only the particular copy that he or she owns.

A copyright gives the holder the right to exclude others from reproducing the work, preparing derivative works, distributing copies of the work, and displaying the work in public. Copyrights last for the life of the holder plus 70 years, after which they go into public domain; however, under the Sonny Bono Copyright Extension Act of 1998, the first existing copyrights will enter the public domain in 2019 no matter how old they are. Works for hire and works published anonymously now have copyrights of 95 years. To secure copyright protection and give the author the ability to sue an infringer, the author must put the work in a tangible form, in other words, a form that can be seen or heard. Although it is not required by law, a copyright notice should also be affixed so that someone who violates the copyright cannot claim that they did not have notice. The notice should appear as follows:

© Copyright 2008 by [name of copyright holder]

To obtain the full protection of the law and provide a paper trail in the event of litigation, the copyright should be registered at the Copyright Office of the Library of Congress in Washington, D.C. A complete copy of an unpublished work or two complete copies of a published work must also be submitted. In general, copyrights can be handled without the use of an attorney if the rules are carefully followed.

DIGITAL MILLENNIUM COPYRIGHT ACT

Copyright law and the issue of dissemination of information are undergoing their most strenuous test as a result of the knowledge economy and the Internet. The ease with which others can infringe on someone's copyrighted material on the Internet has led to the Digital Millennium Copyright Act (DMCA). The DMCA was signed into law in 1998 in response to the threat of the Internet on the works of authors and artists. This law makes it illegal to "manufacture, import, distribute, or provide products or services that are primarily designed or produced for the purpose of circumventing technological measures, such as encryption, scrambling, or other methods, used by copyright owners to protect their works."[9] The law also contains a safe harbor clause to protect Internet service providers from damages if they unknowingly infringe on someone's rights by transmitting or storing infringing material they did not create or by linking users to sites containing infringing material.

For example, recording companies and music distributors continually fight against the disruption of their business models by Internet users who digitize, copy, and distribute copyrighted music over the Internet. The most famous case to be affected by the new law was that involving Napster, the Internet company that had developed a technology to enable users to share and download music for free using software that temporarily turned the user's computer into a server for the purpose of swapping MP3 files. Napster did not qualify as an Internet service provider, and although it did not host or share copyrighted material directly, virtually all of the content available at the Napster site (www.napster.com) was copyrighted material. On September 3, 2002, Napster was forced to liquidate its assets in bankruptcy.

FAIR USE

Fair use is a concept that applies limits to copyright protections in that it permits someone to use another's works without permission. For example, using someone's words for criticism, education, or scholarship is acceptable as long as the original author or artist is credited. However, using another's work to endorse a commercial product is not acceptable. The Internet has created some challenges to the concept of fair use. For example, if a message is posted to a public e-mail list, a receiver can, by implication, forward or archive that message without obtaining permission from its original author as long as the original meaning of the message is not changed.

TRADEMARKS

An invention that cannot be patented can be marked with a brand or trademark that indicates that the inventor originated the idea. A trademark is a symbol, logo, word, sound, color, design, or other device that is used to identify a business or a product. At its most fundamental level, a trademark is a brand. The term *trademark* is regularly used to refer to both trademarks and service marks, which identify services or intangible activities "performed by one person for the benefit of a person or persons other than himself, either for pay or otherwise."[10] Under the terms of the Lanham Act (1946) and its various amendments, three requirements must be met for a trademark to be valid:[11]

- The mark must consist of a device, symbol, name, work, or combination thereof that the USPTO has defined as valid.
- A manufacturer or merchant must adopt and use the mark.
- The mark must distinguish goods sold or manufactured by one party from another.

Table 5-1 depicts some unique or unusual trademarks. The holder of a trademark has the right to exclude others from using confusingly similar marks to protect a trademark against (1) counterfeiting and misappropriation, that is, using a mark that is basically indistinguishable from another mark; (2) infringement, when a mark is likely to cause confusion, that is, when it is too similar to another mark; and (3) dilution, when the use of the same or similar mark, even in a noncompetitive situation, reduces the value of the mark to its owner.

TABLE 5-1 Unusual Trademarks	
Some of the more unusual trademarks include sounds, colors, scents, motions, and holograms.	
U.S. Reg. No. 186,828	Configuration of a molded, conically shaped candy piece
U.S. Reg. No. 1439132	The color pink used in the entirety of home insulation fibers
U.S. Reg. No. 1395550	The sound of a lion's roar used in connection with applicant's movie production
U.S. Reg. No. 2463044	The scent of cherry used in connection with applicant's automotive lubricant
U.S. Reg. No. 2710652	Holographic logo used in connection with baseball trading cards

The case of *American Express v. American Express Limousine Service* [771F. Supp 729 (E.D.N.Y. 1991)] presents a good example of a situation where the owner of a famous mark experiences dilution because another company uses its mark for its service. In this case, a limousine service used the American Express mark for its business. Although the two companies were not in competition with one another, the court found that the defendant limousine company's use of the mark would have a deleterious effect on American Express, the financial services company.

For a trademark to be in effect, the holder must show intent to use or that the trademark is actually in use in interstate commerce. A potential trademark applicant is not required to search for potentially conflicting marks prior to filing an application, but this is easily done on the USPTO public search library at www.uspto.gov or by doing a quick search on the Internet using a search engine such as Google. Before a trademark is registered, an intent-to-use application is filed and TM (or SM for services) is placed after the name or logo. After the trademark is registered, the symbol ®, which means it is a registered trademark, is used.

There are some marks that cannot be trademarked. These include:

- Immoral or deceptive marks.
- Marks that use official symbols of the United States or any state or municipality, such as a state flag.
- Marks that use a person's name or likeness without permission.

The USPTO determines whether a mark can be registered. If it rejects the application, the applicant has 6 months to respond. In theory, once someone owns a trademark, he can own it forever if he follows the post registration formalities and the mark remains in commercial use. Trademarks actually become more valuable with age as the amount of goodwill they create increases.

Under the General Agreement of Tariffs and Trade (GATT), the United States has assumed the obligation for registering trademarks internationally under Section 44(b) of the Trademark Act 15 U.S.C. §1126. Consequently, all countries that are party to the agreement respect these trademarks.

TRADEMARKS AND THE INTERNET

The Internet has spawned a number of new trademark-related legal issues that arise out of technologies used on the Internet. One of the most common areas for dispute is domain names. Domain names, the addresses for Web sites, have created many problems because under federal trademark law, similar businesses may have similar names if they do business in different geographic regions (15 U.S.C. sec. 1057c, 111565–6). However, the Internet does not have geographic boundaries, and simply registering a domain name does not constitute use under the rules of the Lanham Act, which prevents trademark uses that might cause confusion in the marketplace.[12] For example, under trademark law, General Motors and General Mills can both exist because they are in different industries, but the Domain Name System (DNS) allows only one general.com. Similarly, a generic name cannot be registered as a trademark, but a generic domain name such as business.com can be registered. Furthermore, a domain name that simply serves as a locator for a Web page and is not the actual name of the company cannot be trademarked [*In re Eilberg,* 49 USPQ2d 1955 (TTAB 1998)]. Prior to filing for a domain name trademark designation, it is wise to check the list of exclusions found in the U.S. Department of Commerce's Examination Guide No. 2–99.

PATENTS

The most powerful form of protection for IP is the patent, which grants the holder the right to exclude others from making, using, or selling the invention during the term of the patent. In other words, a patent grants defensive rights, not offensive rights—it does not give the patent holder the right to make, use, and distribute the invention, but it does allow the holder to prevent others from doing so. It is also important that the patent holder defend the patent during its life or risk losing it. At the end of a patent's life, the patent is placed in public domain and anyone may exploit it.

The U.S. patent system, as we know it today, was designed over 200 years ago by Thomas Jefferson. He planned it with the express purpose of providing the independent inventor with a brief legal monopoly during which to get the invention into the market and recoup development costs before facing competition. The first patent was issued in 1790, and more than 7 million U.S. patents have been granted to date. Curiously, the mousetrap has received more patents than any other invention. Still manufactured by the Woodstream Corporation of Pennsylvania, it goes by the trademarked name Victor. Since it was first patented in 1903, the mousetrap has been the source of at least 40 patent applications a year. However, only 24 of the total 4,400 patents for mousetraps have actually made money. With so many applications, the USPTO has divided mousetrap inventions into nine categories, including smiting, choking, squeezing, electrocuting, and exploding.

In FY 2006, the USPTO received more than 417,000 non-provisional utility, plant and reissue patent applications, 25,000 design applications, and more than 52,000 PCT (for international applications) applications. In addition, the office received 121,307 provisional applications.[13] Today, about 80 percent of all U.S. patents are filed by large corporations, universities, and federal and private labs. However, the USPTO is mindful of the special needs and limited resources of independent inventors and has established the Office of the Independent Inventor to serve them. In addition, the courts have generally sided with independent inventors in cases where large corporations have infringed on their interests. See Chapter 6 for more information on patent infringement.

WHAT CONSTITUTES A PATENTABLE INVENTION?

The Supreme Court of the United States has stated that "anything under the sun that is made by man" falls into the statutory subject matter for patents (*Diamond v. Chakrabarty,* 1980).[14] However, although it may appear that virtually anything can be patented, the truth is that the USPTO has four specific criteria for determining the patentability of an invention:

- **It must fit into one of the five classes** established by Congress (see the next section).
- **It must have utility.** It must be useful with a practical purpose.
- **It must not contain prior art.** It must be novel in an important way that is not known by others and not previously published for public consumption. U.S. law requires that an invention must not have become public or available for sale more than one year prior to the filing for a patent.
- **It must be nonobvious** to someone with ordinary skills in the field of invention. For example, it cannot be the logical next step in a known process.

THE FIVE CLASSES OF PATENTS

The U.S. Congress has established five categories of patentable inventions, and any patent application must address at least one of these classes.

- Machine or something with moving parts or circuitry (e.g., fax, rocket, photocopier, laser, electronic circuit).
- Process or method for producing a useful and tangible result (e.g., chemical reaction, method for producing products, business model).
- Article of manufacture (e.g., furniture, transistor, diskette, toy).
- Composition of matter (e.g., gasoline, food additive, drug, genetically altered life-form).
- A new use or improvement of something from the first four categories.

If it appears that an invention might fit into more than one category, the inventor is not required to determine in which categories the invention should rightfully be included. There are also some very specific exclusions to patent filings; for example, laws and phenomena of nature, naturally occurring substances, abstract mathematical formulas, and ideas. However, if an inventor alters something found in nature, as in the case of genetically altered tomatoes, the inventor may file for a patent. In *Diamond v. Chakrabarty,* Chakrabarty engineered a bacterium that broke down components of crude oil. No such bacterium existed in nature; thus, the Court ruled that this bacterium was the product of human ingenuity and could be patented. It is important to note that if an inventor obtains a patent on an improvement of one of the first four categories, he may not be entitled to manufacture the whole device without risking infringement of the original inventor's patent.

TYPES OF PATENTS

The USPTO offers three basic types of patents: utility, design, and plant. Of the three, the utility patent is the most commonly sought and is the source of the majority of the growth in the number of patents granted in the information age.

In particular, utility patents on software make up a large portion of this increase. In addition to utility, design, and plant patents, the business method patent has been a rapidly growing subcategory of utility process patents.

UTILITY PATENTS

Utility patents protect the functional part of a machine or process. A mathematical formula that describes the launch trajectory of a rocket may not be entitled to patent protection, but the software that actually makes the rocket leave the launch pad may be entitled to patent protection.[15] Gene patents also fall into this category. The first gene patents were issued in the 1970s, but since then, more than 1,000 genes have been patented, and thousands more await patent approval. In many cases, the company applying for the patent has no idea what specific purpose the gene sequence that is being claimed will serve. It is important to remember that scientists can patent laboratory-generated gene sequences and alterations of human genes, but they cannot patent individual human genes occurring in nature. Utility patents last for 20 years from the date of application with the USPTO.

BUSINESS METHOD PATENTS

The business method patent is actually a type of a utility patent under the classification of a process. That process has included such concepts as bidding on airline tickets, diagnosing problems, and processing insurance claims. To date, the courts have not defined what differentiates a business method claim from a process claim.[16]

Traditionally, U.S. courts have held that an invention must involve a physical transformation to be patented, drawing on various courts' interpretations that laws of nature, natural phenomenon, and abstract ideas are not patentable. However, in 1994, the Federal Circuit Court ruled that abstract ideas could be patented if, when reduced to practice, they produced a "useful, concrete and tangible result" [In re Alappat, 33 F. 3d 1526 (C.A.F.C. 1994)]. Accordingly, the USPTO revised its guidelines and opened the door to what is now known as the business method patent. From 1996 through 1999, the USPTO experienced an explosion in business method patent applications, from 700 to 1,300 in that time frame. It became the fastest growing patent category.[17] In an effort to curtail the rush to patent any business activity on the Internet, on March 29, 2000, the USPTO issued a statement declaring that the business method patent will only apply to fundamentally different ways of doing business, and that the embedded process must produce a useful, tangible, and concrete result.[18]

The flood of business method patent applications began with *State Street Bank & Trust Co. v. Signature Financial Group,* 149 F.3d 1360, in 1998. Signature Financial Group applied for a patent on its proprietary application software designed to automate its portfolio management system. State Street Bank wanted to license the application, but when negotiations failed, it sued Signature on the grounds that the patent violated the business method patent eligibility requirements. The Federal Circuit Court ultimately upheld Signature's patent rights. The State Street Bank case served to expand the concept of what constitutes physical transformation as a requirement for patentability to include manipulations of electronically stored data. It also eliminated the business method exception to patentability. A number of other well-known cases have emphasized the problems with business method patents. In October 1999, Internet giant Amazon.com sued bookseller Barnes and Noble alleging infringement of its one-click patent. The case was settled in January 2001 with undisclosed royalty payments.[19] Several lawsuits are still pending against eBay claiming infringement of patents on automated auctions.

DESIGN PATENTS

A design patent protects the "visual ornamental characteristics embodied in, or applied to, an article of manufacture" but not its structure or utilitarian features.[20] A protected design has no function but is simply part of the tangible item with which it is associated. The design cannot be hidden or offensive in any way, nor can it simulate a well-known or naturally occurring object or person. Examples of design patents include eyeglasses, a design on a vase, or the design of a door handle. A design patent application may only have a single claim (37 CFR §1.153). A separate application must be filed for each independent design, as multiple designs cannot be supported by a single patent claim. (Claims are discussed in the section on the patent process.) Design patents are valid for 14 years from the date of application.

It is important to note the existence of Invention Development Organizations (IDOs), which are consulting and marketing businesses that claim to help inventors bring their inventions to market. Some of these organizations are legitimate, but, unfortunately, most are not. They often encourage the inventor to pursue a design patent without considering the merits or the market feasibility of the invention. The design patent protects only the appearance of an article of manufacture, not its functionality. So once an inventor gets a design patent, someone else can create the same article of manufacture, alter the design, use the same functionality, and also receive a patent. It is wiser to seek the counsel of a qualified IP attorney than to work with an IDO.

PLANT PATENTS

Plant patents protect new and distinct varieties of asexually reproducing plants. The plant for which a patent is being sought must be uniquely different from any plant existing naturally in nature. This patent is good for 20 years from the date of application.

FILING FOR A PATENT

The USPTO Web site clearly describes the patent application process and it is briefly depicted in Figure 5-2, but any inventor should still consult with a qualified IP attorney when applying for a patent because much of the USPTO's decision on whether to grant the patent depends on how the claims are worded. Claims are statements about the portions of the invention the inventor believes to be novel. In the United States, only the original inventor or inventors have the right to apply for a patent. However, the original inventor may subsequently assign the patent to a company or individual. If a patent has joint owners, any single owner can make,

FIGURE 5-2   The Patent Process

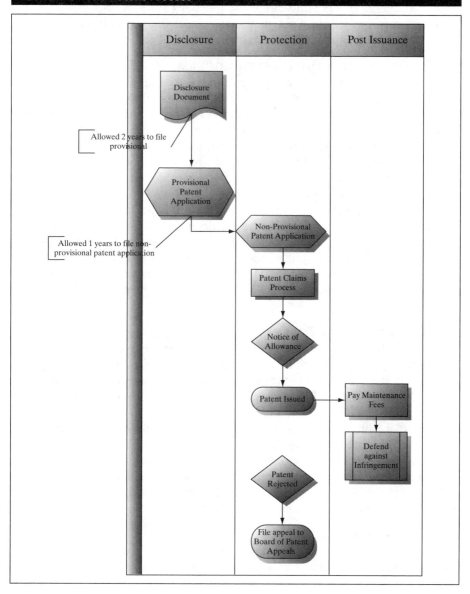

use, or sell the invention without consulting with or obtaining permission from the other owners. Therefore, if two inventors jointly apply for a patent, they should have a written agreement that discusses the distribution of equity in the patent and potential proceeds from royalties or sale.

It is always wise to conduct a preliminary patent search or seek the services of a patent attorney or firm that specializes in patent searches. As most patents are not commercialized, it will be difficult to know for sure if the invention is novel without doing a patent search. The following sections briefly describe the typical process for securing a patent, which includes filing a disclosure document, a provisional patent application, and a nonprovisional patent application.

THE DISCLOSURE DOCUMENT PROGRAM

Inventors often protect their inventions in the earliest stages of development by taking advantage of the USPTO's Disclosure Document Program.[21] The disclosure document merely serves as evidence of the date of conception of an invention; it does not grant any rights like those granted by patents, and it does not take the place of a formal patent application. However, the disclosure statement could become an important document should two inventors find themselves working on the same idea at the same time. The inventor who filed the disclosure statement could be in a stronger position to be declared the one who can file for a patent. It is important to note, however, that the date of receipt of the disclosure document is not the effective filing date for a patent application. Furthermore, the disclosure document does not substitute for a conventional, permanently bound, witnessed, and notarized laboratory notebook or record.[22] The document will be kept in confidence for 2 years, after which the USPTO will consider it abandoned if no patent application is filed.

THE PROVISIONAL PATENT

The provisional patent allows an inventor to complete a first patent filing in the United States at a much lower cost than that required for a formal patent application. The purpose of the provisional patent is to give inventors an opportunity to speak with manufacturers and others about producing the invention without fear that they will take the invention as their own. It does not, however, take the place of a formal, nonprovisional patent application. The inventor is given only 12 months from the date of filing the provisional patent application to file a nonprovisional patent application before the application is abandoned, and that time period cannot be extended. This approach should definitely be considered as it is legally more powerful than a disclosure document and permits the inventor to label the invention as patent pending.

NON-PROVISIONAL PATENT

A nonprovisional patent filing includes all types of patents and establishes the filing date on which the 20-year patent life is based. The application will require a technical description, known as the disclosure of the invention. It must contain enough detail for an ordinary person skilled in the relevant technology to make and use the invention. Although it does not need to include blueprints or original source code, it should use flowcharts and text to describe each step of the process of making the invention.

The claims in the application serve to define the scope of the protection requested. Every patent application must contain at least one claim of novelty, utility, and nonobviousness. The inventor's attorney will word the claims so that they are broad enough to cover all the potential applications of the technology, but specific enough to demonstrate uniqueness. When the patent application is received by the USPTO, it conducts a search of its patent records for prior art. It then issues an office action that normally includes objections to the claims contained in the application. During this time, the patent application is described as "patent applied for," which establishes the claim and dates relative to prior art. During the examination process; the patent application is not available to the public. It is very common for the USPTO to reject one or more claims on the first pass, frequently because of prior art or nonobviousness. Several communications between the inventor's IP attorney and the USPTO examiner assigned to the patent application will argue the merits of any claims that may have been rejected by the examiner. Once the USPTO accepts the revised claims, it issues a notice of allowance that announces that the patent will be issued. The inventor may market and sell the invention during this process, but must clearly label it patent pending and provide the number assigned to the patent application. Once the patent is issued, it becomes public record and anyone can view it.

If the patent is rejected, even after modifications, the inventor may appeal to a Board of Patent Appeals within the USPTO. Failing to overturn the rejection here, the inventor may appeal to the U.S. Court of Appeals for the Federal Circuit. As this process may take years, an inventor may want to weigh the cost of undertaking the appeal against the value of getting the invention to market without a patent.

FOREIGN PATENTS

U.S. patent rights extend only to the borders of the United States. They are not valid in other countries; every country has its own laws regarding IP. There are two important differences between international and U.S. procedures in patent filing. The European Patent Convention (EPC) gives patent rights to the first person to file for the patent, whether or not that person is the original inventor. By contrast, the United States permits only the original inventor the right to file an application.[23] Furthermore, in the United States, an inventor can make an invention available for sale up to one year before filing a patent application. This is not the case in other countries, where publication or availability for sale before the date of filing will bar the right to apply. In addition, most countries other than the United States require that the invention be manufactured in that country within 3 years of receiving the foreign patent.

The Patent Cooperation Treaty (PCT) of 1970 permits an inventor to file a PCT document or blanket application in his or her home country and then designate the countries in which the patent is requested.[24] The inventor has 30 months to begin the process of filing a formal patent application in every country they have listed in the PCT. Similarly, the EPC offers a blanket application and grants an inventor rights in all member countries. The clock now stops for a year if an inventor files a patent application in any member country.[25] This means that the second country in which the inventor files a patent will treat that application as though it were filed on the initial date of application in the first country, giving the inventor the earliest date of invention. However, enforcement of patent rights is still on a country-by-country basis.

When deciding whether to file patents in another country, entrepreneurs should consider the following:

- Has the invention been published before the date of application? If so, in many countries the entepreneur would be barred from filing?
- Is the entrepreneur prepared to manufacture in the country in which the patent is being sought?
- Can a reasonable profit be made in the country in which patents are filed?

It is very important to consult with an IP attorney with experience in foreign patents because the laws differ country by country. The attorney can help the inventor determine if the time and expense of foreign patents is essential to the success of the potential business.

Summary

Intellectual property consists of proprietary rights in the form of patents, trademarks, copyrights, and trade secrets. These rights give the holder the right to exclude others from making and using the property under protection. Trade secrets are the easiest form of protection to obtain but provide the weakest level of protection. All they require are documents specifying that something is a trade secret that must not be disclosed. These documents often take the form of NDAs and contracts. Copyrights protect the original works of authors, artists, musicians, and programmers and last for the life of the holder plus 70 years. To secure copyright protection, the work must be in a tangible form and contain a copyright notice. Trademarks protect symbols, logos, words, sounds, colors, designs, or other devices used to identify a business or a product in commerce. Trademarks must be in commercial use to be valid and are renewable every 17 years. Patents are the most powerful form of protection for IP. They grant the holder the right to exclude others from making, using, or selling the invention during the term of the patent. An invention may qualify for a patent if it fits into one of five classes established by Congress, has utility, does not contain prior art, and is nonobvious.

Discussion Questions

1. An inventor has just developed a new type of collapsible furniture that will be useful for students in college dormitories where space is limited. What kinds of protections should the inventor consider for this product and the business that would be developed to commercialize it?
2. Why would an inventor choose to file a provisional patent application rather than a disclosure document?
3. For what reasons might an inventor decide not to patent an invention that is clearly patentable?
4. What kinds of things are best protected through trade secrets?

Gordon Gould: The Father of Laser Technology

When your childhood heroes are Marconi, Bell, and Edison, it is not surprising if you become an inventor. Gordon Gould knew before he entered high school that he would someday be an inventor, but he did more than just wait for that day to come; he prepared for it by studying how things work. Gould experienced his "eureka" discovery on November 9, 1957, when he was 37 years old. A Columbia physicist, Charles H. Townes, had invented a means of amplifying microwave energy, which he called the "maser," but Gould was interested in finding a way to do this same thing with light. The idea for his invention came to him in a rush that evening of November 9, and he spent the entire night writing down all his thoughts, designs, and potential applications for the invention. The next day he immediately had his notebook notarized. Gould's invention was a way to amplify light and use the resulting light beam to cut and heat substances and to measure distances. Gould realized that this discovery was going to be his life's work.

Gould consulted with a patent attorney; but, unfortunately, he misunderstood what he was told. He thought that he had to build a working prototype of his laser to acquire a patent, but the USPTO only requires that an inventor describe his invention in such a way that a person skilled in the art can replicate it. So excited was Gould to begin work on a laser application that he left Columbia university without finishing his dissertation and took a position with Technical Research Group, Inc., a small New York company. Upon winning a $1 million government grant in 1959, he finally filed for an historic patent that disclosed more than a dozen interrelated inventions covering fundamental laser technology. Meanwhile, Charles Townes had already applied for a patent on his optical maser. To make matters worse, the government declared Gould's research top secret, and because he did not have a government security clearance, his notebooks were confiscated. Fortunately, he had kept copies of them and retained the primary know-how for the project in his mind.

Townes and his partner, Arthur Schawlow, received the patent on their optical maser in 1960 and for the next 17 years, theirs would be the only laser patents on which royalties would be paid. In 1973, Gould received a decision from the Patent Office that declared that his original application had no disclosure of an operable laser technology. This decision also effectively invalidated his pending applications. Gould would not give up; he was battling for his patents, but the cost was becoming unbearable. At one point, Gould was referred to a well-known patent attorney, Richard I. Samuel who, after much investigation, believed that Gould was the true inventor of the laser. His firm agreed to fund Gould's patent fight for up to $300,000 in exchange for 15 percent of future royalties. The firm that agreed to act as the licensing agent for Gould's patents, REFAC, would take 25 percent of future royalties, leaving Gould with 35 percent.

In May 1977, the patent office announced that it would issue a patent to Gould for a device that amplified light. Over the next few months, Gould filed for several more patents and also filed an infringement suit against Control Laser International Corp., which had been paying royalties to Townes for the maser patent for nearly 17 years.

(continued)

(continued)

On the strength of the first patent, issued in 1979, Gould and his attorney won enough financial backing from private investors to start Patlex Corp., which they later took public. What was unusual about this new company was that its primary asset was its equity stake in the outcome of various lawsuits. Gould and Samuel had filed suits against about 90 percent of the laser companies in existence at that time.

What followed were years of battles with the USPTO and the various companies Patlex had sued. In many instances, the Patent Office behaved in rather unusual ways, because, as it claimed, any Gould patents could potentially be enforced against the government as well. Still, the Patent Office is supposed to be an independent body, not an advocate, and this atypical behavior in the end worked in Gould's favor. On December 19, 1985, the courts stated that the Patent Office had made many errors in evaluating Gould's patent claims and ruled in his favor. That ruling started an avalanche of rulings in Gould's favor. In the end, more than 100 laser makers signed licensing agreements with Patlex, including such giants as Ford, General Electric, and National Semiconductor. Gould was finally recognized for his historic invention. He died in 2005 at the age of 85.

Sources: Mike Hofmann (December 1, 1997). "Patent Fending," *Inc.,* www.inc.com, accessed September 11, 2008; Erik Larson (March 1, 1989). "Patent Pending," *Inc.; Gould v. General Photonics Corp.* 534 F. Supp. 399 (N.D. Cal. 1982); *Gould v. Mossinghoff,* 229 U.S.P.Q. 1 (D.D.C. 1985).

Endnotes

1. Eisenberg, R.S. (1989). "Patents and the Progress of Science," *University of Chicago Law Review* 50: 1017–1086; Kitch, E.W. (1977). "The Nature and Function of the Patent System," *Journal of Law and Economics* 20: 265–290; Merges, R.P., & Nelson, R.R. (1990). "On the Complex Economics of Patent Scope," *Columbia Law Review* 90: 839–916.
2. Kesan J.P. (November 2000). "Intellectual Property and Agricultural Biotechnology," *American Behavioral Scientist* 44(3): 464.
3. Cohen, W., Nelson, R., & Walsh, J. (2000). "Protecting Their Intellectual Assets: Appropriability Conditions and Why U.S. Manufacturing Firms Patent (or Not)," Working Paper 7552, National Bureau of Economic Research, Washington, DC; Stern, S., Porter, M., & Furman, J. (2000). "The Determinants of National Innovative Capacity," Working Paper 7876, National Bureau of Economic Research, Washington, DC.
4. Sanyal, P. (2004). "Intellectual Property Rights Protection and Location of R&D by Multinational Enterprises," *Journal of Intellectual Capital* 5(1): 59.
5. Bessen, J., & Maskin, E. (January 2000). "Sequential Innovation, Patents, and Imitation," MIT Department of Economics Working Paper No. 00–01.
6. "The Uniform Trade Secrets Act with 1985 Amendments," (February 11, 1986). Drafted by the National Conference of Commissioners on Uniform State Laws and approved by the American Bar Association. http://www.law.upenn.edu/bll/archives/ulc/fnact99/1980s/utsa85.htm, accessed September 11, 2008.

7. Fishman, S., & Stim, R. (February 4, 2002). "Trade Secret Basics," *NOLO Law for All,* www.nolo.com/encyclopedia/articles/pts/trade_secrets.html, accessed September 11, 2008.

8. 2001 Duke L. & Tech. Rev. 0018, May 31, 2001.

9. U.S. Copyright Office (December 1998). *Summary of the Digital Millennium Copyright Act of 1998* (Washington, DC: U.S. Copyright Office), p. 4, http://www.copyright.gov/legislation/dmca.pdf, accessed September 11, 2008.

10. 15 U.S.C. §1127.

11. Kopp, S.W., & Suter, T.A. (Spring 2000). "Trademark Strategies Online: Implications for Intellectual Property Protection," *Journal of Public Policy & Marketing* 19(1): 119–131.

12. Brown, J.D., & Prescott, J.E. (2000). "Product of the Mind: Assessment and Protection of Intellectual Property," *Competitive Intelligence Review* 11(3): 60.

13. "Performance and Accountability Report, Fiscal Year 2006," *United States Patent and Trademark Office,* p. 16, www.uspto.gov, accessed September 11, 2008

14 *Diamond v. Chakrabarty,* 447 U.S. 303 (1980).

15 United States Patent and Trademark Office, http://www.uspto.gov/web/offices/pac/doc/general/index.html#whatpat, accessed September 11, 2008.

16. *State Street Bank & Trust v. Signature Financial Group Inc.,* 149 F.3d 1368, 47 USPQ2d 1596 (Fed. Cir. 1998).

17. Williams, R.L., & Bukowitz, W.R. (2001). "The Yin and Yang of Intellectual Capital Management," *Journal of Intellectual Capital* 2(2): 96–108.

18. Love, J.J., & Coggins, W.W. (2001). "Successfully Preparing and Prosecuting a Business Method Patent Application," Paper presented at annual meeting of AIPLA, www.uspto.gov/web/menu/pbmethod/aiplapaper.rtf, accessed September 11, 2008.

19. Hall, B.H. (2003). "Business Method Patents, Innovation, and Policy," Institute of Business and Economic Research, Department of Economics, University of California, Berkeley, p. 24.

20. U.S. Patent and Trademark Office: Design Patents, www.uspto.gov/web/offices/pac/doc/general/design.html, accessed September 11, 2008.

21. U.S. Patent and Trademark Office: Disclosure Document Program, www.uspto.gov/web/offices/com/pac/disdo.html, accessed October 2007.

22. U.S. Patent and Trademark Office: Disclosure Document Program, www.uspto.gov/web/offices/com/sol/notices/disdo.html, accessed September 11, 2008.

23. Oddi, A.S. (1996). "Un-unified Economic Theories of Patents: The Not-Quite-Holy Grail," *Notre Dame Law Review* 71: 267–327.

24. Patent Cooperation Treaty, 28 U.S.T. 7645 No. 8733 (1970).

25. Paris Convention for the Protection of Industrial Property, 21 U.S.T. 1,583,828 U.N.T.S. 305 (1967).

CHAPTER 6

PATENT AND TRADEMARK STRATEGY

Intellectual property (IP) is a source of wealth and risk for companies of all sizes. With more patents and trademarks being filed than ever before, the chances of developing something without inadvertently infringing on someone's patent or trademark are decreasing. In an Internet world, it's even more likely that an entrepreneur's business will suffer infringement of its IP. For example, a company Web site can be hacked and proprietary software shared around the world. That's exactly what happened to John Anton, who in 2006 discovered that a company in India had hacked in and stolen the software code that enabled his customers to design their own apparel online. Not only had the company, Infogate, stolen proprietary graphics and images, it was creating sites to compete with Anton's company, Anton Sport, and selling Anton's software to unsuspecting customers.[1]

However, IP strategy is not just about protecting assets against infringement; it's also about creating wealth for a company and its owners. Since the 1980s when companies first began looking at IP as a way of creating wealth, rising R&D and production costs, increased competition, and an uncertain economy have spurred entrepreneurs to diversify their company's revenue streams so as not to rely solely on revenues from sales, but to also consider revenue from the licensing of their intellectual assets.[2] Harley-Davidson reaps millions of dollars a year from licensing its famous motorcycle brand to appear on a variety of products. Restaurant Technologies, based in Eagan, Minnesota, licenses telemetry systems to restaurants that use their cooking oil to determine when they're running low and to track usage of a number of items that can save the restaurants a lot of money. Today, more than ever before, entrepreneurs can generate significant revenue from the various forms of intellectual assets they create.

This chapter explores strategies for protecting patents and trademarks and then considers licensing of intellectual assets to create wealth.

PROTECTING PATENTS

Today, it is unlikely that a company will be able to protect its products with a single IP vehicle (patent, trademark, copyright, or trade secret). The competitive, global environment requires a barrier of protection to safeguard a product from those who would seek to co-opt it for their own purposes. The barriers that entrepreneurs must create have become large and complex. For instance, Figure 6-1 depicts an example of some IP barriers that may need to be constructed to protect an integrated circuit invention and its potential applications. It is important to note that if the inventor does not identify all possible applications of the technology in its patent claims, a competitor could patent an application not accounted for in the inventor's original application and then demand royalties from the original inventor's customers.[3]

FIGURE 6-1   Sample Protection Net for an Integrated Circuit

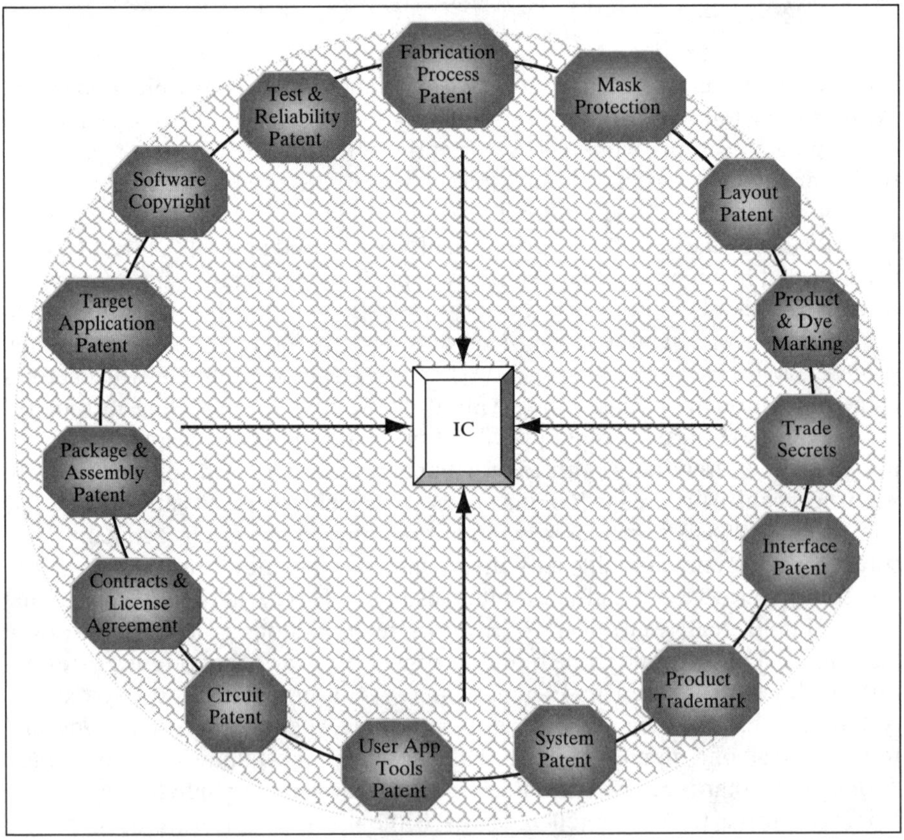

An effective patent strategy will improve a company's chances for success in three important ways: providing a temporary monopoly, enhancing financial performance, and increasing competitiveness.[4]

ESTABLISH A TEMPORARY MONOPOLY

The most important benefit of a patent is that it lets a company take advantage of a first-mover strategy in a market with no immediate competitors; that is, it enables the company to stake out a temporary monopoly. An effective patent strategy also protects core technologies and enables the entrepreneur to leverage them to create a family of branded products. Cogent Systems accomplished that by building a family of products around its unique fingerprint matching system. Xerox held a monopoly on the copier market for almost 20 years before it was forced by a federal court to license its technology. So important is the first-mover advantage that some firms focus their R&D efforts on areas where they can gain the strongest patent protection and avoid litigation.

IMPROVE FINANCIAL PERFORMANCE

Today, the majority of a company's assets reside in IP, and these assets are often underutilized and undervalued, usually because no market for them has been identified, so no revenue stream is possible. Patents have the potential to be important revenue generators through licensing royalties on their use. They also save companies money when they're used as bargaining chips for strategic partnerships and cross-licensing agreements, or where the patent is used as payment for the use of another company's patent. Because the cost of maintaining patents is relatively high due to maintenance fees charged by the USPTO (see Figure 6-2) and the opportunity cost of not commercializing the patents, it is important that entrepreneurs either commercialize the patents they have or donate unneeded patents to universities and other nonprofits such as the National Institute for Strategic Technology Acquisition and Commercialization (NISTAC) in Kansas City, which works to find new commercialization opportunities for patents donated to it. These donated patents become a write-off against taxable income for the company.

An audit of a company's patent portfolio can yield a veritable treasure trove of potential revenues and cost savings; therefore, any patent strategy should include due diligence on the company's existing patent portfolio. The following are some actions that should be taken during a patent audit:

- Map the patents in the portfolio to determine expiration dates, maintenance fee schedules, strength of patents, and interrelationships among patents.

- Determine if there is access to the know-how associated with the patent either in the form of documents or the original inventor(s).

- Check how often other companies cite these patents or target them for acquisition. If those citations are declining in number, it may mean that the patent is becoming obsolete and the pace of innovation in that area has slowed.

FIGURE 6-2 It Costs Small Businesses Money to Hold a Patent

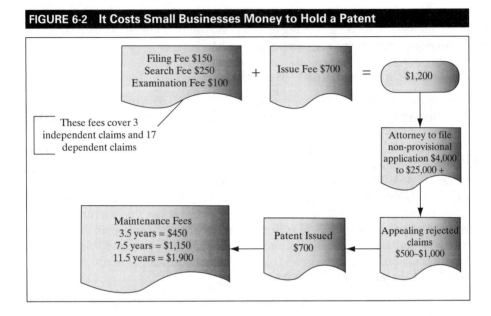

- Evaluate the financial worth of the patents. This can be accomplished by separating the patents into critical and noncritical patents according to their impact on company goals. Those that are critical typically involve core technologies used in the company's current and future products. Noncritical patents represent technologies that will be licensed and are not used in current or future products.

INCREASE COMPETITIVENESS

Patents can be a source of competitive advantage for the entrepreneurial companies that hold them. In addition to giving the entrepreneur a first-mover advantage with its temporary monopoly, patents can be licensed, creating a competitive advantage through customer and vendor relationships that are not easily circumvented. Furthermore, the patents of competitors are tools that enable the entrepreneur to gather intelligence about a competitor's strategy so that the entrepreneur can make more effective decisions about his company. In 1998, for example, a small, graphic chip design firm, S3, realized that it was very quickly going to run into Intel's patent wall and have to pay enormous royalties to do business. After conducting some patent research and using an anonymous bid, it managed to acquire the patents of a chipmaker that had filed for bankruptcy. Having done its homework, S3 knew that within that portfolio of patents it had acquired was the patent that pre-dated the Intel Merced chip patent. Now S3 was in a position to hold Intel hostage to potential infringement of the patent. Instead, S3 chose to reveal itself to Intel and require that Intel cross-license its patents in exchange for the vital patent S3 now owned.[5] The strategy was successful, and S3 is now a global company with more than 300 engineers and a long list of world-class clients such as Nokia and Motorola.

Although patents provide a strong competitive advantage, research has found that companies typically build an arsenal of weapons to support their patents. These weapons include secrecy, first-to-market and integrated product/process strategies, trademarks, and supply chain control strategies, all of which are designed to strengthen the patent position and put up barriers wherever a competitor tries to go.[6] The need for a diversified portfolio of strategies comes from the very nature of competitive advantage in high technology. Some of the tactics used to create a competitive advantage for technology entrepreneurs include patent walls, running, and coalitions.[7]

CREATING A PATENT WALL

Companies with proprietary consumer products that are easy to design around often attempt to create a patent wall, a barrier of multiple, interlocking patents that prevent another company from duplicating the product without infringing on multiple patents. Gillette, the shaver company, has taken this strategy to superior heights. For example, it has surrounded its Sensor shaver with 22 interlocking patents that cover everything from the twin, independently moving blades to the design of the handle. It even patented the container in which it comes because it gives off a masculine sound and feel when the package is ripped open.

A similar strategy is *bracketing,* which is when derivative inventions that surround the original patent effectively lock a competitor out of the market. For example, suppose a company has developed an innovative high-intensity light and has patented the filament. Now suppose that the filament requires a more durable glass bulb and socket housing to absorb the additional heat from the high-intensity bulb and special packaging because the bulbs are vulnerable to the oil on human hands. The company holds the patent on the filament, but if another company develops and patents the socket housing, the glass bulb, and the packaging, it has effectively locked the original company out of the market unless it goes through the competitor.[8] So the developer of the filament must also capture the components surrounding the filament to insure the ability to commercialize the invention. If he does not, a large company can respond by "wallpapering" around it through a series of closely related patents. Then the large company sues the entrepreneurial company for patent infringement because the entrepreneur can't commercialize his technology without going through the wall that the large company has erected. Because the entrepreneur cannot afford to fight a multimillion dollar battle given its limited resources, she backs off and agrees to license the technology to the big company for less money than she rightfully should have gotten.[9] Studying the patent landscape around the invention is critical to avoiding this type of situation.

RUNNING

If a company sets up a barrier, a competitor will eventually find a way around it, or at least that is the premise behind the run strategy. Inventors who sit behind their patent barriers in a defensive posture actually give their competitors time to catch up on the learning curve and overcome any barriers the inventor may have erected. To avoid this problem, entrepreneurs must plan to introduce a constant stream of patented innovation, always staying at least one step ahead of the competitor. By doing so, the inventor gains first-mover advantage and a greater degree of control over the competitive environment over time.[10] The inventor-entrepreneur employs the running strategy by decreasing the cycle time on next-generation products through parallel development: a new technology enters the market, another is in development, and another is on the drawing boards. Successful technology companies such as Intel use this strategy.

BUILDING A COALITION

A competitive strategy that runs counterintuitive to traditional thinking is when a company lowers barriers to entry and invites competitors to use its technology, creating a coalition of companies all using the same technology. Innovators choose this approach for several reasons: (1) to increase the likelihood that their technology becomes the dominant design by having more companies develop applications and use it, (2) to increase demand from distributors and end users, (3) to enhance the company's current capabilities by partnering, (4) to take advantage of the network effects of more people using the technology, and (5) to enter markets that were previously unattainable.[11] These coalitions are often created through licensing. In the 1970s, Intel licensed its microprocessor to several semiconductor companies in an effort to ensure that customers had an adequate supply of microprocessors and system support. In turn, these licensees then developed complementary chips, which worked to ensure that Intel became the dominant design. Once Intel's design was established as the dominant technology in the industry, Intel kept future generations of chips proprietary to insure its dominance.

Entrepreneurs can take advantage of a number of ways to leverage the patents their company holds in advantageous ways, but one of the critical decisions relative to patent strategy is determining when and if to patent.

DECIDING WHEN AND IF TO PATENT

In some instances, a market opportunity demands that a company commercialize its technology prior to seeking or achieving patent protection. Usually this is a case where technology development is moving quickly and the opportunity could be lost if delayed by the patent process. During the feasibility analysis portion of the commercialization process, an entrepreneur investigates the market to determine if the business concept developed around the technology has merit. This process takes time, money, and effort, but is an important task to undertake prior to spending substantially more time and money developing a prototype and completing the commercialization process. Feasibility analysis reduces some of the risk of a technology launch by helping the entrepreneur decide if a patent is warranted and the timing is correct.

CHOOSING WHETHER TO PATENT

In general, positive answers to several questions will help an entrepreneur decide that an invention should be patented, assuming that it meets the

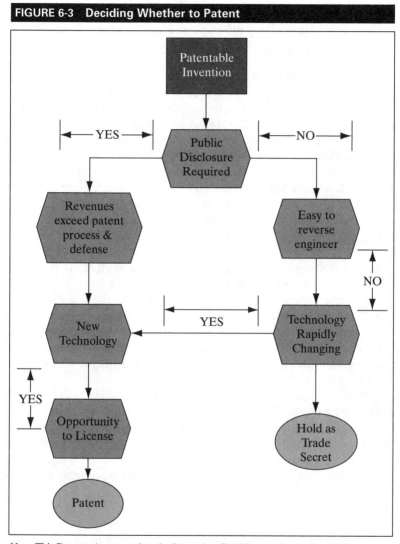

FIGURE 6-3 Deciding Whether to Patent

Note: This Process Assumes that the Invention Qualifies for Patent Protection.

requirements of the U.S. Patent and Trademark Office discussed in Chapter 5. This decision-making process is depicted in Figure 6-3.

- Does this invention solve key challenges in the market?
- Does the invention fall under the oversight of the FDA? FDA regulations require that therapeutics and small-molecule drugs be disclosed publicly when they're marketed.
- Will revenues exceed the potential cost of litigation and patent enforcement?

- Is the invention easily reverse-engineered?
- Is the field of use evolving too rapidly to take the time to patent?
- Is there an intent to license the technology?

Sometimes choosing not to patent an invention is the best strategy. The independent inventor with a small company needs to carefully consider whether filing for a patent is worth it. The only right that is gained from a patent is the right to sue an infringer, and the entrepreneur may not have the financial wherewithal to do so. If an entrepreneur holds critical know-how that is essential to the implementation of the invention, she may decide not to patent it and retain the invention as a trade secret. It will be very difficult, even for a large company, to duplicate that tacit knowledge. If, on the other hand, a patent is absolutely necessary, the inventing entrepreneur should consider partnering with a larger company looking for new technology. The chances of actually getting the technology to market without having to deal with infringement lawsuits will be much greater.

Consider a situation where a company has no significant competition and its R&D costs represent less than 2 percent of the selling price of its product. The company would incur little risk in simply forgoing the expensive patent process in favor of building its brand quickly in the marketplace. By contrast, consider a company that has a huge R&D expense to recoup from its initial sales. It needs time to do that, and, if it has a successful product, competitors will flock to replicate it. In this case, the company might be wise to seek patent protection.

Another instance where choosing not to patent might make sense is where there is no way to create an impenetrable patent barrier or doing so would be too costly and time consuming. Again, the better strategy may be to get the product to market quickly and keep improving it to stay ahead of follow-on competitors. In general, in situations where the real life span of the patent is uncertain because of market fluctuations, and the profit potential is also uncertain, it may not make sense to spend the time and money filing for a patent.

TIMING THE PATENT

During the feasibility process, entrepreneurs need to be careful to not run afoul of one important rule: the on-sale bar. The courts have specifically prevented inventors from describing their inventions in a printed publication in the United States or in a foreign country or from putting their inventions in public use or on sale more than a year prior to filing for a patent (35 USC § 102b). What constitutes "on sale" is subject to question, and what bars a patent application depends on: (1) clarification of the minimum type of activity that comprises "on sale" and (2) identification of the point at which a process becomes an invention. Nevertheless, this is an important rule that has kept many an inventor or university researcher from seeking patents on their research. In particular, university researchers are under pressure to publish to meet their tenure requirements, but publishing too early may bar a patent. To avoid being subject to the on-sale bar, entrepreneurs should do the following:[12]

- Disclose to the USPTO any sales so that they are considered "of record." This permits the USPTO to study the sales to determine if the patent application is still valid and increases the chances that the examiner will allow the claims.

- At a minimum file a provisional patent application prior to undertaking any commercial activity to establish a priority date. The application should fully disclose the invention that will be put on sale.

- If conducting an "experimental sales program," to judge the efficacy of the invention, the product should be given at no charge and the customer informed that the product is a "beta."

UNDERSTANDING PATENT INFRINGEMENT

Patent infringement occurs when a party other than the inventor holding the patent or a legal licensee makes and sells a product that contains every one of the elements of a claim in that patent. The issuance of a patent gives the holder the right to defend that patent against infringers in a federal court. In fact, an inventor must defend a patent or risk losing it in a challenge from a competitor. If a patent holder is successful in prosecuting the infringer, he or she may receive a reasonable royalty and an injunction to prevent further manufacture and use of the infringing product. If the infringer refuses to pay the required royalty, the inventor can enjoin or close down the infringer's operation. Alternatively, the court may choose to mediate an agreement between the parties that allows the infringer to pay an agreed-upon royalty in exchange for permission to use the patented invention.

Surprisingly, it is quite difficult to prove that a patent is invalid because the courts generally side with the USPTO, assuming that it made the proper decision. This means that defendants in an infringement suit bear the burden of proving with "clear and convincing" evidence that the patent is not valid. This is a much higher burden of proof than the typical "preponderance of evidence" found in civil litigation. Additionally, the U.S. Supreme Court has established the "doctrine of equivalents," which assets that a product will infringe an existing patent claim even if it lacks a component listed in the claim if it contains a similar component that is "insubstantially different." This was done to prevent infringers from using insignificant differences to circumvent a patent. However, the federal circuit court has recently defined the doctrine more narrowly, saying that if a component was added after the original filing of the patent application (and that is often the case), that component is not entitled to protection under the doctrine of equivalents [*Festo Corp. v. Shoketsu Kinzoku Kogyo Kabushiki Co.* 187 F.3d 1381, 1381–1382, 51 USPQ2d 1959, 1959–1960 (Fed. Cir. 1999)]. What this means is that if a patentee fails to claim a particular item, the patentee now has the right, within two years of the grant of the original patent, to file a reissue application to enlarge the scope of the original claims. This can only be done to correct an error "made without any deceptive intention," but which resulted in the patent being wholly or partly invalid" [35 U.S.C. § 251 (2000)].

Patent infringement actions are costly and very difficult to prosecute, primarily because the infringer often makes the case that the patent was invalid in the first place and that assertion presents a far more complex issue. The average cost of patent litigation today is reaching $4 million and growing.[13] Moreover, many companies regularly challenge their competitors' patents in court as a business strategy to drain their competitor's resources and make it difficult for the patent holder to compete. A patent infringement warning, which generally comes in the form of a strong letter from the patent owner's attorney, should never be ignored. If an entrepreneur receives a cease and desist letter for patent infringement from a competitor's attorney, it's important to consult with an attorney to determine if infringement is actually taking place. If an entrepreneur finds that his company is infringing another company's patents, it should take immediate steps to stop the infringement and seek a resolution from the owner.[14] If, on the other hand, an inventor's patent has been infringed upon by another company, the inventor may recover damages for a period of up to 6 years before he files the suit against the infringer. If the inventor waits too long to file a suit, however, he may be barred from filing at all, because it is presumed that if the inventor knew about the infringement and did nothing, he probably was unable to defend his patent.

The courts tend to favor the inventor and often file injunctions against alleged infringers even before the case is tried. The courts can also triple the damages if they determine that the infringement was willful (see Case Study: Settling Patent Infringement Can Be Lucrative). Enormous awards in the hundreds of millions of dollars are not uncommon. In 1996, independent inventor Gilbert Hyatt received a patent on the basic microprocessor, astonishing the semiconductor industry. He then assigned his rights to Phillips Petroleum Co., which helped him collect $100 million in licensing fees from the computer industry.[15] This case was not an overnight success, however; Gilbert had fought for this patent for 20 years.

CASE STUDY

Settling Patent Infringement Can Be Lucrative

Jerome Lemelson was one of the most prolific inventors in U.S. history, but his fame comes from the rewards he reaped from aggressively defending his patents against major corporations. In 1989, he received his first favorable verdict when a jury awarded him $24.8 million against toy manufacturer Mattel, Inc., which had infringed on his patent for a flexible toy racetrack. The judge later raised the amount to $71 million because he believed that Mattel had willfully infringed on the patent, but in 1992, an appeals court overturned the ruling. That did not stop Lemelson, who went on to file

(continued)

(*continued*)

lawsuits and threaten companies such as Motorola, Eastman Kodak, and Apple. By the time of his death in October 1997, he had received about $200 million in settlement compensation. In an effort to support the efforts of independent inventors and to encourage people to invent, Lemelson used the money to establish a foundation to "stimulate the U.S. economy and secure its position in the global marketplace by creating the next generation of inventors, innovators, and entrepreneurs."[16]

PROTECTING TRADEMARKS

Companies are now taking greater care in protecting their trademarks because trademarks are more than simply a way to distinguish one company or one product from another. They can actually bestow inimitable associations and meanings to a product that set it apart from competitors. This competitive value often results in other companies intentionally or unintentionally infringing on a trademark holder's rights. The standard for judging trademark infringement is the likelihood of confusion,[17] and similarity between trademarks is the most common cause of trademark infringement cases.[18] Trademarks cause confusion if they result in the same connotation in the minds of consumers, for example, the confusion between Play-Doh and Fundough *(Kenner Parker Toys Inc. v. Rose Art Industries Inc.)*, or when one trademark is very similar to another, so much so that it appears that they come from the same source, for example, Roach Inn and Roach Motel insect killers *(American Home Products Corp. v. Johnson Chemical Co., Inc.)*.[19]

Many companies exacerbate the problem by misusing their trademarks in print. In the following example, notice that in the first case, *Mywidget* is used as a noun, in the second as an adjective to describe software.

Incorrect usage: *Mywidget*™ is the future of Web 2.0 businesses.
Correct usage: *Mywidget*™ software will help customers build their Web 2.0 businesses.

Trademark names by definition are adjectives that describe a product or service. They are not the actual product or service and should not be used as such. Furthermore, the trademark should always be used consistently in the same typeface or style.

As a company grows and develops a portfolio of trademarks, these trademarks will need to be managed. It's often useful to divide the trademarks into three buckets: strategic trademarks (essential to the mission of the company), sub-brand trademarks that help differentiate the company, and tactical trademarks, which are not essential and might be abandoned or held under common law protection. By categorizing the trademarks, an entrepreneur can better understand and allocate the resources required to maintain them.

TRADEMARKS AND THE INTERNET

The growth of the Internet has made the protection of trademarks much more challenging. In 1998, MARQUES, the European association of trademark-owning companies, surveyed 350 IP specialists to examine the issue of trademark infringement on the Internet. In just 3 weeks, it received 60 responses and found that at least 85 percent of companies had experienced IP infringement, 78 percent had suffered domain name infringement, and 40 percent had experienced copyright infringement.[20]

So how does a company protect its trademark against infringement on the Internet? The World Intellectual Property Organization (WIPO; www.wipo.int) suggests the following tactics:

- Conduct an Internet audit of domain names and trademarks on the Web using an Internet search engine such as Google. Examining UseNet (user groups) and the company's e-mail system to learn the extent of infringement is also important.

- Monitor the company's domain name portfolio on a monthly basis; that is, check every site the company owns to make certain that it is accurate. Domain name registrations should be renewed promptly.

- Perform a monthly audit of the Internet, UseNet, and any other areas where infringers are likely to operate. Systems can be purchased that will do these searches and provide reports on a daily basis.

- Check to make sure that appropriate trademark and copyright notices are posted.

- Make certain that the company is entitled to use any images or content that appear on its Web site and that it has appropriate permissions where required.

LICENSING INTELLECTUAL PROPERTY

Licensing is simply a grant to another party that permits that party to develop, manufacture, distribute, or otherwise use the licensor's IP in the marketplace whether that IP is technology, a process, or a trademark. Examples of licensing deals range from the very complex, such as licensing the breakthrough Contour Crafting robotic technology that will construct a whole house in 24 hours,[21] to a simple trademark cross-licensing deal such as the one that publisher HarperCollins created with coffee roaster Leaves-N-Beans Roasting Co. to promote paperback books with bags of coffee.[22]

Although the largest dollar revenue volumes from licensing go to large corporations (IBM generates approximately $1 billion in licensing revenues annually),[23] most licensors and licensees are actually smaller entrepreneurial companies that have learned that royalty revenues provide a significantly higher return on investment than many other sources of revenue.[24] There are a number of reasons why licensing may make sense for both the licensor and the licensee. First, it is often more profitable for the owner of a patent or trademark to become a licensor than to try to develop and market all the possible applications of the invention or trademark. Some technology inventions, particularly platform technologies from which many derivative applications are possible, are too large in potential scope and require too many resources for any one company to commercialize them alone. In fact, frequently the inventor company cannot identify all the possible applications of its invention. In this situation, licensing to other companies that have established manufacturing and distribution capabilities speeds the adoption of the technology and stimulates further innovation.[25] In the United States, manufacturing is historically the largest recipient of royalty income, at about 76 percent of the country's total royalty income. This is not surprising when one considers that about 73 percent of all R&D is performed by manufacturing businesses. However, nonmanufacturing royalties are increasing, particularly in the areas of communication services, computer programming and related businesses, and testing services.[26] For example, an entrepreneur may develop a proprietary process that can be licensed to noncompeting industries, producing a valuable new revenue source.

There are also nonfinancial reasons for entrepreneurial companies to have a licensing strategy in place. For example, many software companies prefer to have another company handle distribution. They do this by licensing their core software product to developers who can then customize it to meet the needs of particular customers. This enables the original software manufacturer to enjoy the benefits of reaching multiple markets without the expense of setting up distribution channels. The licensee (in this case the distributor) benefits from gaining access to new technology and increasing its product offerings. Another example is the benefit of cross-licensing technologies as a way to avoid what is known as a patent thicket—where multiple blocking patents held by various competitors prevent innovation from taking place. By creating patent pools and cross-licensing each other's technologies, competitors are effectively able to continue to innovate while stopping new competition with substitute technologies from entering their space.[27]

Licensors of trademarks, such as the Walt Disney Company's licensing of its characters, benefit from taking its brand into markets that it does not have the capability to access, such as apparel and electronics. Entrepreneurs with products that would benefit from the association with a globally recognized brand such as Disney stand to gain from licensing the trademarks.

Finally, in-licensing, or purchasing the IP of another company to complement existing technology or to improve processes, is an excellent, but often unrecognized, way for entrepreneurs to augment performance and spur growth without investing in significant research and development.[28] Of course, in-licensing can include not only technology and systems but trademarks as well. Often the association of the entrepreneur's brand with an established and respected brand increases the value of the entrepreneur's product. As a young start-up with a proprietary fingerprint matching technology, Cogent Systems licensed its technology to TRW (later acquired by Northrop Grumman) and partnered with that company so that it could bid on lucrative government contracts that required an association with a prime contractor.

It is important to note that independent inventors who become entrepreneurs and launch companies sometimes choose to hold their IP in their own name and then license it to their company. In this way, the entrepreneur insures that he or she controls the IP in the event that something happens to the company. However, when entrepreneur-inventors seek investor capital, this approach will probably not fly. Investors will no doubt want the IP to reside in the company and will ask that the inventor assign the patents to the company so that the company owns them. The reason is, if the inventor retains ownership, he or she could potentially license it to competitors.[29] Consulting with an attorney on the pros and cons of doing this would be essential.

Although licensing revenues are critical to entrepreneurial companies with relatively small patent portfolios, these same companies are also facing significant challenges from piracy, infringement, and globalization, which can make it more difficult to grow their portfolios.[30] A 2006 PricewaterhouseCoopers (PWC) study on technology licensing revealed this new licensing environment for smaller, entrepreneurial companies and suggested that these companies may need to position themselves for acquisition by a larger company or risk that their licensing revenues decline in favor of companies with revenues of over $100 million and portfolios of more than 250 licenses. PWC attributes this advantage of larger companies to network effects—the value of a network increases with the size of the network. What entrepreneurs can learn from this research is that their ability to create networks of partners will increase their chances of dealing effectively with these new challenges.

In the next sections, we consider licensing strategy from the perspectives of the licensor and the licensee and then examine what it takes to create an effective license agreement. Figure 6-4 depicts the process from both perspectives.

THE LICENSOR'S PERSPECTIVE ON THE LICENSING PROCESS

The licensor is the individual or company that grants license rights to another individual or company for the use of an invention. A successful licensing process will include a number of steps that should be followed to ensure that the needs of both the licensor and the licensee, who will depend on each other during the term of the agreement, are met in a mutually satisfactory way.

DECIDE WHAT WILL BE LICENSED

An individual entrepreneur or a company can license a product, process, know-how, a brand, and the rights to manufacture, market, distribute, or use a product in the production of another product. Every situation is different; therefore, the best combination of rights for the technology an entrepreneur wishes to license must be determined so that the highest value possible can be achieved. The licensor must also decide whether the licensee will have the right to further develop or modify the technology and whether those modifications will be granted back to the licensor.

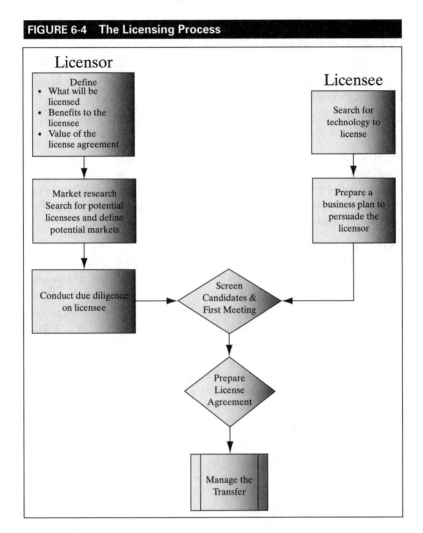

FIGURE 6-4 The Licensing Process

DEFINE THE BENEFITS TO THE LICENSEE

As with any purchase, licensees will be purchasing benefits that they need. These benefits must be identified; in other words, what makes the license valuable to the licensee? The licensor's ability to achieve the highest value for IP is a function of the benefits the customer perceives to be associated with the technology, as well as the associated benefits of any know-how or tacit knowledge that is transferred with the IP. Benefits are easily defined from the licensor's perspective, but the licensee's perspective is critical to achieving the valuation that the licensor seeks.

DETERMINE THE VALUE OF THE LICENSE

Several factors determine the ultimate value of a license:

• The economic life of the IP, that is, how long it can potentially provide a revenue stream to the company. This is often not based on the remaining term of a patent but rather on how long the IP can produce revenue before it is rendered obsolete by new technology.

- The potential for direct competition by companies that design around the IP.
- The potential for government legislation or regulation that might damage the marketability of the IP.
- Changes in market conditions that might render the IP obsolete or depress its value.

Unfortunately, no formula can perfectly determine the value of a license agreement because each deal is unique. Issues such as whether to license on a percentage of gross sales basis or on a use basis will affect value. Whether or not geographic exclusivity is important will also affect the structure of the deal. Valuation of technology is discussed in more detail in Chapter 7.

CONDUCT MARKET RESEARCH

It is important to make certain that the potential market into which the licensee will take the product is sufficiently large to ensure a reasonable profit from the effort. If the licensor's IP is new, that is, not well known, the licensor will have to build a case for the feasibility of the market to attract potential licensees. Potential licensees will have conducted their own research, and the results of that research will be presented to the licensor as part of their business plan; however, it is always wise for licensors to do their own research as well. Because licensees are trying to make a case for the market they have chosen for the licensor's technology, they may avoid bringing up negatives. Therefore, licensors will want to find out for themselves what those negatives might be and if they can be overcome.

SCREEN CANDIDATES AND THE FIRST MEETING

It is often the case that a licensor will receive initial interest from several candidates, some who might simply be testing the waters and are not very serious about following through. To avoid wasting time on unqualified prospective candidates, licensors often ask for a refundable evaluation fee. Upon receiving an inquiry from a potential licensee about a licensor's IP and a request to schedule a potential visit, the licensor should perform several tasks as described in the following sections.

Prepare for the First Meeting. Before the first meeting with a potential licensee the licensor should:

- Provide the potential licensee with a comprehensive nonconfidential disclosure about the IP that is available for licensing.
- Elicit additional information from the licensee candidate about the company's capacity, staffing plans, technical capabilities, and financial strength.
- Prepare a secrecy agreement for the licensee candidate.
- Prepare employees for the visit, its purpose, and the need for nondisclosure of certain elements of the IP.
- Do due diligence on the licensee before the meeting.

From this point forward, the task descriptions are focused on the licensing of technology since it is a more complex process. However, the fundamentals can be applied to the licensing of trademarks as well.

Conduct the First Meeting. The first meeting should take place at the licensor's site so that the licensor maintains control of the discussion and disclosure. The licensor should present a professional presence and avoid unprepared remarks. If language is a problem, an interpreter will ensure that the parties understand each other correctly. The licensor should make clear that any technology advancements undertaken by the licensee are granted back to the licensor. In addition, license payments must be tied to performance and the licensor should discuss the impact of secrecy obligations.

Undertake Due Diligence on the Licensee. License agreements, the contracts that detail the relationship between the licensor and licensee, usually extend for several years; therefore, it is vitally important to ensure that any potential licensee possesses the resources, knowledge, and skills to fulfill the terms and conditions of the license agreement and successfully commercialize the technology. Any potential licensee candidates should provide contact information for previous license agreements they may have had. The licensor should then follow-up on those contacts to find out if the candidate was reliable in the payment of royalties and achieved performance targets. This will be a good indication of how the licensee will behave under a new license agreement. License agreements are discussed more fully in a later section.

MANAGING THE LICENSE

Licensors must develop a strategy to effectively manage the transfer of technology so that the IP can be protected during the licensing process. The following sections present some guidelines for managing the transfer of technology.

SECRECY AND NEGOTIATION

The licensor should define the plans for disclosure of the technology to the licensee, which typically is accomplished in stages until the final agreement is signed. During the negotiation period, the licensee may designate a "Typhoid Mary" in her organization who receives the technology disclosure information but is contractually constrained (in effect, quarantined) from revealing it to others in the company (or outside the company) for a specified period of time.

The license agreement that will spell out the terms of the license arrangement is a negotiated document, and the party who wields the most clout is the one who brings something critical to the table. Licensors typically possess power when they own a radical technology that no one else has. Licensees hold the power when the innovation is so radical that there are few, if any, potential licensees willing to take the risk of developing and commercializing it. To entice the first licensee, the licensor may have to provide preferential treatment in the form of a lower royalty rate, a lower up-front fee, and the first right of refusal on new markets. To effectively negotiate with the licensee in this or any other scenario, the licensor needs to understand the other party's decision-making processes because this information will affect the timeline for transfer of the technology and its ultimate commercialization in the marketplace.

THE POINT OF CONTACT

The licensor should establish a point of contact with the licensee's business and assign someone in the company as the licensee's point of contact to reduce the possibility of communication problems. It is likely that the licensor will also need to provide some in-house technical support over the term of the agreement. Companies often place one of their own employees inside the licensee's company during the development phase to oversee and facilitate a smooth transfer of the technology.

THE LICENSEE'S PERSPECTIVE ON THE LICENSING PROCESS

With more and more companies acquiring technology to speed up their R&D processes and remain competitive, in-licensing has become big business. However, the very speed that has induced companies to acquire technology rather than develop it themselves has made the due diligence prerequisite that much more important. The licensee must investigate the licensor's track record. Has the licensor successfully executed other license agreements? What has been the company's success rate with new products? What kind of relationship has the company had with its licensees?

Potential licensees should insist on direct access to the owner/CEO of the company with which they intend to do business. The owner/CEO represents the vision of the company and embodies its culture and attitudes. If the licensee does not have good feelings about this person, chances are she will not enjoy working with the company. Two clues to the potential success or failure with the licensor are whether or not the owner/CEO prepared for the first meeting and their attitude at that meeting. A lack of preparation could signal that the company is not familiar with the licensing process or that it does not take the licensee seriously. If the licensing company employs a full-time licensing professional with expertise in tech transfer, the whole process will go much more smoothly.

SEARCHING FOR THE RIGHT TECHNOLOGY

Evaluating the technology that the licensee wishes to acquire is critically important because the consequences will be long term and any mistakes will be costly. Table 6-1 presents some of the sources for licensing that will assist the entrepreneur in the search.

Once a technology is identified, some of the questions that should be answered when evaluating a technology are:

- Does the technology work in the way the licensor claims?
- On what measures are the performance data calculated? Watch out for data based solely on lab performance because there is usually a decline in performance from the laboratory to the real world.

TABLE 6-1 Resources for Licensees	
Free Software Foundation: http://www.fsf.org/licensing	A useful site for entrepreneurs dealing with open source software licensing.
Google patents: http://www.google.com/patents	A simple intuitive approach to patent search.
IP world: http://ipworldonline.com/	A global resource on issues related to patents and trademarks as well as news on IP.
NISTAC: http://www.k-state.edu/tech.transfer/NISTAC	A non-for-profit associated with Kansas State Universities with technologies donated from Fortune 50 companies that are available for licensing.
University Tech Transfer Offices	Go to the university's home page and search on "university tech transfer."
U.S. Patent and Trademark Office: http://www.uspto.gov	A searchable database of all issued patents and registered trademarks.
Yet2.com: http://www.yet2.com	A clearinghouse for technologies that inventors and companies want to license. Also, a place where licensors promote their technologies.

- Will the licensor provide any guarantees of the technology's performance?
- Is the technology completely owned by the licensor or does the licensee also have to be concerned about another party and their role in the process?

To add order to the often chaotic world of licensing, some companies, such as Yet2.com, have created license exchanges, which are matchmaking sites for licensors and potential licensees. Yet2.com believes that most companies exploit only about 20 percent of their R&D ideas because they cannot find value in the remainder.[31] It also claims a clientele that includes Boeing, Honeywell, Microsoft, Toshiba, and Sony Corporation among others.[32] The problem is that most companies rely on the grapevine to find licensees, and that technique is often not very fruitful. For example, 3M holds the patent on a polymer that they use in adhesives. They know that the polymer could also be used in chromatography, but 3M does not do work in that area, so they do not know any potential licensing candidates. By putting the patent on a license exchange, 3M might be able to find an entrepreneurial company that can commercialize it.

Yet2.com places anonymous descriptions of licensors' technologies on its site. The licensors pay a modest fee per entry, and the potential licensees view the descriptions for free. If they would like to view more complete descriptions, earlier uses of the technology, patent status, and licensing forms, they pay a small fee. To go to the next level of access, the potential licensee must pay an earnest fee and then the licensor is revealed to them. If a deal is brokered and a license agreement executed, Yet2.com receives a commission.

PREPARING A BUSINESS PLAN

The licensor will want to know that the licensee has studied the market and has a plan for how to commercialize the technology. The licensee will be asked to provide a business plan that demonstrates her company's ability to execute, in other words, that the company has the resources—human, financial, knowledge, and facilities—to commercialize the technology. Information about how to construct this business plan can be found in Chapter 3.

NEGOTIATING THE TYPE OF LICENSE

From the licensee's perspective, the technology for which the licensee is seeking rights should be uncoupled from the business itself. What this means is that the licensee should only pay for the value added by the new product associated with the license agreement. Furthermore, if the licensee must do some additional development to get the technology ready for market (and most do), the licensee would be wise to seek an exclusive license for the markets in which the technology will be exploited. Licensees generally do not benefit from a nonexclusive license that gives all competitors the same advantage. With a nonexclusive license, only the licensor and the customers of the licensee benefit. From a licensee's perspective, an exclusive license, even for just one industry, is preferable to a nonexclusive license for products in several industries. However, licensors who grant exclusive licenses typically do so only to an established industry player because a larger company will be able to pay the higher royalty rate associated with an exclusive license. Licensors typically grant exclusive licenses only in fields in which the licensee has a demonstrated capability and they grant global rights only to companies that have global experience. Nonexclusive licenses are most appropriate for technologies that have broad applications in many areas such that no one company could possibly cover them all. Genetic therapy is one example of a field where nonexclusive licensing or exclusive licensing in one industry is advantageous because at this early stage of the technology, it is nearly impossible to predict all of its possible applications in medicine, agriculture, and the chemical industry.

THE LICENSE AGREEMENT

The license agreement is the contract between the licensor and the licensee that spells out the terms and conditions of the license over its life. Because this agreement will likely last for several years, both parties should consult an attorney with experience in license agreements. The following sections describe some of the clauses typically found in license agreements. A qualified attorney will structure the agreement with the appropriate clauses for the particular situation.

GRANT CLAUSE

The grant clause describes what is being delivered to the licensee through the license agreement, that is, the right to manufacture, distribute, use, and so forth.

To accomplish the transfer of the technology, this clause will typically grant the licensee the right to practice the technology and the right to receive the knowledge and know-how of the licensor, which may be transferred via design sessions, training, and so forth. The grant clause also states whether the license is exclusive, which gives the specified rights only to the licensee, or nonexclusive, which means that others may enjoy these rights as well. It may contain an immunity-from-infringement clause to protect the licensee from potential patent infringement by the original inventor. This clause will also specify if the licensee has the right to grant rights to sub licensees, which may be necessary if the licensee outsources some of its functions.

PERFORMANCE CLAUSE

A performance clause states the dates by which the licensee should have achieved certain agreed-upon goals, such as development of the commercial application of the technology, first customer, or sales targets. Performance clauses are like preventive medicine. They help the licensor avoid a situation where the licensee ties up a technology in an exclusive agreement but never actually commercializes it or never achieves the projected sales levels.

SECRECY CLAUSE

A secrecy or confidentiality clause restricts disclosure and use of the information being transferred and specifies who may know the details of the IP and for what period of time. It also spells out when and under what conditions the person may share the details with others in the licensee's business and for how long. Typically a secrecy obligation lasts for between 5 and 10 years.

PAYMENT CLAUSE

The payment clause discusses the method of payment for the license. The licensor often charges an up-front commitment fee that ensures that the licensee has a financial stake in the venture. Then there is a running royalty that is typically based on a percentage of gross sales and is charged over the life of the license agreement. A significantly higher royalty rate can be commanded with an exclusive license that gives the licensee the advantage of a temporary monopoly in which to establish the new product.

If the license agreement involves a foreign licensee, this clause will also designate the currency in which royalties will be paid. U.S. licensors typically want payment made in U.S. dollars, but sometimes the licensor and licensee agree on a combination of both currencies. Because foreign currency fluctuates over the life of the agreement, royalty payments will vary as well, which could result in more or less income for the licensor, as well as higher or lower payments for the licensee. These factors should all be taken into consideration when structuring the royalty portion of the agreement.

GRANTBACK CLAUSE

A grantback clause is sometimes called an improvement clause. It permits the licensee to improve on the product with the stipulation that the rights to any improvements are granted back to the licensor. The agreement may also have a grantforward clause, which gives the licensee the right to use improvements made by the licensor or original inventor.

TERM

Every license agreement, like every contract, must specify a term for its existence at the end of which the agreement no longer binds the parties. It is possible to specify in the agreement that the license agreement may be renewed or extended by mutual agreement of the parties.

ADDITIONAL CLAUSES

Some license agreements involve equity instead of royalties or even a combination of the two. Other agreements entail cross-licensing between the two firms party to the agreement. In yet other situations, the agreement contains a "most favorable licensee" clause where the first licensee of a new technology receives additional benefits and more favorable financial terms for the risk of being the pioneer than those given to subsequent licensees.

More and more software companies are including escrow clauses in their licensing agreements. The software companies place their source code into escrow with a neutral third party to serve as documentation if there is an IP lawsuit and to protect themselves and their customers should the company go bankrupt. In one instance, an Internet company had its entire Web site copied by a foreign competitor. Fortunately, the company had placed the text, photos, and graphics in an escrow account, so when the case got to court, the company would be in a better position to prove that theirs was the original site. As of 2000, one of every four business software licenses had an escrow clause in it.[33]

Because of the complexity and ramifications of the license agreement, it is imperative that entrepreneurs see the counsel of a qualified attorney who specializes in these types of agreements. A well-constructed license agreement is the capstone in a process that begins with the disclosure of the invention or the registering of a trademark.

Summary

IP is increasingly a source of wealth and risk for companies. The potential for new revenue streams from patents developed and never commercialized is enormous. At the same time, the need to defend IP against infringers has never been greater. An effective patent strategy will provide a temporary monopoly, enhance financial performance, and increase competitiveness, all of which contribute to a company's success. As with a patent strategy, a trademark strategy can build a strong brand and protect it. Rising R&D and production costs, increased competition, and an uncertain economy have spurred companies to diversify their revenue streams through licensing IP so as not to rely solely on revenues from sales. Licensors need to decide which of their technologies they want to license. Then they must define the benefits of the technology to the licensee and conduct market research to determine if what the potential licensee says about the market for the technology is reliable. Conducting due diligence on the licensee is important to ensure that the licensee has the resources, knowledge, and skills needed to fulfill the terms and conditions of the license agreement and successfully commercialize the technology. Valuing the license agreement is a difficult task that is based on the economic life of the IP, the potential for direct competition, the potential for government legislation, and changes in market conditions that could affect the value of the technology. The licensee, on the other hand, will want to do a comprehensive search for technology that will fit with their company and then prepare a business plan that will be shared with the licensor to demonstrate the licensee's understanding of the market and what is required to successfully commercialize the technology. Every company should have a licensing strategy that is supported by everyone in the organization, that contains a plan for managing the company's IP, and that allows the company to identify the best licensees.

Discussion Questions

1. In what ways can an effective patent strategy contribute to the success of a technology venture?
2. What is the value of developing a trademark strategy?
3. What steps should a company take if it suspects that an infringer is violating its patent?
4. Why is it important today for any technology company to have a licensing strategy?
5. From the licensor's perspective, what would be important to have in place prior to speaking to potential licensees?
6. Suppose you have found a core technology that you want to license to develop and sell applications in your industry. In addition to the technology, what would you want to have transferred under the license agreement?

CASE STUDY

Skycar—Licensing a Dream

Ever since the cartoon series "The Jetsons" became a household world in the 1970s, people have fantasized about owning a car that could fly. Today, with traffic problems in major metropolitan areas on the rise, the dream of rising above it all has the potential to become reality. At least that's the plan at Moller International in Davis, CA where the

(continued)

(*continued*)

company has been testing the M400 Skycar, which will transport four people at speeds similar of those of small planes. Successful commercialization of this invention will require "highways in the sky" that are controlled electronically and sanctioned by the Federal Aviation Administration (FAA). For now, that part of the dream is still at a distance.

However, in July 2007 after 20 years and $200 million in R&D, Paul Moller, a former UC Davis professor, began production on the M200G Volantor, a tiny two-passenger vehicle that can take off and land vertically like a helicopter. With the capability to stay in the air for between 45 and 90 minutes, it can fly at speeds up to 50 mph and stay at 10 feet off the ground to steer clear of FAA regulations. Reliability is a critical factor in the introduction of new technology, and that certainly is the case for an airborne vehicle such as the M200G. Customers want to know that the vehicle will perform as promised and not put them in greater danger than their car might. Being a pioneer in an industry is a long and arduous path with no guarantees. Pioneering technologies typically exert an enormous cash drain on a company and when finally they are launched, they tend to exhibit mediocre performance that only improves over many iterations or versions of the technology. The M200G is no exception. In 2007, Moller strategized that the company needed to move ahead quickly with projects that could immediately generate revenue to sustain the completion of the M400 Skycar, so the original plan to test fly the Skycar was delayed to 2008. Instead, Moller plans to produce the M200G at a rate of about 450 vehicles over three years and sell them at prices that range from $95,000 to $145,000, depending on options selected. Moller envisions the M200G as the "perfect all-terrain vehicle (ATV)" because it can operate over water, land, snow, crops, and so forth. Potential customers for such a vehicle include ship-to-shore transportation, ranching and farming, and paramilitary operations, to name a few.

Another technology that has the potential to bring in additional revenues to the company is their Rotapower® engine, which has been found to be a perfect power plant for plug-in hybrid electric vehicles. With their manufacturing partner Freedom Motors, which holds the worldwide exclusive license to distribute, manufacture, or sublicense engine production for any applications of the Rotapower engine except aircraft, Moller is planning to sublicense manufacturing of the engine to companies in China and Eastern Europe where the labor intensive process of engine assembly can be completed more economically.

Moller understands that adoption of radically new technology is never an easy path. Initially it is ridiculed (the same thing happened with the telephone, the airplane, and personal computers, for example); then people try to prevent its introduction, and finally it becomes obvious to everyone that the technology is going to take hold. Moller firmly believes that the M200G will pave the way for his Skycar eventually to take flight.

Sources: Jasmin Aline Persch (September 14, 2007). "Flying Car Guru Gets more Down to Earth," *NBC News,* www.msnbc.msn.com, accessed September 11, 2008; (August 2007). "Skycar Status Update," *Moller International* 7(2); Jordan Hultine (July 20, 2007). "Jetson-Like Flying Car in Production," *ABC News Internet Ventures;* (August 6, 2004). "Skycar Inventor Keeps Working on His Dream," *NBC News,* www.msnbc.msn.com, acessed September 11, 2008.

Endnotes

1. Dahl, D. (December 2007). "A Hacker in India Hijacked His Website Design and Was Making Good Money Selling It," *Inc Magazine,* http://www.inc.com/magazine/20071201/a-hacker-in-india-hijacked-his-website-design.html.
2. Goodwin Procter LLP (July 1, 2001). "Patent Licensing: Another Way to Enhance Return on Investment," *IP/Tech Advisor* 1(3): 1.
3. Kevin Klughart (July 1999). "Protect Your Intellectual Property," *Test & Measurement World* 15–22, http://www.tmworld.com/article/CA187500.html, accessed September 11, 2008.
4. Ibid.
5. Ibid.
6. Wesley Cohen, Richard Nelson, & John Walsh (2000). "Protecting Their Intellectual Assets: Appropriability Conditions and Why U.S. Manufacturing Firms Patent (or Not)," Working Paper No. 7552, National Bureau of Economic Research, Washington, DC.
7. Allen Afuah (1999). "Strategies to Turn Adversity into Profits," *Sloan Management Review,* 40(2): 99–109.
8. Kevin G. Rivette, & David Kline (January–February, 2000). "Discovering New Value in Intellectual Property," *Harvard Business Review,* p. 6.
9. Brad Mead (March 2001). "Patents: An Idea Whose Time Has Gone?" *Inc.,* pp. 43–44, www.inc.com, accessed September 11, 2008.
10. Afuah, *op. cit.*
11. Ibid.
12. William E. Hickman, & Michelle Saquet Temple (2003). "The On-Sale Bar After *Pfaff,*" *OKJOLT Rev.* 4: 18, www.okjolt.org, accessed September 11, 2008.
13. Kelly C. Hunsaker (August 30, 2005). "Taking Care of Business," *Open Forum, San Francisco Chronicle,* www.sfgate.com, accessed September 11, 2008.
14. Ralph A. Mittelberger (June 2001). "Patents: What Every Engineer Should Know," *Civil Engineering* 71(6): 58–63.
15. Mike Hofman (December 1997). "Patent Fending," *Inc.* 19(18): 111–114.
16. Lemelson Foundation Web site www.lemelson.org/, April 13, 2002, accessed September 11, 2008.
17. Michael J. Allen (1991). "Who Must Be Confused and When? The Scope of Confusion Actionable Under Trademark Law," *Trademark Reporter* 81(2): 209–259.
18. Ellen R. Foxman, Philip W. Berger, & Joseph A. Cote (March–April 1992). "Consumer Brand Confusion: A Conceptual Framework," *Psychology And Marketing* 9: 123–141.
19. Richard C. Kirkpatrick (1998). *Likelihood of Confusion in Trademark Law* (New York: Practicing Law Institute,); *Knorr-Nahrmittel A. G. V. Reese Finer Foods, Inc.* (1988), 695 F. Supp. 787 (D.N.J.).
20. Nicholas Wood, "Protecting Intellectual Property on The Internet. Experience and Strategies of Trademark Owners in a Time of Chance," *International Review of Law, Computers & Technology* 13(1): 21–28.
21. Contour Crafting, http://www.contourcrafting.org/, accessed September 11, 2008.
22. Johannes, A. (December 17, 2007). "HarperCollins, Coffee Co. Team for Packaging Deal," *International Licensing Industry Merchandisers' Association,* http://promomagazine.com/contests/news/harpercollins_coffee_team_deal/, accessed September 11, 2008.

23. Rajiv P. Patel (April 25, 2007). "A Patent Portfolio Development Strategy for Start-up Companies," *Fenwick & West LLP,* www.fenwick.com, accessed September 11, 2008.

24. Shiara M. Davila (July–August 2001). "Rent-A-Brand," *The Advisor,* pp. 34–36.

25. William J. Baumol (November–December 1999). "Licensing Proprietary Technology is a Profit Opportunity, Not a Threat," *Research-Technology Management* 42(6): 10–11.

26. Stephen A. Degnan (March–April 1999). "The Licensing Payoff from U.S. R&D," *Research-Technology Management* 42(2): 22–25.

27. Katherine J. Stranburg, Gabor Czardi, Jan Tobochnik, Peter Erdi, & Laszlo Zalanyi (2006). "Law and the Science of Networks: An Overview and an Application to the Patent Explosion," *Berkeley Technology Law Journal* 21(4): 1322.

28. Meagan C. Dietz, & Jeffrey J. Elton (May 18, 2005). "Getting More from Intellectual Property," *The McKinsey Quarterly,* wwww.mckinseyquarterly.com, accessed September 11, 2008.

29. Webb, M.S. (February 2005). "Your Patents: What Will the Investors Think?" *The Metropolitan Corporate Counsel,* p. 22.

30. Ibid. p. 8.

31. John Pullin (March 22, 2000). "Ideas Exchange in Site," *Professional Engineering* 13(6): 28–29.

32. Yet2.com, Inc., Company Overview, (October 8, 2007). *BusinessWeek,* http://investing.businessweek.com/research/stocks/private/snapshot.asp?privcapId = 94689, accessed September 11, 2008.

33. Bill Roberts (February 1, 2000). "Safe Keeping," *Electronic Business* 26(2): 44.

CHAPTER

HIGH TECHNOLOGY PRODUCT DEVELOPMENT STRATEGIES

Entrepreneurs today face real challenges in successfully introducing new technology products to the market and these challenges plague them throughout the initial development of the technology as well as during new product development (NPD) when the technology is turned into a commercially viable product or application. A global economy produces a highly intense competitive environment and with the shortening of product development and product life cycles brought about by technology, not all technology launches are successful. Given that companies spend an average of 46 percent of their resources on designing, developing, and launching a new technology product, and given that one in every four projects started never sees the marketplace, it is easy to see why entrepreneurs are looking for ways to improve their success rate.[1]

Many reasons exist for the failure of new technologies, chief among them are a lack of effective market research and limited resources. On the market research side, new technologies fail due to not understanding customer needs, not conducting in-depth intelligence on the competition, insufficient market research, poorly defined product concept, lack of financial planning, and failure to test the market.[2] Recent research has found that small to mid-sized entrepreneurial companies do a poorer job of executing market-related activities than technical activities with respect to NPD.[3] Part of the reason for this is the inventor's arrogance about the value of the invention. With typically several years invested in the invention, the inventor is unwilling to consider the possibility that the invention has no commercial

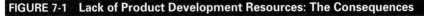

FIGURE 7-1 Lack of Product Development Resources: The Consequences

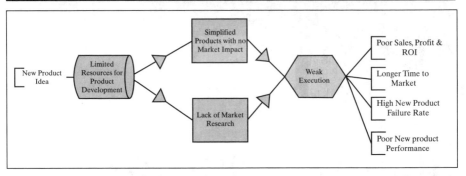

value. Even with high-potential new technologies, the requirements in terms of market expertise often exceed the capabilities of the entrepreneurial team.[4]

Entrepreneurial firms also face the serious challenge of limited resources for NPD. Because product development is a high-risk stage in the launch of a new venture, investors typically prefer to enter when the product is ready commercially. Therefore, funding for technology and product development often must come from other sources: government funding, grants, and strategic partners, to name a few. The lack of sufficient resources for NPD has significant ramifications for a new company as illustrated in Figure 7-1.[5] These unintended consequences include:

- Resorting to more simplified products that avoid more costly design and development.
- Not conducting sufficient market research to determine customer needs and preferences. Research has learned that about 75 percent of new products were not supported by critical market research.[6]
- Moving too quickly through the process, often resulting in redesign, rework, and poor execution, which can mean that first-to-market opportunities are missed.

Having an effective strategy in place can make it possible for entrepreneurs to avoid many of the more egregious problems of technology and product development. This chapter considers an entrepreneurial product development model that makes it possible for start-up technology companies to compete effectively in a global marketplace. It also looks at ways to manage the risk and expense of R&D through outsourcing and partnerships. Going forward, we will use NPD to encompass both technology and new product development.

ENTREPRENEURIAL PRODUCT DEVELOPMENT MODEL

New product development is an iterative process with many feedback loops that result in constant tweaking of the technology and its product or application until it is commercially ready. This process is depicted in Figure 7-2 and although the

FIGURE 7-2   New Technology Product Development Process

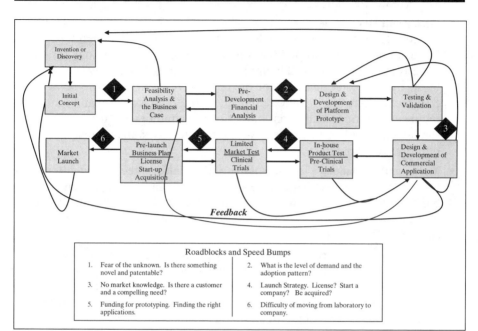

process appears to be linear, in reality it is very much an organic process from start to finish with many activities taking place in parallel or out of the normal order.[7] The various stages depicted in Figure 7-2 are described below.

- **Invention or Discovery.**   This stage is described in Chapter 2 and involves the recognition of a problem or a serendipitous discovery brought about by connecting concepts that are not normally connected.

- **Initial Concept.**   In this stage, the idea for the product begins to take shape, generally from a technical perspective and the groundwork is laid for the physical development of the product later on. The entrepreneur spends a little money to check the technical and competitive landscape to determine if there are any major reasons why this idea shouldn't be developed further. Those reasons could be existing patents or technical merits, for example.

- **Feasibility Analysis and the Business Case.**   Assuming no potential fatal discoveries in the initial concept stage, the entrepreneur then conducts both technical and market feasibility analysis to determine preliminary performance objectives and risks and to assess market readiness and attractiveness. An analysis of the competitive landscape will also be important to assess whether the entrepreneur's technology can find a successful market niche. Chapter 3 discusses feasibility analysis in depth.

- **Pre-development Financial Analysis.**   At this stage, the entrepreneur determines the resources required to develop the technology including building the first prototype and later a production quality version of the prototype that is ready for market.

- **Design and Development of Platform Prototype.** The platform is essentially the core technology upon which all the applications will be built. For example, PhotoBioMed has a patented platform technology for bio-adhesives that can be used in applications ranging from delivering drugs to the eye to cosmetic fillers for the face. Developing a prototype of the core technology is critical to determining the final form, fit, and function of any applications built from it. Platform technologies often arise from fundamental or basic research. Not all technology launches involve platform technologies.

- **Testing and Validation.** The prototype of the platform technology often does not resemble the final marketable product. Early in its development, it must be tested to insure that it will be a reliable foundation for any applications that spring from it. The technology is first tested in alpha form within the confines of the company.

- **Design and Development of Commercial Application.** Once the core technology is developed, it is time to develop the application of that technology that will serve a need in the market, in other words, the product. At this point it is particularly important to include customer input to minimize redesign and insure that the final product meets market needs.

- **In-house Product Test and Limited Market Test.** The application is first tested in-house to insure that it is technically sound. Then field tests with customers are used to refine the design and insure that the customer's needs are being met. Limited product introductions are often used as a "soft launch" to observe the product in its actual customer environment. Many an entrepreneur has been surprised to learn that customers use their products in ways they never expected.

- **Pre-launch Business Plan.** With a marketable technology, the entrepreneur has several launch strategies from which to choose. Three of the more likely are licensing the technology to an established company (see Chapter 6), starting a company to commercialize the technology (see Chapter 3), and being acquired by a larger company.

Throughout the development process there are a number of roadblocks and speed bumps that either slow the process or take it in a new direction. These are illustrated as black diamonds in Figure 7-2. These roadblocks are particularly troublesome for scientists and engineers who have spent most of their time in the laboratory rather than out in the market. Therefore, the points in the technology and product development process where business expertise is required often come as a surprise. Those who do not recognize the importance of understanding the market tend to develop "field of dreams" technologies for which there is no real pain or need in the market. When that is the case, no launch strategy is likely to be effective.

FACTORS THAT AFFECT THE NPD PROCESS

Which factors positively affect the NPD outcome has been the source of much discussion in the research literature. Brown and Eisenhardt proposed that process efficiency and product effectiveness are a function of various agents: team members, project leaders, senior managers, customers, and suppliers.[8] However, Iansiti and Clark contended that a company's ability to perform is dependent on its total capabilities.[9] Capabilities are used to deploy and coordinate various resources[10] and consist of the knowledge within the organization.[11] Technological capabilities such as R&D and manufacturing routines are an important driver of NPD success.[12] Accumulated technological knowledge from previous experience[13] and knowledge of product architecture, aesthetics, and ergonomics are complementary to these capabilities.[14] Market knowledge is also a critical factor in product development success.[15]

The seminal research of Cooper and Kleinschmidt on 161 companies involved in NPD provides important insight into which product development practices lead to high performance.[16] The four primary factors as they relate to new ventures are depicted in Figure 7-3 and discussed here:

- A superior, rigorous new product process is the strongest predictor of profitability. This process must consist of go/no go decision points, research, flexibility, and early sharp product definition. It is important to note that simply having an NPD process in place is not enough. The quality of the process and the commitment to it are what drive success.

- Resources in the form of money and people are critical to performance but they do not drive profitability. Today with open innovation sources like

FIGURE 7-3   Factors Affecting Superior New Product Performance

Product Innovation
Strategy

Product Development
Resources and
Commitment

New Product
Performance

Team Culture
Encouraging
Innovation

Process for
Developing and
Vetting New Ideas

Guru.com making it possible for entrepreneurs to seek technical assistance from any part of the globe, entrepreneurs don't have to take on expensive employees in the early stages of the company.

- The quality of the development team has a major impact on performance, particularly where there is a strong team leader committed to NPD.
- An entrepreneurial culture where innovation and quick failures are supported.

USING TECHNOLOGY S-CURVES

Technology product development has often been framed in terms of traditional S-curve theory, which proposes that early stage technologies display a relatively slow rate of progress in performance. However, as the technology is better understood and diffused into many small markets, the rate of performance improvement escalates. Later, when the technology achieves a mature stage, it reaches an upper limit of performance such that to achieve any improvement requires additional, costly engineering. However, reengineering the technology at the mature stage is generally not cost-effective because generally a new technology platform emerges that eventually makes this technology obsolete. The pattern of this escalation and decline resembles the letter S as depicted in Figure 7-4.[17] Understanding this pattern makes it possible to design an NPD strategy that introduces next generation technology at the appropriate moment—generally when the old technology reaches the top of the S-curve. Many large companies such as Hewlett Packard and Intel have mastered this approach, introducing the next generation technology after the market for the early generation technology has been sufficiently penetrated.

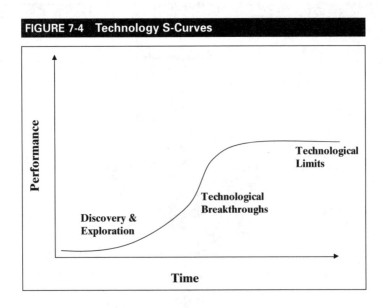

FIGURE 7-4 Technology S-Curves

EVALUATING NEW TECHNOLOGY

All potential technologies should be subjected to careful scrutiny. Table 7-1 presents some of the areas that need to be addressed and the pertinent questions that should be answered when evaluating the potential success of a new technology. Generally this is accomplished during the feasibility stage of NPD. Answering these questions will provide the entrepreneur with a tremendous learning experience and will help to minimize some of the risk associated with any new undertaking.

TABLE 7-1 Evaluating a New Technology		
Role of the Customer	*Role of Company Capabilities*	*Role of Business Development*
How will customers use the technology?	Does this technology extend a current S-curve or begin a new one?	How can an effective job of market research be ensured?
Will customers see this technology as a continuation of previous technology—an improvement—or as discontinuous, a product that will make previous technology obsolete?	If the company does not choose to go ahead with the development of this technology, will someone else develop it?	How long will the market research take and who will be responsible for it?
Will installation be required? If so, what form will it take?	What technical requirements does this project have and does the company have those capabilities?	How will customer input be incorporated?
How much learning is involved on the part of the customer? For which customers is there a higher learning curve?	What are the biggest technical risks? Are there ways to overcome them?	What will happen if the research points to an insufficient market or to product failure?
How will customers purchase the technology? What is the total cost to the customer of purchasing this technology?	Is the technology capable of being manufactured? Can the company do it or will it have to outsource that capability?	What are the intellectual property and regulatory issues associated with this project? Is the technology patentable?
Are there customers beyond the initial targeted customers? Who are they and why will they buy the product?	Does the company have unique capabilities that make it imperative that it be the one to develop this technology?	
What will it take to create customer awareness and stimulate the desire to purchase?	Do competitors have technology that better meets customer needs?	

(continued)

TABLE 7-1 *Continued*		
Role of the Customer	*Role of Company Capabilities*	*Role of Business Development*
What is the potential of this market assuming the success of the technology?	Does the company's technology reflect real customer needs? In what way? If the company must invest in new capabilities, can it justify a return on investment sufficient to make it worthwhile? Can a family of products be built off this technology platform? Is it sustainable for the long term?	

Note that some of the questions in Table 7-1 concern platform development of incremental and disruptive innovations. Incremental innovation is based on an existing platform and presents fewer product development problems than disruptive innovation, which has no precedent and is based on a new platform. With incremental innovation, it is often possible to conduct concurrent engineering or parallel processing during product development, which speeds things up. However, for disruptive innovations, the learning curve is steep, and it is often more advantageous to follow a more sequential process.[18]

REDUCING TIME TO MARKET

In biotech and other life science industries, long development cycles are the norm, typically measured in years. Inefficiencies and delays abound in these industries, costing companies thousands of dollars a day in profits. Reducing time to market can have a significant impact on market success and bottom-line profit. For issues specifically related to biotech and the healthcare industry, refer to the section "Developing a Regulatory Strategy."

The secret to reducing product development time lies in effective teams and better coordination of all the development activities. Some specific ways to reduce cycle time and achieve higher performance in any industry include:

- **Network effectively with external partners and internal resources not on the development team.** The ability to work outside the development team and then integrate new information into the NPD process is strongly related to high-performance teams.[19]

- **Document the workflow associated with the product development process.** Every NPD process consists of a number of tasks, many of which are interrelated or sequential. Creating a flowchart of these activities will help uncover duplicated efforts, potential bottlenecks, and other problems that could slow the development process.

- **Set goals for completion times.**   An interesting phenomenon occurs when team members work together over a long period of time. The time it takes to complete a task actually increases because inefficient routines become internalized. To break out of old routines and increase the speed at which tasks are completed requires setting new performance goals that everyone buys into. These goals should be just beyond the logical reach of the team, causing the team to look for innovative ways to increase their performance.[20]

- **Make the team accountable for its performance.**   All the planning and design will go for naught if no one is accountable for implementing the plan. It is important to find ways to measure improvement and provide incentives for achieving goals.

MEASURING SUCCESS AND RISKS

A number of models for measuring NPD success and risks have been proposed over the past decade: voice of the customer, time-based competition, and maximizing reuse, to name a few. Companies have rushed to adopt these measures as their ace-in-the-hole for success. However, mixed results from the use of these models indicate that no one model used alone can ensure product development success. Recent research has found that organizations that are rated high in R&D effectiveness by their R&D directors are significantly more capable than their less effective counterparts in nearly every area. Moreover, they are far better prepared for fast-cycle product development and are better at developing strategic alliances, understanding customer needs, and commercializing their technology.[21]

Firms that are rated as less effective face several risks. These firms are unable to accelerate their product development process and achieve a faster time to market. They believe that unless they developed the technology, it has no value—called the "not invented here" syndrome—and this keeps them from taking advantage of partnering with other technology companies. They are not effective at comprehending the needs of the customer or identifying future needs that customers currently don't recognize. Finally, they do not have the mechanisms in place to convert basic technology to market applications.

MANAGING THE RISK OF R&D

Research and development occur at the intersection of engineering or science and market research in an effort to provide something that customers want. Because most NPD involves a combination of software, hardware, tooling, prototyping, or clinical trials, the risks associated with the process are derived from the nature of the technology, the investment required, and the expertise of project management.[22] Each of these will be considered separately.

TECHNOLOGY RISK

Technology risks are those associated with the technology itself including such things as obsolescence, complexity—which makes costs too high to produce a profit—and product definition. The following are some ways to reduce risk during the NPD process.

- **Use off-the-shelf or proven components whenever possible.** Where a particular component has worked well in a previous product, it should be used in the new product if possible.
- **Don't force a solution.** Sometimes two options appear workable, and the risk of choosing one and being wrong is more costly than producing both. For example, Black & Decker was attempting to determine the best handle size and shape for a battery-powered screwdriver. Certainly, this was a critical decision. Should the company go with the thinner handle that held two cells and was more comfortable for smaller hands or with the thicker handle that held three cells and provided more power? Ultimately, Black & Decker decided to continue designing both until further market research could prove one more valuable than the other.[23]
- **Talk to the customer.** The best way to reduce risk in any technology screening and product development process is to get continual input from the customer. That means letting customers talk directly to design engineers. Pelco, Inc., a leader in video surveillance systems, brings its customers to the manufacturing floor and creates rapid prototypes of their ideas on the spot. This saves design time and gives the customers a vested interest in Pelco's success.
- **Tackle the riskiest issues first.** When screening a technology idea, the natural tendency is to focus on the issues that carry the lowest risk and save the tougher issues for last. It is always more prudent to identify the highest risk with any development project first and make sure there is a way to reduce that risk. Otherwise, it could put the entire project in jeopardy after time and effort have been spent taking care of less critical risks.

INVESTMENT RISK

R&D is one of the most expensive aspects of technology commercialization. When a company plans to allocate a large portion of its budget to R&D or an outside investor considers investing in a company's R&D, the decision to do so is based on assumptions the company and investors have made about the market and the customer. If those assumptions come from outdated or secondary sources of information, the risk of error increases. Some of the questions that any company or investor should ask prior to considering an R&D opportunity include the following:

- Is the purpose for undertaking R&D consistent with the firm's business goals?
- Are the data upon which decisions will be based current and from reliable sources?
- Has the company collected primary data from potential customers?
- How realistic are the initial estimates of volume, price, and cost?
- What is the opportunity cost of this project?
- Why should this project be done over others?

PROJECT MANAGEMENT RISK

The goal of risk management is to avoid failure. To accomplish this difficult task, it is the job of the entrepreneur to achieve a balance among three resource constraints: time, funds, and product requirements.[24] Entrepreneurs must consider what compromises, if any, must be made to deal with cost, quality, safety, and the environment and which risks are inherent in this product development process and how they will be handled? In addition, the plans for product launch to the market—including design and documentation release, supply chain management, and process documentation for manufacturing, installation, and service—must be detailed.[25] Issues such as volume, price, and costs are critical, as well as how the entrepreneur plans to respond to competitor actions. Looking to the future, it will be important to consider how the company can anticipate technological changes and estimate when to introduce a next generation technology.

However, there is a downside to risk management. If an entrepreneur is too concerned with avoiding failure, he or she may not take the appropriate risks necessary to achieve great successes and grow the company. Failure produces invaluable information that may never have been learned otherwise. Product screening and development are inherently iterative processes that rely on fast failures—trying one thing, testing another, and continually moving in a forward direction based on lessons learned.

INCREASING R&D EFFECTIVENESS

Recognizing that R&D is an expensive proposition for any company, but also realizing that it is a vital component in a company's competitive strategy, it is important to find ways to increase the effectiveness of R&D in those areas that have a significant impact on overall business performance. Research has uncovered the key areas that entrepreneurs should focus on to increase the effectiveness of their R&D programs.

FORM INTERNAL LINKS BETWEEN TECHNICAL AND NONTECHNICAL GROUPS

In general, R&D and technology personnel are not involved in the nontechnology functions of the business.[26] The tendency in most organizations is to work apart rather than collaboratively, to guard information rather than share it. Entrepreneurs need to bridge the gap between the tech and nontech sides of their businesses by involving each in the other's activities. The most successful firms place business people on product development teams early in the NPD process. Similarly, they place technology staff inside functional groups such as marketing and finance so that the technology people can understand the nature of business problems and business goals and find ways to facilitate them with technology. The case study on IDEO at the end of the chapter is a good example of a company that integrates all the various disciplines represented in its organization.

INVOLVE CUSTOMERS AND SUPPLIERS IN THE BUSINESS

The most effective firms have open and frequent communication between R&D, manufacturing, marketing, suppliers, and customers.[27] No entrepreneurial company can rely solely on internal resources to design and develop new products. Every company must have a link to its customers and other companies in the value chain; however, the problem is that customers are limited by their experience and their ability to describe their needs.[28] If a company is truly seeking to innovate with new, more radical technologies, approaching customers in the traditional way may not do the trick because customers will simply describe incremental improvements based on what they know rather than suggesting a completely new solution. To more effectively use customers to guide the design of new products, the following suggestions are helpful.

- Observe customers in their environment to identify problems they face and how they currently solve them.

- Customers are problem identifiers not solution providers. It is important to remember that customers only ask for what they believe is technically possible, which is normally quite limited. For example, Palm Inc. should be poised to take a major leap in its technology for smartphones. If Palm's engineers want to disrupt the current technology, they need to find out how customers want to communicate without putting limitations on the question. They may find out that customers want to communicate without having to deal with a traditional smartphone; in other words, they may want to communicate solely through their voice. Armed with a problem definition, Palm's engineers can now focus on how to solve that problem using their technical expertise. Chances are they will arrive at a solution that will excite customers and not simply be a modest addition of features.

OUTSOURCING TECHNOLOGY INNOVATION

Today's fast-paced innovation and shorter windows of opportunity require resources that few companies have in-house. It is unlikely that one company, acting alone, can sustain a technological advantage for very long relying solely on its own creative talent and capital resources. More and more companies are seeking technology from external sources, from about 20 percent of their total technological base in the 1980s to over 50 percent in the 1990s.[29] In the biotech industry, for example, the top 20 pharmaceutical companies depend on in-licensing for about 20 percent of their sales.[30] Niklas Zennstrom, a Swedish entrepreneur, with his Danish partner Janus Friis, outsourced product development of their Internet telephony company Skype to a company in Estonia. "There is a spirit there that fosters change and advancement."[31] Outsourcing product design and R&D is a relatively new phenomenon. More common has been the outsourcing of manufacturing, tech support, and programming. Many entrepreneurs have found that outsourcing is the only way to find the knowledge talent who will work quickly for reasonable fees. Devin Green, founder of ESP Systems, which developed a technology that lets restaurant patrons control the speed of their meals, knows firsthand that finding a domestic manufacturer that can meet the time frame and resource constraints of an entrepreneur is almost impossible. Green used Flextronics, a contract manufacturer with many foreign design centers.[32]

Fortunately, several forces have come together to make the outsourcing of innovation possible and even more cost-effective than doing it in-house. First, economists report that the gross national product in the largest world economies is doubling every 14–16 years.[33] This environment has spawned hundreds of new, focused niches of sufficient size to invite innovation. Second, the number of technologists and knowledge specialists has increased at an exponential rate. The knowledge products they have developed have made it possible for small businesses to compete alongside large companies. The software-based communication, analytical, and modeling tools they have created have inspired new products and services in fields as diverse as biotech and food services. Finally, entrepreneurs are encouraged to develop and exploit new technologies because of the availability of investment capital and the lower capital requirements to start new technology ventures.

Today, technology companies reduce risk, lower costs, and decrease cycle times by factors of 60–90 percent through the strategic outsourcing of innovation.[34] Moreover, outsourcing provides a firm with a network of expertise that it could not afford to hire in-house. Consider industries dependent on software, for example, manufacturing, where 15 sequences of programming can be combined in 10 million ways, each producing the potential for a new product or process. It is difficult to conceive of a company that could fully exploit all of those possibilities using in-house resources.[35] Third party vendors can apply their expertise to specific areas of the business to reduce costs and produce more efficient operations.[36] Many firms have discovered innovative marketing solutions by outsourcing to firms that specialize in customer relations. For example, Jordan Neuroscience leverages its relationships with hospitals so that it is able to plant observers inside the hospital to find and solve problems that hospital personnel, such as trauma care physicians, do not see while they are performing their duties.

DEVELOPING A REGULATORY STRATEGY

In the next decades, every industry will face common challenges stemming from limited capital and human resources that affect which new technologies get developed. The life sciences industry, including biotechnology and biomedical technologies, however, faces additional risks that do not generally impede product developers in other industries. The primary risk is related to the highly regulated nature of the industry, which imposes significant costs and time delays on new product developers. Figure 7-5 depicts the typical time frame for pharma biotech development and ag biotech development. Note that the extraordinary length of time from idea conception to commercialization is due largely to FDA regulatory requirements.

FIGURE 7-5 Time-to-Market for Pharma Biotech and Ag Biotech

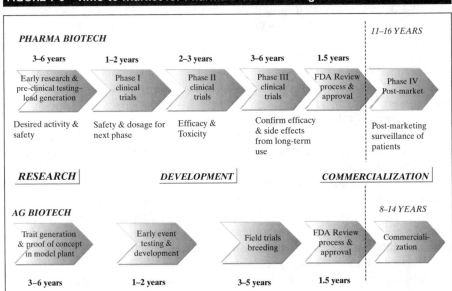

A survey conducted in 1999 by the editors of *Drug Discovery & Development* found that, in general, clinical trials and FDA approval were the biggest time delays experienced by researchers.[37] But when asked to identify specific tasks that slow the development process, researchers cited writing reports and proposals (50 percent of respondents), management duties (35 percent), and testing too many compounds that would never be used to make drugs (35 percent).[38] Table 7-2 presents the general development process for pharmaceuticals and the challenges to getting through the process in a timely fashion. It has been estimated that a clinical cycle has 204 discrete activities that must be completed to produce the clinical report.[39] An example will help to clarify and summarize the process. Suppose that a researcher is studying molecules with the hopes of developing a drug to deal with colon cancer. In the discovery phase, thousands of molecules are investigated for their ability to provide a curative effect on a target. These active molecules are then tested to determine if the activity can be increased, followed by testing in rats or mice to determine toxicity. If none is found, the process moves to the development phase where the lead molecule is tested in humans through a series of clinical trials on both those who are healthy and those who are suffering from the targeted disease.

Simultaneous with this testing is work on designing a commercial operation to produce a product and studies in animals to look for effects at various dosage levels. If the drug is sanctioned by the FDA after these clinical trials, the process moves to the commercial phase where it is produced for target markets and then later ramp up to full-scale production.[40] Because it is common that multiple lead molecules will be identified in the discovery phase and become candidates for development, the researcher has the difficult problem of attempting to determine

TABLE 7-2 The Pharmaceutical Development Process and Its Challenges	
The Process	*Loss of Time in the Process*
1. Discovery of a pharmacologically active chemical entity	• Determining the test protocol • Identifying a site for the investigation
2. Toxicology testing	• Preparing the test product • Testing the clinical product for stability
3. Formulation of the drug	• Filing an investigative new drug application with the FDA
4. Clinical development	• Creating and publishing case reports • Gathering data from the investigative site • Developing computer programs to record data • Analyzing the data • Summarizing the findings • Coordinating investigators and contractors

Source: Adapted from Boggs, R.W., Bayuk, L.M., & McCamey, D.A. (September–October 1999). "Speeding Development Cycles," *Industrial Research Institute.* 42 (50): 33–38.

which lead to follow first, given that following all of them simultaneously is not financially feasibile. It becomes necessary to weigh the options based on the probability of technical success (bringing the right molecule through development and the rewards and risks associated with developing that molecule). In general, the following are some of the considerations in choosing which molecule to develop:

- How many different diseases can be treated by the molecules (more is better)?
- How difficult will the development be? The degree of difficulty will affect the cost.
- What are the estimated sales should the drug reach the market?
- How quickly can the chosen molecules be pushed through the pipeline?

The difficulty in choosing the most promising molecules becomes evident when one considers that, on average, 5,000 compounds emerge from discovery and animal testing (preclinical). Of those, approximately five compounds make it to human testing, and only one to market. Even if a drug makes it to market, there is no guarantee of success. In 2001, the FDA required Bayer Pharmaceutical to pull its cholesterol-lowering drug Baycol off the market when 31 people died from fatal muscle toxicity.[41] In 2004, Merck was required to remove its arthritis drug Vioxx from the market.

Today combinatorial research methods enable researchers to produce and screen thousands of compounds at a time through an automated process. Combinatorial analysis results in better compounds because thousands of variables can be tested virtually instantaneously. It also achieves faster time to market, produces more market launches, and permits the use of premium pricing, all of which increase the value of R&D.[42]

Combinatorial research is useful in industries other than biotech as well. The research of John Busch provides an example in the area of materials R&D. In the plastics industry, a new concept will typically take 3–4 years of R&D, another 1–2 years of pilot testing to scale out the operation, and then a full-scale launch that will not return a profit for at least 5 years. Part of the reason for this extended time to launch is the time it takes to conduct all the experiments to arrive at the most effective material compound. Combinatorial methods can produce at least a tenfold increase in R&D productivity, reducing the time in R&D from 4 years to 3, and the time in the pilot test from 3 years to 2. Bringing the new product to market earlier also permits a 15 percent price premium. The financial consequences of all this are to increase the value of such a development program from $10 million to $37 million taking into account the up-front costs of the combinatorial facility.[43]

In today's environment, most biotech start-ups begin their lives as R&D operations being funded by government and foundation grants. However, when they reach the clinical trials stage, they typically partner with larger companies for late-stage clinical development and marketing. In doing so, they give up a large share of the equity in what they have developed, but with subsequent technologies, they are able to retain more rights because their resources have enabled them to take the technology farther along the development path before seeking an investment partner.

Summary

The NPD environment has been changing rapidly. Today, companies are focusing on growth through R&D innovations because they see that intangible assets such as patents and trademarks now form the basis for the highest market capitalizations. However, many new technologies fail, primarily because the companies that launch them do not do the necessary market research to learn what customers want. The NPD process is nonlinear and iterative. It generally begins with a discovery or recognition of an opportunity followed by a period of technology screening and platform identification to determine which project the company intends to undertake. Once the technology is determined, technical and business activities begin to take place simultaneously. As the business team develops a business concept and investigates the market through feasibility analysis, the technology team is designing, developing, and testing the technology platform and then the product family. Then comes a period of in-house and limited market testing. If all goes well, preparations for product launch begin with the development of a business plan and marketing strategy. Research has found that forming internal links between technical and nontechnical groups and involving customers and suppliers in the business can enhance the effectiveness of the R&D process. Furthermore, outsourcing aspects of the R&D process and working with strategic partners can make the process more cost-effective.

Discussion Questions

1. As a new product developer, what are the three most important things that should be remembered when formulating a product development strategy?
2. In what ways can a company increase its chances of designing right the first time?
3. Every R&D project carries with it some degree of risk. Suppose an entrepreneur is proposing to develop a wearable PDA that is unobtrusive and responds to voice commands. What are some of the risks in the development of this product? How should they be managed?
4. What are the major advantages and disadvantages of outsourcing innovation?
5. What are the unique challenges facing entrepreneurs in highly regulated industries such as biotech?

CASE STUDY

IDEO — Where Innovation Is the Culture

If you want to produce over 90 new products a year, try turning your company into a living laboratory. At least that is the approach that IDEO founder David M. Kelley takes. IDEO, based in Palo Alto, California, is one of the most important design companies in the world, with offices in San Francisco, London, and Tokyo. Some of the more familiar products to come out of the company include the PalmV PDA, Crest's "Neat Squeeze" toothpaste container, and Levolor blinds.

Because the world in which Kelley and his employees work is stressful and driven by unreasonable deadlines, Kelley believes that the environment must be flexible and freewheeling. Employees work in project teams for weeks or months at a time and then switch to another project team with different members. The IDEO culture also recognizes differences in tastes and preferences. For example, the younger employees love to play loud music while they work, so Kelley designated a special area for them called the Spunk Space where they will not disturb their more conservative coworkers. It is a noncompetitive environment where the customer is the boss. Their 26-person team of human-factors experts, industrial designers, electronic engineers, interaction designers, mechanical engineers, software programmers, and manufacturing engineers work together to produce smart products. Everyone is expected to be up-to-date in their area of specialty, but employees are also encouraged to explore outside of their disciplines.

IDEO's brainstorming sessions follow five guidelines: (1) stay focused on the topic, (2) encourage wild ideas, (3) defer judgment, (4) build on the ideas of others, and (5) only allow one conversation at a time. Their motto is "fail often to succeed sooner." Consequently, IDEO constantly builds and tests prototypes, identifying failure points early in the product development cycle. How a company deals with failure is often a sign of how innovative it is. In fact, the biggest reason that more companies do not have a product development culture like IDEO is their fear and disdain of failure. Once they have given a new product idea the go-ahead, everyone is expected to believe in the

(continued)

(*continued*)

product and work to make it happen. The problem with this approach is that no one is identifying failure points along the way, so when problems are finally discovered at the end, it is a far more costly process to redesign and rework the product. At IDEO, failure points are identified early and often so that teams can quickly learn from them and move on. IDEO teams also design and test multiple components of a product simultaneously. For example, while they are working on the electrical components of a new product, they will also be testing its waterproof case or testing its circuit board's resistance to heat. For products that require Federal Communications Commission (FCC) certification, testing is done early in the process instead of waiting until the end.

Satisfying customers' needs is the prime directive at IDEO. For example, one health care network was looking for an appliance that would let medical caseworkers monitor elderly patients at home without having to physically visit them each day. IDEO sent its human-factors experts into patients' homes to learn what the important needs were. By doing this, they found out everything they needed to know to give users what they needed, from how the user opens the monitor box to the size of the buttons the user must push to make it work. Taking an unconventional approach to market research is how the great minds at IDEO come up with unique solutions. For example, when the SSM DePaul Health Center in St. Louis, Missouri wanted to update its emergency room, the IDEO team got "up close and personal." One of its anthropologists secretly took the role of a patient and was able to videotape his emergency room experience. That approach led to solving a longstanding problem that patients were having with what they viewed as a very chaotic emergency room. Giving patients a simple "map" that spelled out the seven activities that would take place when they came to the emergency room lowered the level of stress for the patients, which made the staff's job less stressful as well.

AT IDEO, no innovation ever disappears. All ideas, whether they have been used in a product or not, go into a virtual museum called the Tech Box, also called the toy box, which is really a metal filing cabinet with five drawers, each housing a different category of innovation, for example, thermo and optical innovations, manufacturing processes, and amazing materials. In each drawer are a variety of strange gadgets, each one prototyping some innovation. Anyone can take one of these to test it for use on a product that is being developed. The Tech Box has been such a success in inspiring ideas that IDEO has replicated it in 10 other offices, including customer–partner Steelcase, a manufacturer of office furniture. The physical Tech Box is only part of the picture. IDEO has also developed an intranet that links all of its offices, provides everyone with data on each of the 150 materials in the filing cabinets, and connects the user with the person who placed the gadget in the Tech Box.

IDEO seems to have found the solution to sustaining innovation in a corporate environment by redefining the way R&D looks. Rather than relying on the rigid structure and process orientation of most R&D companies, it has chosen to create an environment where creativity and innovation are natural by-products of the company culture.

Sources: Pethokoukis, J. (October 2, 2006). "The Deans of Design," *US News and World Report;* Brown, T. (June 2005). "Strategy by Design," *Fast Company* 95: 52; Bill Roberts (December 2000). "Innovation Quotient," *Electronic Business,* www.e-insite.net/eb mag/; John Teresko, (August 21, 2000). "R&D Serves Dual Purpose," *Industry Week,* www.industryweek.com/; Paul E. Teague (January 17, 2000). "A Toy Box for Ideas," *Design News,* www.manufacturing.net/dn/.

Endnotes

1. Griffith, A. (1997). "Drivers of NPD Success" *The 1997 PDMA Report* (Chicago: Product Development & Management Association).
2. Fields, M., Gilbert, P., & Udell, G. (2003). "Reasons New Products Fail: An Examination of Selected Product Development-Related Shortcomings and Oversights," *Business Journal for Entrepreneurs* 4: 114–142; Fields, M., Udell, G., & Gilbert, P. (2004). "More Reasons New Products Fail: An Examination of Planning, Development, and Implementation Oversights," *Business Journal for Entrepreneurs* 1: 177–201.
3. Huang, X., Soutar, G.N., & Brown, A. (2002). "NPD Processes in Small and Medium-Sized Enterprises: Some Australian Evidence," *Journal of Small Business Management* 40(1): 27–42.
4. Crawford, M., & DiBenedetto, A. (2003). *New Products Management* (New York: McGraw-Hill).
5. Cooper, R.G., & Edgett, S.J. (2003). "Overcoming the Crunch in Resources for NPD." *Research Technology Management* 46(3): 48.
6. Cooper, R.G. (1993). *Winning at New Products: Accelerating the Process from Idea to Launch,* 2nd ed. (Reading, MA: Addison Wesley Publishing Company), p. 33.
7. Mankin, E. (2004). "Is Your Product-Development Process Helping—or Hindering—Innovation?" *Strategy & Innovation* (Boston: Harvard Business School Press), p. 4.
8. Brown, S.L., & Eisenhardt, K.M. (1995). "Product Development: Past Research, Present Findings, and Future Directions," *Academy of Management Review* 20: 343–378.
9. Iansiti, M., & Clark, K. (1994). "Integration and Dynamic Capability: Evidence from Product Development in Automobiles and Mainframe Computers," *Industrial and Corporate Change* 3: 557–605.
10. Amit, R., & Schoemaker, P. (1993). "Strategic Assets and Organizational Rent," *Strategic Management Journal* 14: 33–46.
11. Iansiti, & Clark, *op. cit.,* 557–605.
12. Camuffo, A., & Volpato, G. (1996). "Dynamic Capabilities and Manufacturing Automation: Organizational Learning in the Italian Manufacturing Automobile Industry," *Industrial and Corporate Change* 5: 813–838; Hayes, R.H., Pisano, G., & Upton, D.M. (1996) *Strategic Operations: Competing Through Capabilities* (Cambridge, MA: Harvard Business School Press).
13. Helfat, C.E. (1997). "Know-How, Asset Complementarity, and Dynamic Capability Accumulation: The Case of R&D," *Strategic Management Journal* 18: 339–360.
14. Ulrich, K.T., & Eppinger, S.D. (1995). *Product Design and Development* (New York: McGraw-Hill).
15. Hunt, S.D., & Morgan, R.M. (1995). "The Comparative Advantage Theory of Competition," *Journal of Marketing* 59: 1–15.
16. Cooper, R.G., & Kleinschmidt, E.J. (May–June 2007). "Winning Businesses in Product Development: The Critical Success Factors," *Research Technology Management* 50(3): 52.
17. Christensen, C.M. (Fall 1992). "Exploring the Limits of the Technology S-Curve. Part I: Component Technologies," *Production and Operations Management* 1(4): 340.
18. Miller, W.L., & Morris, L. (1999). *Fourth Generation R&D,* New York: John Wiley & Sons, Inc. p. 300.

19. Gladstein Ancona, D., & Caldwell, D. (September–October 2007). "Improving the Performance of New Product Teams," *Research Technology Management,* Industrial Research Institute, Inc. pp. 37–43.

20. Ibid., p. 38.

21. Gupta, A.K., Wilemon, D., & Atuahene-Gima, K. (May–June 2000). "Excelling in R&D," *Research-Technology Management,* www.Iriinc.org/webiri/index.ctm.

22. Leithhead, B.S. (October 2000). "Product Development Risks," *Internal Auditor,* 59–61. http://findarticles.com/p/articles/mi_m4153/is_5_57/ai_67590524, accessed September 13, 2008.

23. Smith, P.G. "Managing Risk as Product Development Schedules Shrink," *Industrial Research Institute, Inc.* 42(5): 25–32. http://www.europa.com/~preston/R-TM9–99/R-TM9–99.pdf, accessed September 13, 2008.

24. Ibid.

25. Ibid.

26. Gupta, & Wilemon, *op. cit.* "Changing Patterns in Industrial R&D Management," 497–511.

27. Gupta, Wilemon, & Atuahene-Gima, *op. cit.*

28. Leonard, D., & Rayport, J.F. (November–December 1997). "Spark Innovation Through Empathetic Design," *Harvard Business Review,* Reprint 97606, p. 103.

29. Slowinski, G., Stanton, S.A., Tao, J.C., Miller, W., & Mcconnell, D.P. (September–October 2000). "Acquiring External Technology," *Research-Technology Management* 43(5): 29–35.

30. (October 2005). "Licensing Strategies: Trends in the Top 20 Pharmaceutical Companies Activity," *Datamonitor,* http://www.datamonitor.com/industries/research/?pid=DMHC2139, accessed September 13, 2008.

31. Buchanan, L. (May 2006). "The Thinking Man's Outsourcing," *Inc. Magazine,* www.inc.com.

32. Ibid.

33. United Nations, Statistical Yearbook (1998). New York, www.un.org/depts/unsd/sd_databases.htm.

34. Quinn, J.B. (Summer 2000). "Outsourcing Innovation: The New Engine of Growth," *Sloan Management Review,* www.findarticles.com.

35. Quinn, J.B. (Summer 1999). "Strategic Outsourcing: Leveraging Knowledge Capabilities," *Sloan Management Review* 40: 9–21.

36. Ibid.

37. Studt, T. (January 1999). "Drug Development Bottlenecks Not Cured by Technology Alone," *R&D Magazine,* p. 40.

38. Ibid.

39. Boggs, R.W., Bayuk, L.M., & McCamey, D.A. (September–October 1999). "Speeding Development Cycles," *Industrial Research Institute* 42(5): 33–38.

40. Blau, G., Mehta, B., Bose, S., Pekny, J., Sinclair, G., Kuenker, K., & Bunch, P.R. (2000). "Risk Management in the Development of New Products in Highly Regulated Industries," *Computers and Chemical Engineering* 24: 659–664.

41. "Baycol Information," *U.S. Food and Drug Administration Center for Drug Evaluation and Research,* http://www.fda.gov/cder/drug/infopage/baycol/, accessed January 2, 2008.

42. Busch, J.V. (March–April 2001). "Combinatorial Analysis—How Much Is It Worth?" *Research-Technology Management* 44(2): 38–45.

43. Ibid.

CHAPTER 8

TECHNOLOGY TRANSITION AND ENTRY STRATEGIES

As if the challenges of R&D were not enough, a daunting task awaits a technology team when it is ready to start a company and launch a product, whether that be through a tech transfer licensing model, a start-up, or a strategic partnership. The move from laboratory to business operations is not an easy transition because operations demand different skills from the technology team than did product development. In fact, often scientists and engineers forget to consider the types of organizational processes and infrastructure that must be in place to launch a new technology product.[1] They are not helped by the fact that most depictions of the commercialization process simply show an arrow between product development and operations, making it appear as if it just happens. Although research has addressed such things as designing for manufacturing, assembly, and packaging to characterize the transition to operations, the issue of people and skills has not been addressed adequately.[2]

The reality is that an operating business does not happen overnight; it takes a lot of planning; and during that process, lingering technical and market issues continue to emerge, pulling the team in a multitude of directions. If manufacturing processes were not designed in parallel with the development of the product, figuring out how to most efficiently and effectively design those processes could now stall the product launch. Furthermore, even a late-stage prototype of the product is not the same as a production quality unit, and if the team has not completed the sourcing of all components and raw materials for production, that too could delay the launch of the product.

Unfortunately, these issues are only the beginning of the challenges that face technology entrepreneurs when they're ready to commercialize their technologies. This chapter will look at the transition from R&D to operations and consider some of the major challenges.

TRANSITIONING FROM PROJECT TO OPERATIONS

In their research on high-technology companies, Leifer and team found a number of issues that regularly plague project teams during the final phases of product development just prior to launching a new product.[3] For example, assembling a prototype typically uses different processes than will likely be used to manufacture the final production model. These differences introduce technical and process uncertainty during the transition.

Business partners who worked with the team during R&D may not be appropriate partners for a full-scale ramp up of the operations, and the decision becomes whether to continue to outsource some operations to another entity or keep a process in-house and develop it into a core competency for the company, meaning that it will become a critical skill for the company. The R&D team, which is comprised primarily of technical people, does not always understand the objectives of the business team that is charged with getting the product out and generating revenues. Because the R&D team was focused on design issues, it had the luxury of experimentation, fast failures, and continual improvement; the operations team has none of those luxuries.[4] Instead, it is under pressure to generate cash flow for a business that has been burning cash during the entire course of product development.

Another concern during this transition period is how applications and markets will develop. The assumptions made during product design and development, even with customer input, often do not hold up when the product is out in the market. The personal digital assistant (PDA) market in 1995 provides a good example of this dilemma. During the design and development phase, engineers loaded the units with communications functions because these functions were perceived by the engineers as the most critical features for customers. However, as customers began to use the products, manufacturers learned that the calendar scheduling function was the most critical need for the customer and, in fact, the communications functions were not even being used. This is an example of the importance of understanding real customer needs.

BUILD A FIRST-CLASS TEAM

A successful transition from product development to business operations requires three different groups of individuals: (1) the technology people who undertook the product development, (2) people from the operations team (manufacturing, marketing, finance), and (3) the entrepreneur, who can guide the team to a successful start-up, strategic alliance, or transfer of the technology to a larger company.[5] The original team that took the technology through the product development and feasibility stages may not be the same team that is needed to launch the venture and secure the first customer. Particularly in cases where the R&D team was comprised solely of engineers or scientists, the team may not have the business skills and experience to suddenly shift gears and begin focusing on the market. Long before the technology is ready for launch, the entrepreneurial team must make sure that it has all of the skills required to deal with the business side of the business. That may mean bringing one or two people on board with management, marketing, and/or financial capabilities. If the team secured first-round funding from private investors for product development and is now seeking venture capital for a second round, the venture capitalists may be able to assist in securing the right management for the company.

Some of the critical tasks to be undertaken during the transition include finalizing the product and its first applications as well as refining the business model. A plan will need to be developed that details the readiness of the company in terms of personnel, systems, and resources to launch the product. If this expertise is not available in the founding team (and it usually isn't) it will need to be acquired in some manner, usually through consultants or board members who have taken technologies to market.

Every team needs a leader, and most entrepreneurial teams have a lead entrepreneur who embodies the vision for the company. Whether that lead entrepreneur comes from the technical or the business side of the venture does not matter. What matters is that the lead entrepreneur be the company evangelist, the key person driving the company forward through pauses, temporary halts, and every imaginable problem that it will face. The leader rallies the troops and serves as a role model for what it takes to create a great company. The lead entrepreneur is also responsible for inspiring the culture of the company, which can become a critical competitive advantage for a new venture. One caveat is that if the entrepreneur leader comes from the technical side with no business experience, it will be important to bring in business executive talent to insure that the business does not deviate from its goals. Giving up some control will be difficult for most technical entrepreneurs, but in the end it makes the company more attractive to potential funders.

DEVELOP THE MISSION

One of the most critical aspects of planning for the operations of a new venture is identifying and communicating the mission of the company. Research has found a positive relationship between a company's mission statement and its performance.[6] Unfortunately, too many entrepreneurs overlook this aspect of transitioning to operations and end up paying for it later in an unfocused launch effort. Developing a mission statement is a four-part process, as depicted in Figure 8-1. The entrepreneur carries the vision for the business, but to move toward that vision requires discipline, and the mission statement provides that

FIGURE 8-1 The Mission Statement

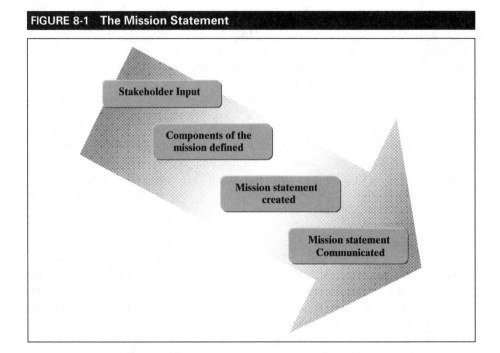

discipline. To construct a mission statement that everyone buys into requires that everyone participate in its formulation, which means including employees and stakeholders, both internal and external.

By communicating with stakeholders during the development of the mission statement, the company can gain a sense of what stakeholders believe they contribute to the performance of the company and how the mission statement is related to company performance. In the second stage, the components of the mission statement are identified. In general, mission statements describe three dimensions of the business: (1) which customer groups are being satisfied, (2) what customer needs are being satisfied, and (3) in what way customer needs are being satisfied.[7] Another approach suggests four components: (1) purpose (why the company exists), (2) strategy (competitive advantage and core competencies), (3) values (what the company believes in), and (4) behavior standards (the behaviors based on the value system).[8]

The third stage of mission development embodies the process by which the mission statement is actually created. A free flow of ideas is appropriate and necessary for the creation of a mission statement that everyone can be proud of. Oftentimes, however, this free exchange of ideas is difficult because the entrepreneur's vision for the company is strong. Consequently, in a new venture, it is likely that the founding team members will actually be the ones to structure the mission statement in such a way that it operationalizes the lead entrepreneur's or the team's vision for the company. In the final stage, the mission statement is communicated to all relevant stakeholders via meetings, the Web site, and by posting it in strategic places in the company's facilities. For example, Google's mission is "to organize the world's information and make it universally accessible and useful."[9] That has been the company's consistent mission since Larry Page and Sergey Brin started the company in their dorm room at Stanford University in 1998.

DECIDING ON A LAUNCH STRATEGY

The launch strategy is a key component of the overall move from R&D to operations. Although the launch strategy will be a function of the expectations of the customer, it will also depend on the capabilities of the company at the time of entry. In general, there are four broad strategies that entrepreneurs employ for commercializing their technologies: tech transfer through licensing, sale of the technology, a start-up, or a strategic alliance.

LICENSE THE TECHNOLOGY

Technology transfer is a process whereby technology and its associated tacit knowledge are transferred to a licensee through a license agreement in the form of rights that permit the licensee to do any of a number of things: further develop, manufacture, and distribute, for example. The licensee doesn't own the technology but has simply purchased the rights conveyed in the license agreement for the specified term of that agreement. Other forms of intellectual property, such as trademarks (brands) and trade secrets, are also frequently licensed. Technology transfer through licensing makes it possible for the entrepreneur to retain ownership of the technology but work with licensees to get the technology into as many markets and as many applications as possible. Licensing is the subject of Chapter 6.

SELL THE TECHNOLOGY

Why would an entrepreneur choose to sell a technology he or she has developed? There are a number of reasons. It may take the company into a market that is very different from other products in the portfolio, so the entrepreneurial team may not have the necessary expertise but a potential buyer may have a strong position in that market. The buyer may already manufacture a similar product using a different technology or it may have raw material position and underutilized capacity, all of which make the buyer better positioned than the entrepreneur to introduce the technology. Selling the technology will require a valuation, which is the subject of Chapter 14.

START A COMPANY

Entrepreneurs who want to keep their technology captive, that is, solely within their own company, will chose to create a start-up company. They may also choose to launch a company when their technology is not easily licensed or there are no companies capable of further developing or producing the applications that derive from the technology. Moreover, it may be advantageous to create a company to prove the technology in the market, increase the company's valuation, and position it for acquisition by a larger firm later on. The subject of start-up is addressed in Chapter 3.

FORM A STRATEGIC ALLIANCE

A strategic alliance consists of two or more companies that join forces to undertake a joint project, share core competencies, or provide resources that one of the companies does not have. Through a cooperation agreement or strategic partnership, the owner of a technology can accomplish several objectives:[10]

- Determine the feasibility of commercializing a particular technology.
- Assess the utility of the technology in terms of applications and modifications of ways to use the technology in the real world.
- Accurately target specific customers for the various applications of the technology.
- Bring together the people who could make commercialization possible — industry partners, financial partners, and so on.

The bottom line is that companies form strategic alliances to gain access to resources, skills, and knowledge that would be too costly to develop on their own and also to establish the standards for an industry. Choosing a strategic partner is a critical decision that must be made as carefully as choosing an investor or a key management employee. It is important to understand why a potential company is willing to partner and what its motives are. Is the entire company behind the alliance or only the person assigned to the partnership? If that person leaves, what does that mean to the alliance? A company that is able to help its partner commercialize a technology should already work in an area that will use applications of the technology; it should also be one of the leading users of that technology and be able to assess the value of the technology to the customer. The strategic partner should see collaboration as a way to gain early access to a technology it needs. For example, a small Scandinavian manufacturer of a new water purification system assembled a panel of leaders in industries dealing with wastewater management and desalination to consider the manufacturer's technology and its potential applications. The panel found several applications, and more than half the panel committed to immediate exploration of a commercial relationship. That commitment resulted in the small start-up that was able to secure government funding for additional development and marketing.

Strategic alliances occur at different points in time in the life of a business. Pre-competitive alliances occur prior to the commercialization of the technology and are usually created for the development of a product, whereas competitive alliances are partnerships that provide competing companies with a common ground and common goals. For example, the Semiconductor Manufacturing Technology Consortium (SEMATECH) was a coalition of U.S. semiconductor manufacturers that formed in 1987 to overcome the threat of Japanese competition in their markets. SEMATECH resulted in firms pooling their resources to design and build chips faster and with more features. The industry, which had been in decline, regained its position 5 years later.[11]

Vertical alliances occur up and down the value chain with suppliers, distributors, or customers. The partners in a vertical alliance seek to acquire a technology or a specific core competency or resource. A technology venture may form a partnership with a supplier to secure better prices and faster access to components and raw materials. Alliances with distributors enable better access to customers, whereas alliances with customers provide important feedback during product development as well as for all the other activities of the business. Customers act as beta testers to check the technology in a real-world environment before it is formally launched to a wider market.

Horizontal alliances are formed with companies in the same position in the value chain, that is, competing firms or firms that produce products that complement the new venture firm's products. In horizontal alliances, the partners want to capture a particular market and collaborate to offer a total solution. For example, Hewlett-Packard and Kodak joined forces to capture the digital photography market by using Kodak's thermal dye transfer process to produce prints on HP printers.[12] During the precompetitive stage, the partners work to develop a common product for a common market. During the competitive stage, the alliances take the form of distribution and cross-licensing agreements, often to establish the standards in an industry by combining the strengths of two or more competitors.

If value chain partners were highly effective, efficient, and reliable, companies would outsource everything but their core capabilities. The reality is that strategic alliances entail risks that include delays, unexpected transaction costs, security breaches, and quality issues. For all the benefits of strategic alliances, recent research has reported that their failure rate is more than 50 percent,[13] whereas other reports put it closer to two-thirds of all alliances.[14] In any case, the problem is that even if they don't fail, they often disintegrate into managerial trauma. Part of the reason for the failure of an alliance is that small technology businesses frequently enter into a partnership agreement from a position of weakness, that is, they need resources to accomplish their goals, and the other firm, which does not really need anything from the smaller business, is placed in a position of power. Moreover, resource dependency when there are only a limited number of potential partners can result in poor performance on the part of the small firm that was unable to find the appropriate partner. Another common reason for failure is that the company that is seeking the specialized capability still tries to dictate how the activity will take place, which undermines the innovative efforts of the strategic partner that was brought on board for its core capability. To improve the chances that a strategic alliance will be successful, a few systems and controls must be in place. See Table 8-1 for some suggestions.

Although the benefits of cooperation are many, the risks are high and should be weighed against the benefits when making any decision to partner with another company. The ultimate success of the launch of a new technology under a cooperation agreement depends on all the parties involved. No one company can ensure

TABLE 8-1	Preparation for a Strategic Partnership
Pre-alliance	1. Study the industry landscape to identify potential partners.
	2. Conduct due diligence on the potential partner to insure that the two firms will be compatible in their company goals and culture.
	3. Talk with firms that have worked with the potential partner to understand the pros and cons of such an alliance.
	4. Put procurement and contract management specialists in place to track the experiences of the alliance and monitor its progress.
During the alliance	5. Develop knowledge systems to collect, evaluate, and monitor what outside suppliers are doing.
	6. Develop feedback mechanisms that make it possible to use the knowledge gained from the alliance to improve other areas of the business and create a better interface between suppliers, the company, and downstream partners.
Post-alliance	7. Evaluate the outcomes against goals.
	8. Check for satisfactory completion of all contracts.

success for all. Consequently, one of the most vexing aspects of strategic alliances is joint decision making and giving up some control to another company, particularly where there is a size disparity between the firms. Research has confirmed that partnerships are more successful and equitable when the firms are of similar size.[15] When a start-up firm partners with a large, established firm to access resources, manufacturing, and distribution capability, the success of the partnership is dependent on the agreed-upon governance structure. In some cases, partners give each other control over specific aspects of the commercialization process; for example, the start-up firm makes decisions regarding design and development and the partner firm has control over manufacturing and distribution. In other cases, decisions are made jointly, which works when the companies have similar cultures and goals.

DECIDING ON AN OPERATIONAL STRATEGY

The operational strategy of a company is a plan for defining and coordinating the various processes inside the organization, in particular those that contribute to the manufacture of the product. Operational strategy is generally associated with a start-up company that plans to manufacture and distribute its technology applications, although some entrepreneurs choose to license some applications to other companies and focus on the application or applications that correspond with their core competencies. Research suggests that market success criteria actually serve to define the manufacturing capability of the firm and the resulting infrastructure that must be constructed.[16] Today, entrepreneurial companies no longer consider themselves as merely a collection of products and services, but rather as a collection of unique capabilities that form the basis for their competitive advantage. Those capabilities that the company does not possess can easily be outsourced. In fact, a Coopers & Lybrand survey of 400 fast-growing small companies discovered that two-thirds of them used outsourcing and this strategy produced higher revenues and growth rates than their non-outsourcing counterparts.

To figure capacity requirements, personnel needs, and to determine where bottlenecks in the company's processes may occur, it's important to understand the process flow of the activities in the business.

PROCESS FLOW

Achieving optimal agility as a company is a function of several factors, including teamwork among workers, suppliers, and customers; similarity of technology lines within product groupings; commonality of parts, components, and product features to save design time and allow for volume purchases; using off-the-shelf parts whenever possible to save time and money; and letting value chain partners participate in the design and manufacture of products. All of these factors involve important processes in the business that the entrepreneur will need to understand.

An important task that every start-up team must undertake is to map out how the business is going to work. This can be accomplished through a process flow chart or imaginary tour of the business. Figure 8-2 depicts a sample process

FIGURE 8-2   Sample Process Flow Chart for a Start-up Technology Product Business

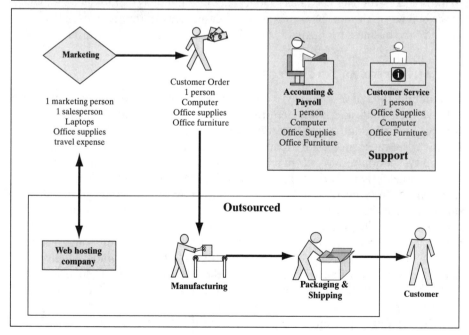

flow chart for a technology product start-up that is saving start-up costs by outsourcing expensive manufacturing and fulfillment tasks. The process flow chart offers a way to visually depict the business and determine personnel and equipment needed as well as capabilities that will be outsourced. Outsourcing these functions means that the entrepreneur can move more quickly because he or she doesn't have to spend time and money acquiring a particular competency.

It is common for entrepreneurs to retain design and development in-house and outsource manufacturing and distribution, two functions that are costly to develop and require significant experience to implement effectively. Entrepreneurs will often outsource human resource functions such as payroll and benefits to companies that specialize in these activities. Again, understanding the complexities of dealing with the IRS and managing benefits is something that many entrepreneurs don't want to attempt because the penalities for doing something wrong are great.

One of the critical functions of any operations strategy is quality management and in small companies—start-ups, for example—the CEO typically assumes the role of quality manager until the company generates enough cash flow that this task can be delegated to a professional quality person. In the meantime, it is vital that everyone in the organization be empowered to solve problems and implement new procedures that result in improvements in quality. The goal of any effective quality management system is for the company to be defect free, which will help achieve the highest levels of customer satisfaction. Many companies employ a PDCA approach to planning for quality. This means that they "plan" for how to improve their processes. They "do" or implement the plan. They "check" the results to verify that the plan actually improved the process, and they "act" or do what it takes to insure that the successful plan becomes routine. The bottom line is that understanding the process flow of the business makes it easier to decide how to most effectively organize the business for flexibility, speed, quality, and optimum performance.

ORGANIZATIONAL ARCHITECTURE

The architecture of a company is the framework through which entrepreneurs achieve their goals and implement the vision for the company. It includes all the formal and informal systems within the organization and how those systems interact. The most successful architectures generally reflect simplicity, flexibility, reliability, economy, and acceptability.[17] Entrepreneurs, particularly at start-up, favor simple designs that are flat in structure to facilitate teamwork and communication. Because entrepreneurs work in uncertain environments, the ability to quickly adjust the way the business operates and responds to its environment is critical, so flexibility is important. Reliability means that the output of the organization is fairly predictable and systems are in place to respond when a failure occurs. Economy reflects the trade-off between efficiency and effectiveness. Entrepreneurs must find ways to produce the highest quality products at a cost that enables them to make a reasonable profit. Finally, an effective organizational architecture must be accepted by all who work within its framework.

One of the important organizational design structures is the Star Model, depicted in Figure 8-3. It addresses all the critical aspects of the organization,

FIGURE 8-3   Star Model of Organizational Design

Source: Based on the work of Edward E. Lawler, III (1997). *From the Ground Up: Six Principles for Building the New Logic Corporation,* Jossey-Bass, and Amy Kates and Jay R. Galbraith (2007). *Designing Your Organization: Using the STAR Model to Solve 5 Critical Design Challenges.* Jossey-Bass.

which are interconnected such that they are all guided by the organization's vision and they all inform the organization's strategies to achieve that vision.

Part of organizational strategy is determining the legal form of organization because it has implications for liability and the management of tax consequences for its owners. Legal forms are considered in the next section.

ORGANIZING FROM A LEGAL PERSPECTIVE

Not only do entrepreneurs need to decide on the operational strategy for their new ventures but also the legal form that organizational structure will take. The legal form of organization is a critical decision that will affect the company for a long time. Choosing the most appropriate legal form is a function of three factors: (1) how much liability protection is required, (2) the company's operating requirements, and (3) the company's tax strategy. In the earliest stages of a new venture—R&D and pre-first-customer—liability is minimal and resources are precious, so the least expensive legal form may be appropriate. However, most technology ventures are characterized by high risk, so the founders will typically seek a legal form that offers protection from liability. The operating requirements of the business also come into play in this decision.

Whether the business has or requires a centralized management structure or is team-based and flexible will need to be taken into consideration. Some legal forms permit more flexibility in the number of owners, for example, or more complexity in organizational structure. The ability to create employee incentives is another operating requirement that must be met by the legal form chosen. The impact of the legal form on the tax strategy of the owners is also important. Some forms allow earnings to be taxed at the owner's personal tax rate (sole proprietorship, partnership, S-Corp, LLC), others require that earnings be taxed at the company level (corporate forms). Determination of the best form for tax strategy depends on the expectation of income and losses, the need to distribute profits, exit scenarios, and the ability to convert from one legal form to another.

This section considers legal forms that are appropriate for the R&D and prelaunch stages of technology firms and those that are more appropriate once firms are launched and have customers. In any case, it is wise to consult with an attorney specializing in legal forms of organization to make sure that the right form has been chosen. See Table 8-2 for a comparison of the various legal forms.

TABLE 8-2   Comparison of Legal Forms

Business Form Issues	Sole Proprietorship	Partnership	Limited Liability Company	C-Corporation	Subchapter S-Corp
Number of Owners	One	No limit	No limit. Most states require a minimum of two members	No limit on shareholders	100 shareholders or fewer
Start-up Costs	Filing fees for DBA and business license	Filing fees for DBA; attorney fees for partnership agreement	Attorney fees for organization, documents; filing fees	Attorney fees for incorporation documents; filing fees	Attorney fees for incorporation; filing fees
Liability	Owner liable for all claims against business, but with insurance can overcome liability	General partners liable for all claims; limited partners liable only to amount of investment	Members liable as in partnerships	Shareholders liable to amount invested; officers may be personally liable	Shareholders liable to amount invested
Taxation	Pass-through; taxed at individual level	Pass-through; taxed at individual level	Pass-through; taxed at individual level	Tax-paying entity; taxed on corporate income	Pass-through; taxed at individual level

TABLE 8-2   *Continued*

Business Form Issues	Sole Proprietorship	Partnership	Limited Liability Company	C-Corporation	Subchapter S-Corp
Continuity of Life of Business	Dissolution on the death of the owner	Dissolution on the death or separation of a partner, unless otherwise specified in the agreement; not so in the case of limited partners	Most states allow perpetual existence. Unless otherwise stated in the Articles of Organization, existence terminates on death or withdrawal of any member	Continuity of Life	Perpetual existence
Transferability of Interest	Owner free to sell; assets transferred to estate upon death with valid will	General partner requires consent of other generals to sell interest; limited partners' ability to transfer is subject to agreement	Permission of majority of members is required for any member to transfer interest	Shareholders free to sell unless restricted by agreement	Transferable (but may affect "S" status); S-corps only have one class of stock (either preferred or common)
Distribution of Profits	Profits go to owner	Profits shared based on partnership agreement	Profits shared based on member agreement	Paid to shareholders as dividends according to agreement and shareholder status	Paid to share holders in proportion to their percentage ownership of company; losses can also be passed through
Management Control	Owner has full control	Absent an agreement to the contrary, partners have equal voting rights	Rests with management committee	Rests with the board of directors appointed by the share-holders	Rests with the board of directors elected by the share holders

R&D AND PRE-LAUNCH FORMS

Any legal form may be used during the R&D and prelaunch phases of the business, but some forms make more sense than others because they are quick, easy, and inexpensive to set up. Two examples are sole proprietorships and partnerships. Although these easier forms do not protect the owners from liability, they can serve the entrepreneur well during the development phase until the point at which the entrepreneur begins to take on liability in the form of employees and customers. Technology companies may attribute the birth of the idea for a technology to a single person but, in reality, most technology companies are started by teams during the product development and pre-launch stage. Whenever two or more people are partnering to launch a company, it is vital that they execute a partnership agreement at inception. There are several reasons for this. For one, the doctrine of ostensible authority holds each partner liable for the acts of the other partner(s) in the course of doing business for the partnership. For example, if one partner enters into a legal agreement with a company on behalf of the partnership, all the partners are bound by the terms of the agreement. This point alone makes clear the importance of choosing partners wisely and drawing up a partnership agreement that spells out the duties and responsibilities of the partners as well as how conflicts will be resolved and how the partnership can be dissolved.

A partnership can be formed by an oral or written agreement or even by implication. For example, the Uniform Partnership Act states that the receipt by a person of a share of the profits of the business is *prima facie* evidence that they are a partner in the business. This means that not only does that partner share proportionately in the profits, but also in the debts of the partnership. The founding team of a new technology venture will most likely all be general partners, which means that they are jointly and severally responsible for the obligations of the partnership. The founding team may decide to take on limited partners, whose liability is limited to their capital investment in the partnership. These limited partners cannot have a say in the management of the partnership or they risk their limited liability status. These types of partners are typically brought in as financial investors.

Like the sole proprietorship, all partnership earnings and losses pass through to the partners, and the partners pay taxes at their personal income tax rates. The partnership does, however, file an informational return with the IRS.

LEGAL FORMS THAT PROTECT THE OWNERS

Most technology ventures choose to use one of the legal forms that protects the owners from liability: the corporation (general and S) or the Limited Liability Company (LLC). It is important to note that while these forms do provide shelter from liability, limited liability status can be forfeited if the entrepreneur treats corporate assets like personal assets or fails to observe required corporate formalities such as rules for board of directors meetings and the recording of minutes. Personal guarantees on loans will also pierce the "corporate veil" and make the entrepreneur liable. In addition to limited liability status, corporate forms provide more prestige for the company and make it easier to raise capital.

There are two types of corporations: the general corporation and the subchapter S-corporation. The general corporation is the only form that is a legal entity, that is, it is chartered or registered by a state and survives the death or separation of its owners from the company (perpetual life). As a result, a corporation can sue and be sued, acquire and sell property and other assets, lend money, and pay taxes. The owners of the corporation are its stockholders who, like limited partners, are liable only to the extent of their investment in the corporation.

A corporation is created by filing a certificate of incorporation and articles of incorporation with the state in which the company will be doing business. It also requires a board of directors that hires the company officers who run the business. Many entrepreneurs choose to incorporate in Delaware because that state has an established body of case law on incorporation issues, a judiciary that is favorable to companies, broad indemnification availability, and fewer opportunities for legal problems. The disadvantage is that for purposes of litigation, if the company is physically located in another state, there will be two venues for litigation. Also, the Delaware corporation will need to register as a foreign corporation in the actual state in which the company is located and may have to pay that state's franchise tax.

Corporations enjoy many benefits. These include limited liability, multiple classes of stock that can be issued to meet the various requirements of investors, status, and the benefits of employee incentive plans. However, they also present many disadvantages. They are fairly costly and complex to form and should not be formed without the assistance of an attorney well versed in corporate law. One serious disadvantage arises from the fact that the corporation is a separate entity for tax purposes. If it makes a profit, it must pay taxes on that profit whether or not the profit was ever distributed to the shareholders. Furthermore, after the corporation has paid taxes on the profit, shareholders are taxed again on any dividends distributed. They cannot, however, deduct losses against their personal income tax liability. Another disadvantage is that the entrepreneur gives up some measure of control (unless the corporation is wholly owned) to a board of directors and shareholders. In a public corporation registered on one of the stock exchanges, entrepreneurs are responsible first to the stockholders and second to customers and employees. As the board of directors represents the stockholders, it has the power to remove the entrepreneur as CEO of the corporation.

The S-Corporation attempts to marry the advantages of the general corporation with the advantages of a partnership. The S-Corp is not a tax-paying entity, but a pass-through entity much like a partnership where the earnings are passed through to the partners and taxed at their personal rates. Losses can also be deducted against the owner's personal income tax liability up to the amount invested in the corporation. Businesses most suitable for the S-Corp are those that do not need to retain earnings for growth. The business should also have sufficient cash flow to cover the taxes that the owners will have to pay at their personal rates, otherwise there could be a situation where the company earns a taxable profit but has a negative cash flow, so the owners have to pay the taxes for the company out of their own pockets. S-Corps have strict requirements: they cannot have more than 100 investors, the owners must be U.S. citizens, and the S-Corp cannot issue more than one class of stock. Furthermore, if the company decides to use venture capital or do an IPO, it will need to convert to a general corporation prior to the IPO.

LIMITED LIABILITY COMPANIES

The LLC offers a flexible alternative to corporations, partnerships, and joint ventures. It combines the limited liability of a corporation with the pass-through tax advantages of a partnership or an S-Corp. It also has the flexibility of a more informal structure. Most LLCs are organized like S-Corporations to take advantage of the pass-through provision. The owners of an LLC are called *members* and their ownership interests are known as *interests*. These terms are equivalent to stockholders and stock. The members create an operating agreement, which is similar to a partnership agreement that spells out the rights and obligations of the members. Members have limited liability unless they have personally guaranteed a debt. Unlike the S-Corp, there is no limitation on the number of members or their status, and the LLC may issue more than one class of stock and have foreign investors. Like the S-Corp, the LLC will need to convert to a general corporation to take on venture capital or do an IPO.

MAKING A DECISION ABOUT FORM

With an understanding of the various legal forms, it is possible to make a more informed decision about which one is most appropriate. Some of the questions that should be asked as part of that decision-making process include the following:

- Does the team possess all the skills and experience needed to operate this venture? If not, the sole proprietorship will not be a good choice.
- Does the founding team have the capital required to start the business alone or do they need to raise it through equity or debt? Raising capital with a corporation is easier than with other forms.
- Is the team able to run the business and cover its living expenses for the first year? Again, this relates to whether or not the team needs to raise money.
- Is the team willing and able to assume personal liability for any claims against the business? If not, a corporation or LLC must be considered.
- Will the business have initial losses or will it be profitable almost from the beginning? If it will experience significant losses, a pass-through legal form will allow the founding team to write off losses against ordinary income.
- What is the team's harvest strategy? If an IPO is in the company's future, a corporation is the best choice.

The answers to these questions will help to narrow the choices. With the advice of an attorney, the right form should be a fairly straightforward decision. The final question about the team's harvest strategy (sometimes referred to as an exit strategy) is important because the form that is chosen should be one that will not have to be changed or one that can easily shift to another form at the appropriate time. The next section deals with the issue of changing the legal form of organization.

CHANGING LEGAL FORMS

As a company grows and evolves, it may reach the point where the current legal form is no longer appropriate for the company's objectives. For example, say an engineer/inventor decides to set up a laboratory in the garage of his home. His spouse is a corporate executive with a good salary, so he is already covered for medical insurance. He plans to work with two other engineers in a partnership structure until they have something that looks like a viable technology with potential applications in the market. In the beginning, the partnership expects losses as it purchases equipment, builds prototypes, and tests them with customers. Sensing that they have something marketable, the team decides to bring in someone with business expertise and form a company. They know that once they launch the product, they will probably incur continuing losses because of all the expenses of start-up—the promotion of the business, finding space to lease, and hiring employees. The team plans that within a year of introducing the product, they will need to seek venture capital to be able to grow as fast as they expect the market will demand. They also see an IPO in their future.

In the beginning, during product development, a simple partnership is usually sufficient as it conserves the limited resources of the founders and the liability to the team's individual assets is small. However, once the partners take on the responsibilities of a lease and employees, they need to consider insurance or moving to a legal form with limited liability. If the company will continue to experience losses, the team may want to use those losses to shelter personal income, which they could do in an S-Corp or LLC. If the period of loss is not long, it might be more cost effective to go immediately to a general corporation because their future plans include venture capital and an IPO. It should be clear from this example that the legal form of an organization is not a static decision, but is based on the company's needs at a particular stage in its life cycle.

Summary

The move from R&D to operations is not an easy transition, as the skills and requirements of the development team are different from those required for operations. An operating business does not happen overnight; it takes a lot of planning. Lingering technical and market issues continue to emerge, pulling the team in a multitude of directions. A successful transition requires three different groups of individuals: people from the innovation team, people from the opera-tions team, and transition management experts. It is the job of the transition team to finalize the product and its first applications as well as refine the business model. The transition team will also need to construct a transition plan that details the readiness of the company to launch the product in terms of personnel, systems, and resources. Part of the organizational model is the operational strategy of the company, that is, a plan for defining and coordinating the various processes inside the organization, in particular those that contribute to the manufacture of the product. Research has learned that the commitment model of organization is well-suited to high-tech companies seeking an eventual IPO. The legal form that a new company team decides to use for its venture is a critical decision that will affect the company for a long time. Choosing the most appropriate legal form is a function of three factors: (1) how much liability protection is required, (2) the company's operating requirements, and (3) the company's tax strategy.

Discussion Questions

1. What are the key challenges a technology team faces when moving from R&D to operations?
2. Why is developing a mission statement so important to the new venture? What is the strategy for constructing a mission statement?
3. Compare the commitment organizational model with the star or engineering model. Which is more effective for a start-up company? Why?
4. Why is the corporate form the most popular for high-tech ventures?

CASE STUDY

Quantum Dots

Starting a new technology company is a challenging task at best, but when the technology is at the cutting edge of a new industry where no one has gone before, there are enormous hurdles to overcome. That was the task that start-up Quantum Dot Corporation took on in 1997 when its founders, Joel Martin and Bala Manian, started the company. They were determined to conquer the field of nanotechnology, manipulating and building materials on the nanometer scale, which is one-billionth of a meter in size. Joel Martin, a physical chemist, and his partner had years of experience in Silicon Valley, having helped launch more than six medical device companies. Institutional Venture Partners supported Martin's notion of finding a technology that would "capture people's imagination" and provided financial backing.

Having money to spend solved only part of the problem. The quest was daunting as most of the technology that Martin found was either "ho-hum" or would require 20 years of development before the market was ready for it. At long last, he found the exciting technology he was looking for in quantum dots. Quantum dots are nanoparticles, semiconducting crystals that are so small that they can only be seen through a

(continued)

(*continued*)

microscope. They are governed by the laws of quantum mechanics, which speaks to the behavior of atoms and molecules. The size of a dot determines its wavelength and color of fluorescence. For example, a 2-nanometer particle glows bright green, whereas a 5-nanometer particle produces longer wavelengths that appear as red. What this means is that scientists can use different size dots to produce a broad spectrum of different colors. Although this was interesting science, it had never been translated into a viable business. No one knew what to do with the dots. However, as scientists began to improve on the dots, the colors became brighter and more refined, and it became apparent that they could be used in biological imaging and diagnostics to provide scientists the ability to image cell and organ behavior at a level of detail never before seen.

About the same time that Martin was looking for a technology to invest in, two scientists at Lawrence Berkeley Laboratory, Paul Alavisatosa and Shimon Weiss, were trying to find a way to exploit the biological potential of quantum dots. Quantum dots are the size of proteins, so it was logical that the two might be compatible. Research in 1998 confirmed that nanoparticles could be used as bio-probes in living systems. One month later, Quantum Dot Corporation was founded, having licensed all the relevant technologies from Lawrence Berkeley Laboratory, MIT, Indiana University, and the University of Melbourne in Australia. Martin basically brought together rival scientists to push Quantum Dot forward. The UC Berkeley Lab also took an equity stake in the company.

The entry strategy was not clear. Martin knew that he did not want to compete with the big diagnostics companies such as Roche, but he also did not want to turn quantum dots into a commodity. Extrapolating from another industry, he settled on Intel's business model. He would make quantum dots an essential element of every diagnostic kit and analytical instrument. The benefit to the customer was that quantum dots would withstand more cycles of excitation and light emission than basic organic molecules, which decompose rapidly, so investigators could track what was happening in cells and tissues for longer intervals of time. Furthermore, quantum dots come in many colors, and those colors are vibrant. The first target market was diagnostic test manufacturers. The second target was instrumentation manufacturers. The company also began work on what it hoped would become its killer app, biological bar codes, which are essentially polymer beads packed with millions of quantum dots. Each bead would have a known color signature instead of the traditional tag, which would be an easier way to recognize gene sequences.

In 2000, the company was experiencing a sense of urgency. It did not yet have a highly successful product despite having raised $7.5 million in the first few months of the business. The company knew that if its killer app was not ready within a couple of years, it would have to find alternatives to support the company financially. At the same time, competitors were nipping at its heels—small companies started by world renowned university chemists seeking to capitalize on the growing interest in nanotechnology. By May 2000, the dot-com bust had occurred and solid technology companies were looking better all the time. Quantum Dot was able to complete a $30 million equity round that month with venture capitalists who were not influenced by the extremes of the market and understood the timeline of biotech companies. Throughout 2000, with one of the few tangible nanotech products in the marketplace,

(*continued*)

(*continued*)

Quantum Dot received several research grants and began developing strategic partnerships with such giants as GlaxoSmith Kline, Genentech, and the National Institutes of Health. The company's strategy was two-pronged: (1) recruit top researchers to develop new technologies (the engineering model) and (2) licensing fundamental quantum dot technology from major universities. The strategy proved successful. By 2003, Quantum Dot Corporation had 137 patents in its portfolio, making it the world leader in semiconductor nanocrystal technology for use in biological, biochemical, and biomedical applications. In 2004, its alliance with Carnegie Mellon University achieved the ability to circulate quantum dots for hours in animals by coating the molecules twice with a polymer. This had important implications for long-term animal studies.

In the fall of 2005, Quantum Dot was acquired by giant Invitrogen for an undisclosed amount. The company had spent significant time and money getting its technology to market and was now out of capital for growth. Speculations at the time were that it was acquired for less than the $45 million in venture capital it had received over the years. Still, many argued that an acquisition by such a large company was a sign that nanotech start-ups had finally come of age.

Sources: (October 13, 2005). "Quantum Dot May be Sold Cheap," http://www.physorg.com/ news7218.html, accessed September 13, 2008; Alivisatos, A.P. (September 2001). "Less is More in Medicine," *Scientific American* 285(3): 66–73; David Rotman (January–February 2000). "Quantum Dot Com," *MIT Technology Review,* http://www.technologyreview.com/Nanotech/ 12035/?a=f, accessed September 13, 2008; (May 16, 2001). "Quantum Dot Corporation Announces Issuance of Patent for Nanocrystal Probes," *BusinessWire,* http://findarticles.com/ p/articles/mi_m0EIN/is_/ai_74559293, accessed September 13, 2008; Robert L. Whiddon (May 1, 2000); Quantum Dot Corporation, www.qdots.com/new/homeB.html., accessed February 17, 2008.

Endnotes

1. Boer, H., & During, W.E. (2001). "Innovation, What Innovation? A Comparison Between Product, Process, and Organizational Innovation," *International Journal of Technology Management* 22(1–3): 83–107.
2. Smulders, F., Calauwe, L.De, & Van Nieuwenhuizen, O. (June 2003). "The Last Stage of Product Development: Interventions in Existing Operational Processes," *Creativity and Innovation Management* 12(2): 109–120.
3. Leifer, R., Mcdermott, C.M., O'connor, G.C., Peters, L.S., Rice, M.P., & Veryzer, R.W. (2000). *Radical Innovation* (Boston: Harvard Business School Press), pp. 134–149.
4. Van De Ven, A., & Polley, D. (February 1992). "Learning While Innovating," *Organization Science* 3(1): 92–116.
5. Ibid., 150.
6. Germain, R., & Cooper, M.B. (1990). "How a Customer Mission Statement Affects Company Performance," *Industrial Marketing Management* 19: 47–54.
7. Abel, D.F. (1980). *Defining the Business: The Starting Point of Strategic Planning* (Upper Saddle River, NJ: Prentice Hall).
8. Shirley, S. (1989). "Corporate Strategy and Entrepreneurial Vision," *Long Range Planning* 22(8): 107–110.

9. Google Corporate Information, Company Overview, www.google.com/corporate/, accessed April 5, 2008.

10. Siegel, R.A., & Hansen, S-O. (1995). "Accelerating the Commercialization of Technology," *Industrial Management and Data Systems* 95(1): 18.

11. Browning, L.D., Beyer, J.M., & Shetler, J.C. (February 1995). "Building Cooperation in a Competitive Industry: Sematech and the Semiconductor Industry," (Special Research Forum: Intra- and Interorganizational Cooperation), *Academy of Management Journal* 38: 113–139.

12. Mohr, J.J. (2001). *Marketing of High-Technology Products and Innovations,* Upper Saddle River, NJ: Prentice-Hall, Inc., p. 75.

13. Dyer, H., Kale, P., & Singh, H. (Summer 2001). "How to Make Strategic Alliances Work," *MIT Sloan Management Review,* 42(4):37–43.

14. Gomes-Casseres, B. (Spring 1989). "Joint Ventures in the Face of Global Competition," *Sloan Management Review* 30(3): 17–26.

15. Bucklin, L.P., & Sengupta, S. (April 1993). "Organizing Successful Co-Marketing Alliances," *Journal of Marketing* 57: 32–46.

16. Sweeney, M.T. (1991). "Towards a Unified Theory of Strategic Manufacturing Management," *International Journal of Operations and Production Management* 11(8): 6–23.

17. Johnson, R.A., Kast, F.E., & Rosenzweig, J.E. (1973). *The Theory and Management of Systems,* 3rd ed. (New York: McGraw-Hill), pp. 144–146.

CHAPTER 9

TECHNOLOGY ADOPTION PATTERNS AND MARKETING STRATEGY

Marketing is about strategies, tactics, and techniques employed to raise customer awareness, generate sales, and build long-term customer relationships. Traditional marketing strategy has been described by the 5 Ps—people (customers), product, price, place (the channels through which the benefit is delivered to the customer), and promotion (strategies for creating awareness and generating sales). Today these factors of marketing strategy have been changed inexorably by the new context in which businesses operate. The shift from a product focus to a customer focus has precipitated major changes in marketing theory and practice. For example, as market diversity increases, it creates fragmented markets that make traditional segmentation less effective and efficient.[1] Diversity, which is found in location, lifestyle, ethnicity, income, age, and other factors, refocuses marketing efforts toward satisfying the needs and wants of individual customers rather than mass markets or market segments.[2] It is a more efficient approach to marketing because it focuses on profitable customers and takes advantage of technology and the Internet to find the right customers for the right products. Customers drive transactions, so marketing today is less concentrated on influencing or inducing people to buy and more focused on responding to demand or creating demand.

Perhaps the most important change in marketing strategy has been brought about by the Internet and the "long tail" phenomenon. Today marketers can reach millions of customers relatively cheaply via the Internet and target them in very small niches. The "long tail" describes a probabalistic statistical function known as a power law distribution. Figure 9-1 depicts such a curve. Note that the "tail" goes

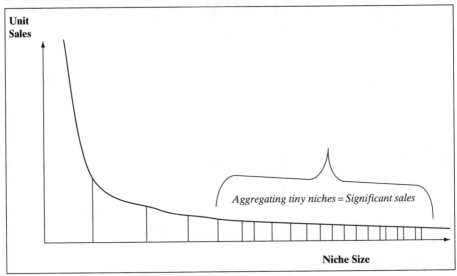

FIGURE 9-1 The Long Tail Phenomenon

Unit Sales

Aggregating tiny niches = Significant sales

Niche Size

to infinity, suggesting that there are an infinite number of tiny niches to be served and that the aggregate of all those niches can account for a significant number of sales.[3] The reason this phenomenon is important is that it describes a unique attribute of Internet marketing. The ability to easily reach and sell to all these tiny niches creates revenues that in the offline world would be difficult to achieve. The Internet and its convergence with video and content production technology, which is now priced within the reach of most people, has given entrepreneurs the ability to produce highly targeted messages to reach these customer niches. Moreover, social networking tools such as blogs, podcasts, vodcast, RSS Readers, and wikis have made viral marketing (word-of-mouth marketing) as common as television advertising. No matter what type of technology business entrepreneurs have, the Internet will play an important role in their marketing strategy because it's generally where customers look first for information.

Traditionally, most technology products are sold business-to-business, but today with online sales capturing 15 percent of total retail sales, many entrepreneurs have chosen to market their technologies direct to the consumer. This chapter explores the unique nature of high-technology markets and some of the most effective ways to create awareness for a new technology and build loyal customer relationships whether those customers are businesses or consumers.

THE NATURE OF HIGH-TECHNOLOGY MARKETS

High-technology markets are unique in that they display a great degree of uncertainty in customers, technology, and competitors,[4] so many marketers believe that a different set of marketing strategies and tactics is required to successfully deal with the dynamic nature of high-technology markets.[5] Moreover, because the margin for error is much smaller with high-technology companies, the execution of the marketing plan must be perfect.[6]

Although specific differences can be found in different industries across the spectrum of technology, from industrial technology to information systems and biotechnology, high-technology environments do share some common characteristics, in particular, market uncertainty, technology uncertainty, competitive volatility, and complexity/velocity. Each of these characteristics will be discussed in more depth in the following sections.

MARKET UNCERTAINTY

Market uncertainty results from the difficulty in correctly assessing customer needs and matching those needs to a particular technology application. The principal source of market uncertainty is customers' resistance to trying a new technology they cannot understand without a significant amount of education and preparation. To exacerbate the situation further, today customer needs are changing at a more rapid pace, often in unpredictable ways. Also, frequently customers will not adopt a new technology until they are fairly certain that it will be the standard in the industry because the switching costs with respect to learning a new technology are high. The classic example of this is the color television, which captured only 20 percent of the market after 10 years because it was expensive and didn't offer enough value over black-and-white television.[7]

TECHNOLOGICAL UNCERTAINTY

Technological uncertainty speaks to the question of whether the new venture can deliver on its promises and meet the needs of customers. This includes the promise of on-time delivery, something that technology companies with new products rarely achieve. Moreover, customers are also concerned about unintended consequences. For example, they may purchase a new technology in the hopes that it will make their business more productive, when, in fact, it often does quite the opposite because of the time involved in training employees, dealing with problems, and taking care of constant upgrades. Customers are also concerned whether the technology will quickly be rendered obsolete by newer technology, given the rapid pace of technological change. The entrepreneurial team is concerned that they will launch an application of their technology only to learn that a different application is more in demand. Deciding which features to include is not a straightforward decision, even with customer input.

COMPETITIVE UNCERTAINTY

If customers are volatile and unpredictable, competitors are equally so. In fact, many competitors for a new technology may come from outside the industry in which the technology was developed. Unfortunately, to their detriment, some entrepreneurs dismiss upstarts from outside the industry who frequently find new ways to create value for the customer that may not be at all related to the original technology but may include bundled services or complementary technology that makes the original technology more desirable to customers.

KNOW-HOW, COMPLEXITY, AND VELOCITY EFFECTS

The combination of know-how or scientific and technical knowledge and tacit manufacturing and sales knowledge can create a significant competitive advantage for a company.[8] Know-how affects market advantage, but so do the complexity of the industry and market, and velocity, the speed at which technology must be developed and brought to market.

Know-how is inextricably linked with R&D expenditures. The U.S. Department of Commerce labels those industries with double the R&D expenditures to sales ratio of other industries as "high tech."[9] When know-how represents a relatively high portion of overall investment, correspondingly high R&D expenditures are typically found.[10] Know-how, unlike products, possesses the unique characteristic that it cannot be used up; it is regenerative and defies the economic principle of scarcity.[11] Know-how increases and becomes more valuable with use, and the speed at which it increases accelerates as more people become more proficient at using it.[12] The cost of producing the first unit based on know-how is high, but the costs of reproduction decline precipitously, in some cases to zero.

What is important to understand about these characteristics of technology markets is that the possibility for value innovation occurs at the intersection of market, technology, and competitive uncertainty. These characteristics provide the disruption in the market that the entrepreneur needs to find a unique niche in which to enter the market. But entering the market is only the first challenge. Understanding customer adoption patterns is also important.

THE TECHNOLOGY ADOPTION CYCLE

The ability to transform an invention into a commercial innovation is a process that generally occurs in two ways: through market research and through the technology itself. The market-driven approach relies on internal and external knowledge to find a solution to a customer need in the market.[13] This approach can cause problems for technical people who have to try to hit a moving target with a single solution. By contrast, the technology-driven approach puts technology in the driver's seat without firm knowledge that a market even exists. This forces the scientist or engineer to develop a solution and then look for a problem. Both approaches come up lacking. A more effective approach is to use a parallel one that combines knowledge about the technology with knowledge about customer needs. This section considers the technology adoption model to describe the unique marketing issues of high-technology ventures and how to determine a marketing approach.

Understanding the adoption–diffusion curve helps entrepreneurs plan for where to target their efforts and what to expect with respect to the rate at which sales will occur. Figure 9-2 depicts the adoption–diffusion curve developed in 1957 at the Agricultural Extension Service at Iowa State College. It was designed to monitor patterns of hybrid seed corn adoption by farmers and it categorized the

FIGURE 9-2   The Technology Adoption–Diffusion Cycle

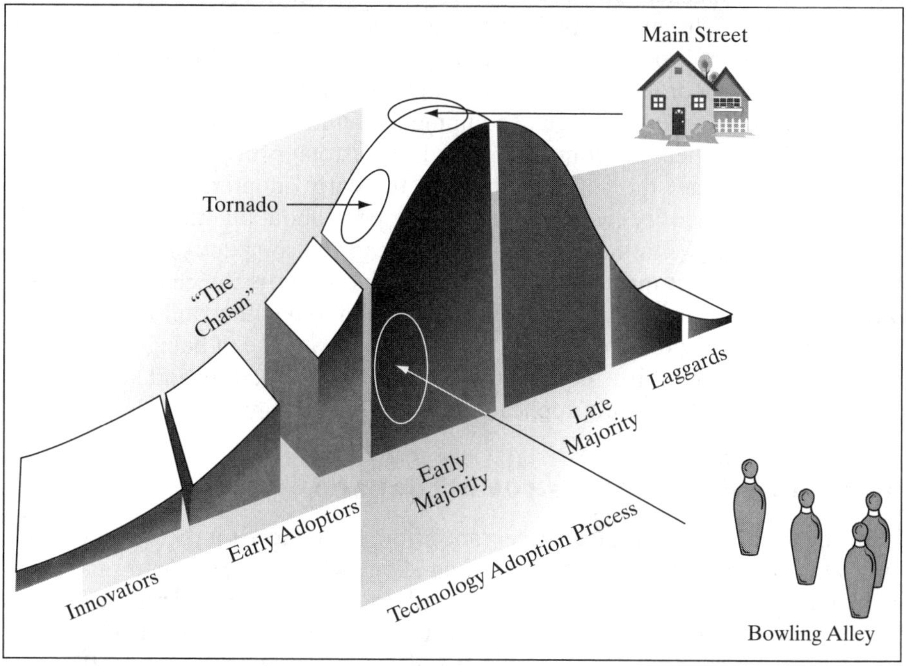

Main Street

Tornado

"The Chasm"

Laggards

Late Majority

Early Majority

Early Adoptors

Innovators

Technology Adoption Process

Bowling Alley

Source: Based on research at the Agricultural Extension Service at Iowa State College, 1957 and Moore, G. (1999) *Crossing the Chasm* (New York: HarperBusiness), pp. 1–11.

farmers based on how quickly they adopted new technologies.[14] More recently, Geoffrey Moore popularized the adoption–diffusion curve and added terms such as *tornado, bowling alley,* and *mainstreet.* These terms are explained below.

What the Iowa State study found was that prior to launching a new technology, an entrepreneur gets feedback from a unique group known as innovators. Innovators are the technical types who are constantly seeking new technologies, particularly before they even reach the market. The importance of the innovators is that they provide the proof of concept for later adopters; that is, they demonstrate that the technology works.

When a company is actually ready to launch a technology, it targets early adopters, those people who are not necessarily technically oriented but who have no fear of purchasing the latest technology. For a new company, this early market presents a time of great excitement. Preannouncements have prepared early adopters for the arrival of the technology, and their enthusiasm to try it is palpable. That enthusiasm, however, may give the company a false sense of confidence if it is not understood that early adopter enthusiasm may not be shared by the mainstream market. Between the early adopters and mainstream adoption lies the "chasm," a black hole of sorts where enthusiasm on the part of the early adopters has waned, but the mainstream market is not yet comfortable adopting the new technology. The vast majority of new technologies languish in the chasm because they haven't satisfied a compelling need on the part of customers. Some examples are artificial intelligence, global satellite positioning, and videoconferencing.

Crossing the chasm is a challenging but essential task for a technology to be adopted by the mainstream market and become the standard in its field. To do this, the entrepreneur must begin to seek out niche markets and encourage early adopters, who are generally original equipment manufacturers (OEMs), to modify the technology to meet the compelling needs of customers in those niche markets. This strategy will get the company beyond the early adopters and enable it to secure the early majority customers, which comprise about one-third of the whole adoption life cycle. With the capture of each niche, the company drives out same-size competition as it marches forward. This drive to cross the chasm requires a fine balance between moving too soon with a technology that still has problems and waiting too long only to lose the competitive advantage of being the pioneer. To be successful, the drive requires the cooperation of vendors and system integrators to craft niche-specific applications of the technology.

BUILDING CRITICAL MASS FOR A TORNADO

Once the technology has gained acceptance from a few niche markets, it finds itself in what Moore referred to as the "bowling alley," where the goal is to rack up as many niches (bowling pins) as possible in order to generate critical mass sufficient to drive the technology into the "tornado." The tornado is a period of mass-market adoption when the mainstream market quickly switches en masse to the new standard. When that happens, everything begins to take place very rapidly. A whirlwind of demand that is impossible to meet requires that the marketing people get out of the way and the operations people take over. All that matters in the tornado is that the company be able to manufacture and ship product as quickly as possible.

To improve the chances of creating a tornado and becoming the ultimate standard, it is important to attack the competition ruthlessly to build a secure foundation. The distribution channel must be expanded rapidly to every type of outlet possible, even at the expense of the customer in the short term, because the price of new technology usually declines rapidly after introduction. Customers will not mind because the technology is in such demand that all they really care about is getting their hands on it. Once the tornado has subsided, there is time to begin building the long-term customer relationships that will be necessary to sustain the company. While in the tornado, it is also important to keep moving the technology to the next lower price point. As the leader, if the company fails to do this, it will lose customers to clones. Consequently, one critical component of an effective tornado strategy is to have manufacturing and distribution partners in place before the tornado occurs. As the new technology becomes the standard, these partners will become standard bearers as well.

AFTER THE TORNADO

Not every company that has experienced the tornado has benefited from it. Nearly 20 years ago, Sony hit a tornado with its Betamax technology for VCRs.

Unfortunately, it attempted to control the tornado by refusing to license its technology to system integrators and application providers, so it was unable to keep up with demand. This attitude forced vendors and others to go around Sony to VHS technology, which was readily available, and VHS became the standard.

If a company survives the tornado, it will arrive at the final stage, known as "main street" to denote its relative calm when compared to the tornado. Main street is where the company immediately has to shift focus to satisfying customers and building sustainable relationships, something it did not do during the tornado when its mandate was simply to get the product out to meet demand. Moore believes that the defining characteristic of main street is that growth no longer comes from selling to new customers, but from niche-specific extensions, in other words, from selling more products to existing customers.[15] To accomplish this requires trusting relationships and more interaction with customers. The bottom line is that entrepreneurs must understand their markets, prepare for demand, and be able to satisfy customers once they have acquired them. All of this demands an effective marketing approach.

DETERMINING A MARKETING APPROACH

The choice of marketing approach will be highly dependent on the market segment that the entrepreneur is targeting. Contrary to popular belief, the largest market is not necessarily the best market to enter first; rather, the market segment or niche where the customer is in the most pain is probably the better choice. The rationale is that if the technology solves a real pain the customer is experiencing—whether that customer is another business or a consumer—that customer will be more likely to purchase. Given that a new venture's primary challenge in the first year is survival, choosing a market segment that will produce sales quickly makes sense.

Determining how to enter a new market is a function of a variety of factors. New ventures with new products have to find a fit with the needs of the new market, and they have to demonstrate to customers that the new venture can provide that fit. It is important that entrepreneurs understand how technology products differ from nontechnology products so they don't choose traditional marketing strategies that may produce poor results because they're not appropriate for technology products. Technology products share some characteristics in common with nontechnology products.

- Benefits to the customer—what problem is the product solving or what customer need is being met? These needs are generally intangible things such as convenience, saving time, and saving money.
- Product attributes that deliver the benefits. These are the aspects of the product that directly address customer benefits and may include cost, value, usability, or reliability, to name a few.
- Product features—the details of the product such as functions, ergonomics, and components.
- Ancillary product features such as warranties, service, and so forth.

It is important to remember that customers purchase benefits, not features. That simple truth explains why a customer might not purchase a technology product with additional features because their problem has been solved with the existing feature set. As an example, many consumers have yet to adopt Microsoft's new Vista operating system because it doesn't solve any significant problems that aren't solved with the existing system.

Technology products have additional characteristics that will affect the entrepreneur's marketing decisions. Because technology products usually go through many "generations" in their development, at any point the information that the entrepreneur provides the customer is time sensitive; that is, its value will not endure. Customers then understand that their technology may soon become out-of-date and decide to "leapfrog" or bypass the current technology in anticipation of later versions.[16] Entrepreneurs also face the decision of whether to make the current generation of their technology "backward compatible," in other words, able to work with previous generations of the technology.

Technology products are often part of a system that is governed by an architecture or rules that make it possible for all the components of the system to communicate.[17] This has implications for customers who may want to use legacy products with the new system. Another important characteristic of technology products is that they are the result of significant embedded tacit knowledge, that is, knowledge not codified or made available to the customer because it's a trade secret retained in the company. Consequently, customers perceive technology products as complex and difficult to understand. The challenge for entrepreneurs when attempting to market these technologies is to be able to convey the benefits in ways that the customer can easily understand without revealing tacit knowledge that might be a competitive advantage for the company. This can be accomplished through easy-to-read instruction manuals with pictures depicting what the customer needs to do.

Entrepreneurs must also understand the difference between introducing an incremental innovation and a radically new or disruptive innovation. An incremental innovation can replace an existing product and provide better performance and lower cost while still offering the same functionality, so it is easily understood and adopted by the customer. However, a radical technology will exact high switching costs from customers by asking them to change their behavior and to learn a new way of doing a particular function with which they are familiar. It is important to note that the radicalness of a technology is not dependent on the technology itself, but rather on the degree of change in customer behavior that must occur to use the technology. For example, the technology for antilock braking systems is substantially different from that of conventional braking systems. Antilock braking employs a microprocessor to rapidly pump the brakes, which is quite different from the mechanical braking process. However, customers do not have to substantially change their behavior when using the antilock brakes in order for them to work. Consequently, antilock brakes are an example of an incremental innovation that is a substitute for existing systems.

The PC is an example of a radical innovation that required a significant change in behavior on the part of customers. Consider the work of accountants prior to mainstream adoption of PCs. Financial information was entered by hand into ledgers, and calculators were used to crank the numbers. It took years before many accountants trusted computers enough to make the considerable effort to learn how to use them and transfer all their record keeping to the PCs. PCs were such a radical concept that a market for them had to be created. Because they affected mission-critical activities of businesses, the adoption rate was relatively slow.

UNDERSTANDING CUSTOMER NEEDS

Most techniques that entrepreneurs and marketers use to understand customer needs are based on existing products with which customers are familiar. With a radically new innovation, there are no existing customer needs being satisfied. However, even with an incremental innovation, it is still quite difficult to collect information from customers about their specific needs because they frequently do not know how to express those needs in ways that aid engineers and marketing people in determining performance criteria. Developing an understanding of customer needs can be achieved by answering several basic questions that include

- What do customers buy?
- When do they buy?
- Why do they buy?
- How do they buy?
- How much do they buy?

To begin to discover the answers to these questions and more, it is important to understand the factors that affect customer-purchasing decisions. Five factors appear to have an impact on the purchasing decision.[18]

1. **Cost/benefit analysis.** Customers tend to consider the benefit of purchasing the new technology relative to its costs. In other words, customers want to know that after they pay the often-higher price for the new technology, it will meet their needs and they will be able to learn to use it quickly and correctly.

2. **Compatibility with existing technology.** Customers will tend to purchase technologies that have similar aspects to products they are currently using and that do not force them to change their current way of doing things.

3. **Difficulty of use.** Customers gauge a purchase on how complex the technology is and how long it will take to learn it.

4. **Readily identifiable benefits.** Customers must be able to see what the benefits are to purchasing the technology without having to understand highly technical terms. Benefits should be intangible like convenience or ease of use and viewed from the customer's perspective. Technology companies frequently tout the features of their products. For example, HDTV has higher resolution than traditional television, but what does this mean to the customer who does not understand what resolution is? It may mean a clearer, sharper picture, but is there enough perceived difference to warrant the much higher price? Only the customer can answer that question.

TABLE 9-1 Adoption Rates for Radical Technologies					
Internet	*Compact Discs*	*Color TV*	*Answering Machines*	*TV*	*Radio*
3 yrs	10 yrs	10 yrs	10 yrs	15 yrs	30 yrs
90 M users	64% mkt	3% mkt	15% mkt	60 M users	60 M users

Source: Hof, R. (June 22, 1998). "The Click Here Economy," *Business Week,* pp. 122–128.

5. **Ability of benefits to be observed.** Are the benefits easily viewed by the customer using the product as well as by people watching the customer use the product? When benefits are easily observed, the desire to purchase is greater.

Considering all of these factors, it is no wonder that it takes time for technologies to achieve mass-market acceptance. Table 9-1 provides the adoption rates for several twentieth-century radical innovations.[19]

It is critical to understand the market into which the new technology will be sold and the nature of technology products in general because they are fundamental to the determination of a pricing strategy, which is discussed next.

PRICING HIGH-TECHNOLOGY PRODUCTS

Pricing new products is one of the most difficult tasks facing an entrepreneur, far more challenging than determining a promotion strategy or deciding on a distribution channel. Pricing strategy must maintain a balance between covering the costs of development and achieving a reasonable profit while at the same time recognizing the price tolerance and value perception of customers. Rarely do entrepreneurs deliberately seek to compete on price because doing so immediately commoditizes their offering and undermines the real value they intended to create for customers. Pricing of high technology is a complicated undertaking for a variety of reasons, not the least of which is the fact that most technologies experience rapid decline of price after market introduction. Some companies have reported price declines of 20 percent or more annually on the technologies they have introduced.[20] The paradox is that businesses can be their most successful when prices are falling the fastest, but this requires exponential growth just to stay ahead.[21] It further requires that a firm lower its costs faster than its prices are declining. Eventually, every technology becomes a commodity—that is, there is demand but the technology is no longer differentiated, so it competes primarily on price. Commodity markets are somewhere that no entrepreneur wants to be because the margins are slim or do not exist, volumes must remain high to compensate for declining margins, and there is no room for error.

As a technology approaches commoditization, entrepreneurs must create new value apart from the value of the original technology so that customers have a reason to pay more for the continued use of the technology. Not only do they have to create new value, customers have to perceive that the value is real and important to them. Many technologies end up being virtually given away while services associated with them and complementary products provide the key to continuing revenues. One factor contributing to the downward spiral of technology prices and competition based on price is Internet search engines such as Google, which enable anyone to easily search for the lowest price on any product.

The goal for the entrepreneur is to achieve the highest price point at market launch and that means getting to market first or at least before that price point begins its downward slide.[22] Perhaps the best way to ensure that products will not quickly become commodities despite low pricing is to develop long-term customer relationships based on a continuing dialogue and to find new ways to sell more products and services to existing customers. Furthermore, the most effective way to counter the price transparency of the Internet is to continually innovate so that customers have choices based on more than price and to create more complex pricing structures, a topic that will be taken up in a later section.

DEFINING THE COMPONENTS OF PRICE

Many factors make up the components of price, including (1) the cost of producing the product, (2) the overall price strategy and goals of pricing, (3) promotions and discounts, (4) the degree of standardization or customization involved in the product, (5) the profit required, and (6) the industry margins. When an entrepreneur focuses solely on covering costs without considering market demand, competition, or the company's marketing strategy, the entrepreneur loses an opportunity to price proactively for competitive advantage. Market-based pricing considers the needs and perceptions of the customer so that the value of dealing with the company and its complement of products are reflected in the price. The overall pricing strategy of the company can be proactive or reactive. A proactive strategy will recognize the value customers perceive from the various benefits offered. For example, one medical device manufacturer developed a technology that would dramatically speed up a number of clinical tests. Customers were excited by the product but sales fell short of projections just a short time after product launch. When the company analyzed its results, it discovered that different market segments perceived radically different value from the product. Pharmaceutical companies recognized the significant cost savings from being able to reduce the number of personnel needed to perform the tests. But university laboratories found that when using this technology their students didn't have enough time to actually learn the testing procedures well. So the company had to modify its pricing strategy to better suit the various customer segments it was targeting. This is also a good example of the importance of seeing the product from the customer's perspective. If customers do not perceive value, they will not pay the price the entrepreneur wants to charge.

Reactive pricing is what happens when a firm is averse to risk and does whatever its competitors do. A risk-averse attitude can also be reflected in the standardization of prices, in other words, offering the same price to all customers. A more proactive approach enables the company to be more flexible in its pricing strategy so that it can price according to its various customer segments to account for buying habits, bundled or unbundled product offerings, and the moves of competitors. Price can also be used to set up entry barriers to competitors and to provide a complex pricing structure that is difficult for competitors to untangle and compare.

CONVERGING ON A PRICE POINT

Today's chaotic market environment means that products move through their life cycles much faster; therefore, management decision making must occur more rapidly and more frequently. As fast as old markets disappear, new ones emerge and competitors become more aggressive in their tactics. Consequently, it is no wonder that companies find that they must stay flexible to adapt to these changes.

Given the nature of pricing for high technology, one solution to the pricing dilemma may be triangulation. Converging on a price point from three perspectives makes it more likely that the price chosen will reflect the real market price, at least for a time. Typically, the three points that converge are 1) cost, 2) competition and customers, and 3) value chain partners

Figuring the direct costs of producing the product is difficult in the very early stages of a new venture because prototype costs typically run about 10 times the cost of the final production-run product. Still, it is important to price the product so that costs can be covered and a profit earned, or the business will not be sustainable. Some technologies—drugs, operating systems, and machines, for example—have extremely high development costs that will probably not be recouped in the first year or even two solely using a premium pricing strategy, generally because of price resistence from customers. Nevertheless, in practice, most technologies are introduced at a relatively high price to speed up the recovery of development costs and bring the company closer to profitability before competitors enter the market and force prices down. The only reason to price very near cost is when cost is the company's competitive advantage and when it is sustainable over the long term against competitors that cannot achieve the same efficiencies.

Customers and value chain partners can provide a wealth of pricing information in the same way that they supplied the entrepreneur with demand information. They both represent the market—customers in a more direct way and value chain partners as intermediaries in the process. Customers generally have no trouble expressing their feelings about price or their intolerance for a particular price point. In calculating the price the customer pays, it is vital to consider the total cost of ownership of the product, which might include delivery, installation, service, and repair. To arrive at a suitable price, the markups along the value chain must also be considered. It is one thing to cover production costs, but the cost of the value added along the channel is ultimately part of the final price as well. If that final price is beyond the tolerance of the customer, the firm must reconsider all the points along the path from the producer to the customer/end user to reevaluate margins, costs, and markups. Many technology companies have had to resort to more direct channels of distribution to avoid the markups of intermediaries that put the final price out of range of the customer.

The competition is certainly another important source of pricing information. However, benchmarking on competitors is a reactive approach to pricing and should only be a guide to determining if the price being considered is even in the ballpark of what the market will accept. If an entrepreneur's technology is superior and creates new value, pricing outside the bounds of competitor pricing may be warranted, especially if it serves to put the technology in a new class all of its own. Radical innovations may appear to have no direct competitors, but there are always alternatives to a new technology, and those alternatives are the competition in the form of substitute products.

CONSTRUCTING A PRICING STRATEGY

The first thing to understand about pricing strategy is that one strategy does not fit all. A pricing strategy will be based on the company's goals and whether the company is a start-up or established; domestic or global; or no tech, low tech, or high tech. Another point to consider is whether the pricing structure is simple or complex. A simple pricing structure will usually result in a lower price because it is easily compared across competitors' products, especially with search engines providing a quick and easy way to compare pricing online. Conversely, a complex structure has many layers of prices and discounts, and it will be more difficult for customers to make direct comparisons. Many companies choose to begin to increase the complexity of their pricing structures by instituting two-part tariff strategies. For example, suppose a company is introducing a new software product that it is hosting via an application service provider (ASP) model. It might charge a monthly flat fee for access to the ASP site and the software and a per-use charge for each time the customer accesses the site and uses the software.

Customer goals will also influence the pricing strategy. If customers are focused on reducing costs, they will probably be looking for the lowest price; conseqently the entrepreneur's margins will be relatively small. On the other hand, if the customer's goal is to solve a problem, the customer will focus more on the bundle of benefits the entrepreneur is offering to solve that problem. Therefore, the price can be higher and the entrepreneur will enjoy bigger margins.

The bottom line is that price should be considered a competitive weapon in the entrepreneur's arsenal of competitive advantages and marketing strategy.

DEVELOPING A MARKETING PLAN

The plan that guides the launch of a new product is as critical to the success of that launch as the product itself. The marketing plan identifies the goals, strategies, and tactics that will be used to create product awareness and reach the customers for whom the benefits are designed. The development of the plan should be an ongoing effort that begins during feasibility analysis. Recall that one of the most important tests of feasibility analysis is the market/customer test. Primary research with the customer helps to refine the product, identify the features and benefits that create value for the customer, and determine demand. Once that information is gathered, it can be applied to developing an overall strategy for market launch and subsequent growth.

CONSTRUCTING A ONE-PARAGRAPH PLAN

Experienced marketers often suggest that it is important to put the most important components of the marketing plan into one paragraph. This forces the entrepreneur to focus on goals, strategies, and tactics to see if they are compatible. The following are the major components of this one-paragraph plan:

- **The purpose.**   What will the plan accomplish? Is it designed to create awareness for a new technology? Keep existing customers? Find new customers?

- **The benefits of the product and any services.**   How will the benefits satisfy a customer need or solve a problem?

- **The target market.**   Who is the first customer for the new technology?

- **The market niche.**   Where does the company fit in the market and how does it differentiate itself from the rest of the market?

- **The marketing tactics.**   Which marketing tools will be employed— advertising, promotion, and so on?

- **The company's identity.**   How does the customer perceive the company?

The following is an example of a one-paragraph marketing plan from a company in the business of fabricating printed circuit boards (PCBs).

The purpose of *PCB Fab's* marketing activities is to establish *PCB Fab's* brand name in the Chinese PCB industry, help potential customers understand *PCB Fab's* services and benefits to customers, and create a market pull for the company's products and services from its target customers. *PCB Fab's* target market segment consists of foreign-owned or top Chinese PCB fabricators that manufacture high-tech, high-end PCB devices. Its initial customers are American and European PCB manufacturers operating in China that are already *PCB Fab's* customers in the United States and Europe. Unlike other PCB fabrication material suppliers in the Chinese market that only offer customers a few limited products, *PCB Fab* provides its customers with the most comprehensive product lines so that customers only need to deal with one supplier and one invoice. In addition, *PCB Fab's* JIT total supply chain management program customizes its products and services to meet customers' specific requirements and eliminate the need for raw materials inventory. In *PCB Fab's* target market segment, the company can potentially create a highly customized, high-margin service that is valued by the target customers. *PCB Fab* will strive to create a brand image of a company that provides its customers with superior services and products with the highest quality and reliability. It also wants to be known as a company with a global reach and the capability of delivering PCB material when customers need it, where customers want it, and the way customers need it. *PCB Fab* will first create the awareness of its products and services in the International Expo of Printed Circuit Industry in Shanghai on March 20. It will then advertise its products and services in Chinese trade magazines. Meanwhile, *PCB Fab* will search and identify local distributors to distribute its proprietary product lines to leading PCB manufacturers in China. Furthermore, the company will leverage its existing strategic partnerships with American and European PCB fabricators to reach their businesses in China.[23]

MARKETING TOOLS

There is a wealth of tools available to entrepreneurs to help them match their message with their market, from newspaper, television, and radio ads to brochures, business cards, and new media tools such as blogs, search engine ads, and social networking sites. It is not within the scope of this book to discuss all these marketing tools and many of the traditional tools like focus groups and mainstream advertising just don't work well for most technology products; however, choosing appropriate marketing tools should be easier if entrepreneurs consider the following:[24]

- Spend time with lead users who are the early adopters of the technology. They can provide important insights into what mainstream customers might desire and through what medium they will want to learn about the technology.

- Don't underestimate the power of network effects. If the value of the technology is only apparent if many people are using it (the fax machine, search engines), then it is important to get the technology into the hands of as many users as possible as quickly as possible, which may mean giving the product or aspects of the product away initially or licensing to other companies to build new applications so that the entrepreneur can penetrate several market niches simultaneously.

- Price for the 20 percent of customers who contribute 80 percent of revenues and target marketing efforts toward the needs of those customers.

- Make certain that the first customer has the highest cost/benefit ratio; that is, the return on investment in that customer in terms of marketing tools is the greatest.

The bottom line is that the tools chosen should target the correct market segment with the right message—one that conveys the value being delivered.

PROMOTING HIGH-TECHNOLOGY PRODUCTS

For whatever changes have occurred in markets and in the practice of marketing, one strategy remains constant—the practice of optimizing the marketing mix. The marketing mix is composed of product specifications, patents, brands, communication strategies, advertising, promotion, public relations, strategic alliances, services, and pricing. Optimization of the of the mix means that getting the maximum return on investment is critical, particularly for entrepreneurs with limited resources. And it's no easy task given the innovations occurring in distribution channels that make finding the best media space or communication tool more difficult. The best advice for entrepreneurs (and the least expensive in the long run) is to deeply understand the first customer for the technology—recall that this customer is the one in the most pain. Understanding how and where customers want to learn about the technology will save time and money and prevent the entrepreneur from mistakenly choosing a tactic or channel that doesn't match customer needs.

Entrepreneurs face an additional hurdle in designing their marketing mix. For decades, innovating firms have faced an enormous problem of appropriability, that is, they had difficulty reaping the fruits of the years of work and heavy investment in R&D.[25] This problem arose out of the fact that innovations are difficult to produce but easy to imitate. Some research has suggested that competitors acquire detailed information on 70 percent of new products within one year of their launch, and that imitating a new innovation costs, on average, one-third of the original cost of development.[26] Today, a company's ability to effectively promote its innovations can serve to moderate the appropriability problem.[27]

The pharmaceutical industry serves as a good example of appropriability and the relationship between innovation and promotion. Firms that produce patented drugs experience high intensity of effort in both R&D and promotion of the drugs at market launch.[28] Because drugs are patented, they also tend to have a high degree of appropriability over the actual economic life of the patent, which is effectively shorter than the 20 years from date of application because of lengthy FDA process requirements. It is difficult to imitate a drug patent because the compound claim is very exacting and includes all formulations or uses of the chemical entity.[29] However, at the end of the patent period, the company experiences intense competition from generic drug manufacturers. Consequently, firms tend to promote heavily during the patent period to establish a secure brand to counteract the competition from generics they will experience at the end of the patent period. They may also choose to lower the price just prior to the end of the patent to discourage generic equivalents. Alternatively, the firm could use a very proactive approach such as licensing or marketing a generic version aimed at hospitals, which tend to be more price sensitive, at the same time they raise the price to pharmacies, as doctors tend to be more brand conscious.

There are a number of promotional tactics that are particularly useful to high-technology product launches and we discuss some of the more successful here: preannouncements, brand building, and publicity.

USING PREANNOUNCEMENTS

Timing is especially critical when dealing with high-technology products. Preannouncements have become a regular tactic, particularly in the software industry, to persuade customers to delay purchasing a product until the new technology is

ready.[30] They are an effective way to give a heads up to suppliers, potential partners, and company stakeholders that a new product launch will be taking place in
the near future and thereby build excitement and momentum for the new technology. They are also ways to maintain a market position until the product actually reaches the market by using a word-of-mouth type of advertising to channel
members and customers so that they can plan their future needs. For example, at
the Consumer Electronics Show in Las Vegas in January 2008, Microsoft
announced its Silverlight video technology to power live and on-demand video
for the 2008 Olympics, but at the time of announcement it was not yet ready for
prime time.

For all of the benefits of preannouncements, they do have their drawbacks.
Announcing far in advance of a launch date is a little like telling the enemy
where the troops will be landing. Competitors have time to react, and generally do so in a big way when and if the product actually launches. This is one
reason why pioneering firms rarely use preannouncements; they want to protect their pioneering advantage.[31] They also want to avoid cannibalizing their
existing products before the new product is ready for market. Announcing
far in advance also raises the probability that the product will not meet its
announced date of launch due to all the normal glitches that take place in
product development and prototyping. If the product is not launched on the
announced date, the firm's reputation suffers and customers may cancel
orders. Preannouncements are known as "vaporware" when they involve software that is announced but does not exist or is years behind in a promised
delivery date.[32] In 2006, *Wired Magazine* named Duke Nukem Forever,
3D Realm's video game, as the top vaporware of the year. The product has
spent nearly a decade in development.[33]

Despite these negatives, preannouncements, if used wisely, can prepare customers for the product launch, stall them from purchasing something else, and
create excitement for purchasing on the day of launch.

DEVELOPING A BRAND PRESENCE

A strong brand is a significant competitive advantage in markets where customers have many choices. Branding is about creating "a deep psychological
affinity to a product or service."[34] The American Marketing Association defines
brand as "a name, term, design, symbol, or any other feature that identifies one
seller's good or service as distinct" from other sellers.[35] In other words, the
customer wants to own the product because the brand has meaning. Compare the
brand recognition versus psychological hold of Google and Intel. Although
Google has brand recognition among Internet search engines, it does not generally elicit an emotional response. People do not feel bad about using another
search engine. However, Intel captures both brand recognition and generates an
emotional response. "Intel Inside" on the front of a PC provokes a feeling of reliability, quality, and strength. Customers think twice about purchasing a product
with a non-Intel microprocessor.

A first-mover strategy requires the development of a strong brand presence, but any technology firm should make branding a significant part of its overall marketing strategy because a successful brand will ultimately bring down marketing costs. A successful brand commands a higher price and enjoys significantly more loyalty from customers. This means that when new products are introduced under the recognized brand, customer acceptance and adoption are almost assured because the customer's array of choices has been simplified. The most effective route to branding is to brand the company and a platform of innovations rather than a particular product or technology. Because of the rapid obsolescence of technology products, it is more important to stabilize the brand in something that will not become obsolete or at least not for a very long time.

Cobranding or joint venturing a product is a common way to benefit from the synergy of two branded companies. For example, entrepreneurial router company Linksys was acquired by Cisco but retained its brand and cobranded it with Cisco. It is important to choose partners carefully when cobranding, as the brands will be inextricably tied together, perhaps for the lives of the companies.

TAKING ADVANTAGE OF PUBLICITY

Publicity is essentially free advertising or word-of-mouth referrals. For any technology start-up with limited resources, publicity is certainly the way to go. If the technology or company is newsworthy, entrepreneurs can get publicity by contacting a newspaper, magazine, or online reporter or editor to share the company's compelling story. With so many cable and network channels looking for content, a very interesting story could even make the evening news. To take advantage of free publicity, entrepreneurs need a press kit that includes a background article on the company, any press releases the company has issued, ideas for stories, and sample of articles that have been written about the company.

Editors typically prefer news items that relate to starting a business, introducing a new product, announcing the promotion of someone key in the organization, awards received, or significant customers acquired, among others. An effective press release should include the date, name of contact person, phone number, release date for the press release, a descriptive headline, and the release information providing the who, what, where, when, and why. A photo, if appropriate, is also helpful in attracting attention and making it easier for the report to create a story. The most important thing to remember about press releases or articles is that they must not sound promotional—in other words, like an advertisement. Several publishing services—for example, PR Newswire (www.prnewswire.com)—are available to gather and distribute information about the entrepreneur's business.

Marketing a new technology product will be difficult or relatively easy depending on how closely the entrepreneur matched a real need or pain in the market with the technology solution he or she is producing. If the technology solves a real and compelling problem, customers won't need much in the way of marketing techniques to help them make the purchase decision. By contrast, a solution for which there is no pain or the pain is not significant will require significant marketing resources to educate and capture customers. An important component of marketing strategy is distribution and that will be covered in Chapter 10.

Summary

Customer-centered marketing is the focus of new ventures today as they struggle to meet rapidly changing customer needs. High-technology markets display a unique blend of market uncertainty, technology uncertainty, and competitive uncertainty. In addition, know-how, complexity, and velocity all affect the market advantage of a high-tech firm. The ability to transform an invention into a commercial innovation occurs in generally two ways: by market research and by the technology itself. The market-driven approach relies on internal and external knowledge to find a solution to a customer need in the market. This approach can cause problems for technical staff that have to try to hit a moving target with a single solution. In contrast, the technology driven approach puts technology in the driver's seat without firm knowledge that a market even exists for it. This forces the technologist to develop a solution and then look for a problem. Both approaches come up lacking. A more appropriate and effective approach is to use a parallel one that combines knowledge about the technology with knowledge about customer needs. Determining how to enter a new market is a function of a variety of factors. New ventures with new products have to find a fit with the needs of the new market, and they also have to demonstrate to customers that the new venture can provide that fit. Pricing is an important part of the bundle of competitive advantages a company has and should be dealt with proactively. All of the issues related to marketing a new technology are brought together in the marketing plan, which is designed to create awareness for the company and its products and consists of goals, strategies, and tactics. The bottom line for any company desiring to develop an effective marketing strategy is to tell a compelling story and solve a real customer need.

Discussion Questions

1. How do the characteristics of high-technology markets affect the marketing strategy of a new venture?
2. What is the most effective strategy for collecting market intelligence?
3. When pricing high-technology products, what factors should be taken into consideration?
4. What is the purpose of a marketing plan? What is the value of compressing the plan into one paragraph?
5. What role does branding play in the promotional strategy of a new high-tech venture?

Finding the Right Formula for Music with Science

In an industry that is troubled with too few big hits and a lot of also rans, Mike McCready believes that he has the solution in a technology he created to predict the hits using science. His company, New York-based Platinum Blue Music Intelligence, gathers enormous amounts of data from every song that has appeared on the Billboard Hot 100 in the United States or the Top 40 in Great Britain. In only 20 seconds, his software can pick up 40 bits of information such as types of instruments used, "fullness of sound," type of melody, tempo, rhythm, and harmony. When McCready studied all this data in a three-dimensional cluster map, he discovered that 80 percent of all the hit songs shared a common structure that could be identified. But what was more interesting was that all the songs in a cluster did not necessarily sound the same. For example, Norah Jones, a jazz artist was found in a cluster with Van Halen, a heavy metal artist. McCready is convinced that he can tell you whether a new song has a high probability of attracting listeners who enjoyed other songs in the same cluster.

Critics of McCready's technology say that because it relies on data from songs that have already been hits, it is not able to recognize a true artistic breakthrough. Furthermore, who is to say that a predicted "hit" that becomes a hit did so because of the science of prediction or because the studios poured enormous amounts of money into its production and marketing. Did it become a hit as a self-fulfilling prophecy? Others argue that high scores that come from music intelligence will encourage recording companies to take a chance on new talent.

McCready has a significant competitor, Polyphonic HMI (now called Music Intelligence Solutions), which developed its technology, Hit Song Science (HSS) while McCready was the CEO of the Barcelona-based company from 2001 until 2005. Producers who have used HSS are astounded by its ability to separate the potentially great from the not-so-great. In 2006, Polyphonic brought in revenues that exceeded $1 million and is now serving the Indian music industry.

The customers for Platinum Blue's technology Music Xray™ and Song Seeker™ go beyond record producers to radio playlist-programmers who seek to create a more effective flow of music by grouping mathematically similar songs. And mobile phone companies such as Vodafone are using this music intelligence to create ringtones. Not to be outdone by the music industry, legal professionals in intellectual property are interested in learning if this technology can help them in their pursuit of copyright infringers.

At launch, the technology faced strong resistance, even from customers who saw the value in the benefits offered. The music industry is slow to change (recall the slow response to the threat of Napster file-sharing technology) and reluctant to adopt new technology that might conflict with its existing methods and norms. When a technology is adopted, the diffusion process is typically slow. In this case, it may be due to a combination of factors that include incompatibility with existing practices and values; complexity, therefore it's not easy to understand; can't be tried easily on a limited basis; and it's not easily observed until the company has established a significant success rate with

(continued)

(*continued*)

its predictions. Diffusion will rely heavily on positive referrals from respected industry leaders. Furthermore, there is a risk in new technology that the underlying assumptions might be challenged. In this case, for example, it is not certain that there is a significant difference between the failed song clusters and the successful song clusters.

The challenges to a marketing strategy for this technology are many and McCready wonders what is the best way to achieve critical mass?

Sources: (November 11, 2006). "How Many Hits?," *The Guardian Weekend*, p. 55; Gladwell, M. (October 16, 2006). "Annals of Entertainment," *The New Yorker* (June 8, 2006). "Sounds Good," *The Economist*.

Endnotes

1. Sheth, J.N., Mital, B., & Newman, B. (1999). *Customer Behavior: Consumer Behavior and Beyond* (New York: Dryden).
2. Sheth, J.N., Sisodia, R.S., & Sharma, A. (Winter 2000). "The Antecedents and Consequences of Customer-Centric Marketing," *Anatomy of Marketing Science Journal* 28(1): 55–66.
3. Anderson, C. (2006). *The Long Tail* (New York: Hyperion Books).
4. Moriarty, R., & Kosnik, T. (Summer 1989). "High-Tech Marketing: Concepts, Continuity, and Change," *Sloan Management Review* 30: 7–17.
5. Rangan, K.V., & Bartus, K. (1995). "New Product Commercialization: Common Mistakes," In V.K. Rangan, B. Shapiro, & R. Moriarty (Eds.), *Business Marketing Strategy* (Chicago, IL: Irwin), pp. 63–75.
6. Mohr, J. (2001). *Marketing of High Technology Products and Innovations* (Upper Saddle River, NJ: Prentice Hall), pp. 7–12.
7. Moore, G. (1999). *Crossing the Chasm* (New York: Harperbusiness), pp. 1–11.
8. John, G., Weiss, A.M., & Dutta, S. (1999). "Marketing in Technology-Intensive Markets: Toward a Conceptual Framework," *Journal of Marketing* 63: 78–91.
9. Shanklin, W.L., & Ryans, J.K., Jr. (1984). *Marketing High Technology* (Lexington, MA: D.C. Heath).
10. John, et al., *op. cit.*, 79.
11. Glazer, R. (October 1991). "Marketing in an Information-Intensive Environment: Strategic Implications of Knowledge as an Asset," *Journal of Marketing* 55: 1–19.
12. Romer, P.M. (1990). "Endogenous Technological Change," *Journal of Political Economy* 98(5): 71–90.
13. Burgleman, R.A., & Sayles, L. (1986). *Inside Corporate Innovation* (New York: The Free Press).
14. The Diffusion Process. Ames: Agriculture Extension Service, Iowa State College, Special Report No. 18, 1957; Rogers, Evert. (1962). *Diffusion of Innovation* (New York: Free Press).
15. Moore, G. (1999). *Crossing the Chasm* (New York: HarperBusiness).
16. Weiss, A. (January 30, 2000). "What Are Technical Products?" http://www.marketingprofs.com/2/techproducts.asp, accessed January 20, 2008.
17. Ibid.
18. Rogers, E. (1983). *Diffusion of Innovations* (New York: The Free Press).

19. Hof, R. (June 22, 1998). "The Click Here Economy," *Business Week,* pp. 122–128, www.businessweek.com.
20. Wysocki, B. (April 13, 1998). "Even High-Tech Faces Problems with Pricing," *Wall Street Journal,* p. A1.
21. Gross, N., & Coy, P. With Otis Port, (March) "The Technology Paradox," *Business Week,* pp. 76–84, www.businessweek.com.
22. Mcdermott, D. (May 3, 1999)."Cost-Consciousness Beats Pricing Power," *Wall Street Journal,* p. A1.
23. This one-paragraph marketing plan was adapted from a business plan drafted by Amanda Wolverton, MBA 2001, University of Southern California. The name of the actual company has been changed.
24. Mohr, J. (January 18, 2001). "Does Marketing of High-Technology Products Require a Different Marketing Took Kit?" *Marketing Guides,* www.marketingprofs.com, accessed January 20, 2008.
25. Arrow, K.J. (1962). "Economic Welfare and Allocation of Resources for Invention," In R. Nelson (Ed.), *The Rate and Direction of Inventive Activity* (Princeton, NJ: Princeton University Press, 1962), pp. 609–624.
26. Mansfield, E. (December 1985). "How Rapidly Does New Industrial Technology Leak Out?" *Journal of Industrial Economics* 34(2): 217–224.
27. Aaker, D.A. (1991). *Managing Brand Equity* (New York: The Free Press), pp. 1–33.
28. Vinod, H.D., & Rao, P.M. (Fall 2000). "R&D and Promotion in Pharmaceuticals: A Conceptual Framework and Empirical Exploration," *Journal of Marketing Theory and Practice* 8(4): 10–20.
29. Ibid.
30. Eliashberg, J., & Robertson, T. (1988). "New Product Preannouncing Behavior: A Market Signaling Study," *Journal of Marketing Research* 25: 282–292.
31. Calantone, R., & Schatzel, K. (January 2000). "Strategic Foretelling: Communication-Based Antecedents of a Firm's Propensity to Preannounce," *Journal of Marketing* 64: 17–30.
32. Yoder, S.K. (February 16, 1995). "Computer Makers Defend Vaporware," *Wall Street Journal,* p. B1, B6.
33. Calore, M. (December 27, 2006). "Vaporware '06: Return of the King," *Wired,* www.wired.com, accessed September 17, 2008.
34. Hatlestad, L. (January 2000). "How to Land a High-Tech Brand," *Red Herring,* www.Redherring.com, accessed September 19, 2008.
35. Macinnis, D. (2006). "Just What Is a Brand, Anyway," *Marketing Guides,* www.marketingprofs.com, accessed April 29, 2007.

CHAPTER 10

THE BUSINESS MODEL

Scientists and engineers often are focused like a laser beam on the technology they are developing with hardly a thought to its business potential. However, today with federal funding agencies demanding to know how the research grants they provide will result in goods and services that benefit society, these technologists must attempt to address the important issue of how to make money from the technology they have developed, and, more specifically, how that technology and the company that launches it will create value for its shareholders, investors, customers, and value chain partners.

The process of creating, delivering, and capturing value is embodied in the term *business model,* which has been used in many contexts with some confusion about what it really means.[1] In a recent study of the definitions of *business model,* it was concluded that the fundamental activities associated with business models are the creation and capture of value. Entrepreneurs *create* value by differentiating their technology products from competitors with new or differentiated benefits, or by meeting an unserved need in the market. Entrepreneurs *capture* value by monetizing their offering, figuring out a way to deliver the product and make money from it. In short, business models are about how the entrepreneur converts a new technology to economic value and delivers that value to the customer.[2] Figure 10-1 depicts the relationship of the business model to the technology and the innovation or economic value that is created during the process of commercialization. The business model selected to take a new technology to market will ultimately determine the economic and strategic value that are created. Strategic value relates to the competitive landscape and the business model's ability to provide options for the entrepreneur to navigate it. Sometimes the business model is the actual innovation as in the case of e-Bay's reserve auction model or Apple's digital rights management system delivered through iTunes that made legal downloads easy for consumers and satisfied the music industry's need to protect its creative assets.[3]

FIGURE 10-1 The Function of the Business Model

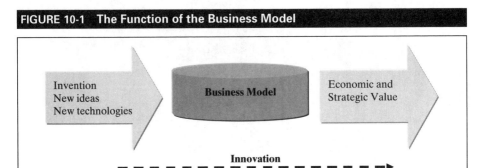

In general, innovation occurs in three major areas: the technology or product/service, the business model, and the process by which the technology is developed and brought to market. A great business model will typically display three vital characteristics: (1) it will create new value that is not currently being offered by competitors, (2) it will be difficult to replicate, and (3) it will be based on accurate assumptions about the customer. This chapter explores business models—how to develop an effective business model and how to avoid issues that cause business models to fail.

DEVELOPING A BUSINESS MODEL

Recall that entrepreneurs convert opportunities to business concepts that they can test in the market (see Chapter 3). A business concept conveys the compelling problem that the business is solving, the customer who is experiencing the problem, the benefit being delivered by the solution, and the means of delivering the benefit. The benefit is the value that the customer perceives and is willing to pay for. In short, the business concept is the entrepreneur's elevator pitch to describe the business. Some entrepreneurs develop technology products that customers don't need, so they won't pay for these products at any price as they don't perceive any value in them. Alternatively, entrepreneurs fail to understand precisely what customers value, so they often use business models that depend on low prices assuming that is what the customer is seeking; this ends up commoditizing their offering and significantly reducing their profit potential.[4]

It is important to understand that business models are not strategy. Rather, they are the implementation of strategy. For example, the business model creates value for the customer and also addresses how the entrepreneurial firm will capture that value through revenues. But the firm's strategy will focus on how to create a sustainable competitive advantage for the firm through intellectual property acquisition, branding, and perhaps an innovative business model. In the latter case, the business model is not the strategy, but one means of implementing the strategy. Developing an effective business model will take into account the value proposition, the company's infrastructure, and the value capture mechanisms. Figure 10-2 depicts the components of a business model.

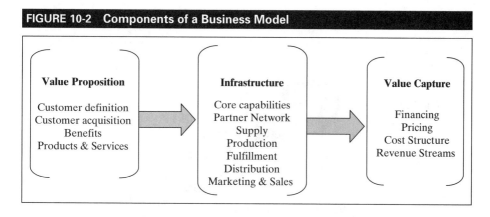

FIGURE 10-2   Components of a Business Model

Development of a business model begins with positioning the firm in the value chain to determine who the customer is. Recall that the value chain is comprised of those activities that add value along the path from raw materials to the customer and include inbound logistics (receiving, warehousing, inventory control), operations (inputs to outputs), outbound logistics (fulfillment, warehousing, transportation), marketing and sales, and after-sales service. Also recall that the customer is the one who pays for the benefit. So if the company is positioned as a retailer, the customer is the consumer. If the company is positioned as a manufacturer, the customer may be the wholesaler or distributor. From positioning the business, the process moves in an iterative manner until the entrepreneur is confident that at least for the present time, the model is sound. Feedback from the market will help to refine the model or even change it over time. In the next sections, we consider the specific steps in developing the business model.

STRATEGIC POSITIONING IN THE VALUE CHAIN

The value chain consists of (1) upstream activities that relate to production and include raw materials, product development, manufacturing, and warehousing; and (2) downstream activities, which are associated with marketing, selling, and distributing the product and includes customer acquisition, sales transactions, logistics, and wholesale/retail outlets. Where a company is located on that value chain is a function of (1) its capabilities, (2) whether its technology is licensed or forms the basis of a new venture, and (3) what kind of business the entrepreneur wants to operate. The goal should be to find a location that will enable the business to make a profit, sustain itself over the long term, and create strategic alliances that will add value to the company and help it achieve its goals.

Figure 10-3 presents an example of the value chain. Note that it consists of primary activities that add value at each step and are the activities responsible for bringing a new technology to market—inbound logistics, operations, outbound logistics, and so forth. These primary activities are then linked to support activities that provide the necessary reinforcement—infrastructure, human resources, and so forth. The result of effective management of the value chain is a profit margin

FIGURE 10-3   The Value Chain

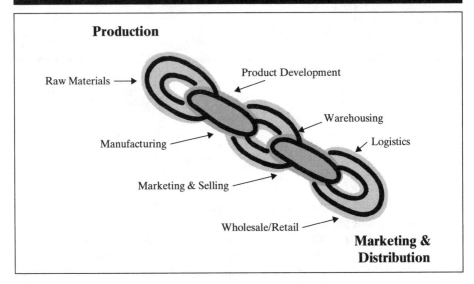

that is in line with the company's goals. For example, if marketing and sales does an effective job of understanding customer demand and delivers relatively accurate sales forecasts to procurement, the correct amount of raw materials or inventory will be ordered and production will be able to be scheduled in a manner that will deliver products to customers when they need them. The profit margin achieved is the difference between the price to the customer and the sum of all the costs incurred in the production and distribution of the product. Since typically not all functions of the value chain are performed by the entrepreneur's company, it is important for the entrepreneur to understand the value added by each value chain member and what each adds to the overall cost of the product.

One of the most disruptive forces affecting value chains today is the Internet, which has influenced business transactions and reshaped collaboration and professional relationships in general. One of the important contributions of the Internet is that is has reduced transactions costs—in some instances to zero. Today, for example, manufacturers who traditionally accrued high transactions costs associated with the purchase of raw materials—finding the best prices, negotiating the best terms, and so forth—have experienced more efficient and lower transaction costs through Internet search engines and linking electroncially to supply chain partners. The Internet has also disintermediated the value chain, eliminating nonessential intermediaries in many industries where they are not adding value to the chain.

An effective value chain has a number of important characteristics that should be identified and considered before developing a business model.

- **Warehousing of inventory.**   At various points in the value chain, materials and products are held or distributed to manufacturers, wholesale, or retailers. An entrepreneur will need to decide whether to hold inventory or outsource that capability to an experienced company.

- **Ownership.**   Entrepreneurs will need to determine if their products will be owned by others in the channel or merely held temporarily and transferred. Entrepreneurs need to understand who owns the product at each point so that someone can be identified if the product is damaged or lost.

- **Financing and payments.**   Effective value chains allow for credit to smooth out cash flow fluctuations and convenient and quick means for collecting payments.

- **Risk management.**   There is always risk associated with movement of goods through the value chain; therefore, entrepreneurs must understand the points of risk and identify third party insurance carriers to mitigate those risks.

- **Member power.**   Often a value chain will produce certain members who have power over others in the system because they might, for example, be the sole supplier of certain raw materials and everyone must use them. They may control the financial resources associated with the value chain or possess information that others don't have. Strong retailers, such as Wal-Mart, can force manufacturers to adopt their supply chain systems.

In addition to value chain characteristics that will affect the entrepreneur's ability to capture value with a business model, entrepreneurs must also decide if market coverage is critical to their strategy and that issue is associated with distribution channels. Distribution speaks to the methods and processes used to take a product from the manufacturer to the consumer or customer (in the case of a business). If the technology must get to market quickly and over many customer segments, it may be necessary to use distribution intermediaries who have the experience and the operational capability to move quickly. How much control the entrepreneur wants over what happens to the product will also determine the distribution strategy. If, for example, the technology requires significant education of the customer or unique marketing tactics, putting the product with a distributor carrying competing products may not be a wise choice. Selling direct to the customer may be preferable.

Also, it will be important to determine whether the distribution strategy chosen will force customers to change the way they acquire and use the product. Will that change be worth it to them? Do the customers being served regularly use the channel the entrepreneur is considering? The answers to these questions will help the entrepreneur refine the business model.

IDENTIFY SOURCES OF REVENUE

The next step is to identify all the potential sources of revenue. Scientists often recognize that they need to license a technology to reach all the potential markets for that technology. For example, suppose an inventor/licensor synthesizes a new molecule and is able to obtain a patent. The new molecule has the potential to become the basis for a drug, a pesticide, or perhaps a food additive.[5] If the inventor has wisely invited people from different industries to learn about the technology, the inventor will quickly see that the technology can be licensed in these three different industries to achieve three distinct revenue streams without the scientist ever having to leave the laboratory and form a company.

An excellent example of the importance of creating multiple revenue streams is the research that Scott Shane did in 1998 on three-dimensional printing technology at MIT.[6] MIT filed for a patent on the Three Dimensional Printing Process (3DP) on behalf of four MIT researchers. The 3DP process produces layers of bonded powder material to form a specified component. Not unlike most researchers, the four were motivated by the pursuit of knowledge and had no intention of starting a company. Consequently, the MIT Technology Licensing Office was charged with finding suitable licensees for the technology. Over the 9 years that this technology was available for licensing, eight teams of entrepreneurs investigated its properties and considered ventures to exploit the technology. They found applications in everything from rapid prototyping and three-dimensional forming of replacement bones to time-release drug delivery and personal sculptures. In all, eight distinct applications were identified that were not recognized by the original inventors. Some of the lessons to be gained from this example are:

- Opportunities usually arise out of industry experience, so it's important to expose a technology to a number of people in different industries.
- Understand and protect the value of the core technology so that it can be licensed for a variety of applications.
- Go beyond the original invention team to find new applications.
- License applications outside the company's core competency to gain critical mass so that the technology might become the standard or dominant technology in its field.

Table 10-1 summarizes four sources of opportunity for new revenue streams that entrepreneurs can consider and potentially apply in their business model.

TABLE 10-1 Sources of Opportunity for New Business Models	
Reposition on the value chain	Look for unserved or underserved niches and customer dissatisfaction.
Reinvent the value chain	Tear apart what currently exists and create a whole new value chain. Extrapolating from other industries is often the inspiration for a reinvented value chain in an industry.
Redefine value-added	If, for example, industry competitors pursue contracts for work from customers, a company may choose instead to study what customers typically want, do the work first, and then sell it to the customer in a turnkey package. The benefit to the customer is speed and convenience. This is what J.D. Powers & Associates did in the market research industry.
Redefine distribution	Think about where customers spend a lot of their time and put a product there. If customers typically are at the end of a long chain of intermediaries, consider selling direct.

IDENTIFY THE COST DRIVERS

In the earliest stages of the development of a new technology, it is extremely difficult to gauge the cost of producing the technology for market. Entrepreneurs must identify those components or processes that will be costly to the development of the final product: supply, production, fulfillment, and distribution, to name a few. When one considers that reducing costs is the fastest way to bring dollars to the bottom-line, it's important to find the lowest cost methods for producing the technology. Some of the things to think about when analyzing cost drivers include how critical success factors (i.e., sales team, marketing strategy, occupancy, and so on) affect revenues, costs, and cash flow. What happens if any of these items change? It is also important to identify the team's core competencies, which are activities that can be accomplished effectively in-house, and those capabilities the team lacks, which can be outsourced. Often outsourcing capabilities such as manufacturing produce a significant saving from not having to invest in capital equipment and labor.

CAPTURE VALUE WITH PRICING, COST, AND FINANCING

The relationship between price and cost is clear—if costs can be keep low, the price to the customer can be lower as well. Lower prices are generally a value to most customers. However, most new technologies frequently enter the market with a premium pricing strategy because the product is new to the market, so the entrepreneur benefits from early adopters' willingness to pay a premium price that enables the recapture of some of the R&D costs before prices inevitably come down. Financing relates to how customers can purchase the product, whether that be with purchase orders, credit cards, or alternative methods such as PayPal. Understanding how the customer wants to pay for the product and giving them that method is critical to capturing value. The subject of pricing is treated in more detail in Chapter 9.

TEST FOR WEAKNESSES IN THE BUSINESS MODEL

The business model is always a work in progress, so it's important to constantly receive feedback from customers and other stakeholders on the validity of the entrepreneur's demand forecasts, pricing, financing options, and value proposition. Typically entrepreneurs will launch their technology products in limited markets to test the business model before spending large amounts of marketing dollars only to discover that the customer is not responding as predicted. An ill-conceived business model can keep a promising technology from succeeding. For instance, not all technologies are appropriate for a business model that involves charging the customer for the technology. Many Web 2.0 (consumer Internet) or new media technologies such as social networking are good examples. The business model that has succeeded in this scenario is giving the technology away free of charge and producing revenue from advertisers who want access to targeted groups of consumers.

A business model is only as successful as its execution, so conducting sensitivity analysis on the model can reveal weak points and identify the critical success factors and their potential impact on the business.[7]

LAUNCH AND MEASURE THE BUSINESS MODEL

With an understanding that there is a high probability that the business model will need to be modified, entrepreneurs can launch their models and track feedback from customers and other value chain members in an effort to determine the most effective model to achieve the best result from the customer. To do that requires the development of metrics to measure success, such as monthly sales, profit per unit, and number of subscribers, to name a few.

In developing metrics, it is important to understand that business models are never static; in fact, they are quite organic, changing as customer needs change, as new competitors enter or leave the market, and as technologies move down the value curve toward commodity status. Some specific examples of how business models change include:[8]

- Expanding the business model geographically, entering new markets, or changing product service offerings. An example might be the entrepreneur who takes his or her technology product into a new region of the global marketplace.

- Selling new products and services to existing customers to keep them from jumping to competitors' products. An example is Apple building on the success of the iPod to offer the iPhone to its customer base.

- Taking the current business model into new product/service areas, which is what Amazon did when it took its successful online bookseller business model and fulfillment process into products that range from clothing to household goods.

- Expanding the current business model through acquisition or strategic alliances. For example, Google's alliance with Skype made it possible for Google to offer its online customers voice over Internet protocol (VoIP) service and Skype tapped into Google's enormous user base.

- Leveraging existing core capabilities to develop new business models. For example, Bombardier, the Canadian snowmobile company, had a business model that included credit financing, so over time it developed an expertise in financial services, which enabled the company to move into capital leasing as a derivative business.

It is important to remember that an effective business model will accomplish two important objectives: (1) inspire complementary products and services, and (2) increase network effects among customers who refer the company and its products to others.

UNDERSTANDING WHY BUSINESS MODELS FAIL

Four major issues tend to doom even the most well-conceived business models, so entrepreneurs must be particularly careful to subject their proposed business model to attack and modification *before* it's implemented in the marketplace.[9]

PREDICTIONS ABOUT THE FUTURE ARE BASED ON FAULTY LOGIC

Entrepreneurs, in their rush to get their technology to market, often make assumptions about future market conditions that have no basis in fact. For example, they may assume that customer demand that their research demonstrated during product development will still exist when the product is ready for market four years later. For example, Napster, the company that pioneered music downloads, incorrectly formulated its business model under the assumption that it would never be held accountable for the copyright violations of its users because the recording industry at the time seemed to be blind to the threat of digitization. However, that assumption proved to be faulty when much later in 2001, the recording industry succeeded in shutting down Napster by court order for copyright violations. Napster incorrectly assumed that the recording industry would not evolve in its thinking.

THE BUSINESS MODEL DOES NOT CREATE AND CAPTURE VALUE

It is common for entrepreneurs to identify a way to create value for customers by solving a problem their customers have. But many times, they struggle to find a way to monetize that value. In other words, customers don't want to pay for the value offered or don't want to pay what the entrepreneur must achieve to recapture the costs of development and make a profit. One university scientist had developed a technology that could track eye movements of consumers as they watched commercials and television programming. The value proposition was that advertisers (the customer) could better position products inside these programs for maximum impact. However, advertisers indicated that they were reluctant to pay for something that would only give them feedback *after* the fact, that is, after the money was spent to develop the commercial. The value they were looking for involved something more predictive before any money was spent. However, this solution was a chicken-and-egg problem for the entrepreneur because to be able to predict the outcome of a commercial, the entrepreneur would need a database of thousands of commercials where the impact of product placement was known and measured. This example demonstrates how some businesses do not create value for the customer. Other businesses cannot capture value in the form of revenues because the numbers don't make sense. Streamline, the defunct online Boston grocer, did not understand the grocery industry and its super thin margins. To successfully operate, Streamline had to spend huge amounts in marketing dollars, service, delivery, and the technology that was the backbone of the business and those costs made it impossible to make a profit.[10]

THE ENTREPRENEUR HAS NOT IDENTIFIED THE CUSTOMER

This is a common problem where intermediaries are the entrepreneur's actual customer. An example is the health care industry where an entrepreneur with a medical device that can significantly improve the lives of patients with a particular chronic problem does not recognize that revenue is not collected from the patient who has the pain and understands the value but from the health care provider whose mission is to reduce costs — a significantly different value proposition.

The bottom-line is that business models fail when entrepreneurs don't sense, respond, and adapt to changing customer needs and market conditions. For many years after its founding, Internet portal Yahoo! struggled to generate a profit despite the fact that it was one of the top sites with respect to unique visitors per month. It wasn't until 2001 when Terry Semel joined the team as CEO that Yahoo! figured out how to create revenue streams from digital music, job listing, online gaming, and premium e-mail accounts.[11] This is a good example of how new business models emerge out of situations where entrepreneurs have to find ways to do more with what they have.

Entrepreneurs should understand that no business model will be effective if the customer does not perceive value in what the entrepreneur is offering. Business models only make sense when the value proposition involves a cure for a real pain in the market.

Summary

The term *business model* has been used in many contexts and there is some confusion about what it really means. In a recent study of the definitions of business model, it was concluded that the fundamental activities associated with business models are the creation and capture of value. Entrepreneurs create value by differentiating their technology products from competitors or by meeting an unserved need in the market. Entrepreneurs capture value by monetizing their offering. The process of building the business model begins with positioning in the value chain. From there the process moves in an iterative manner until the entrepreneur is confident that at least for the present time, the model is sound. Feedback from the market will help to refine the model or even change it over time.

Discussion Questions

1. Why is it important to identify the entrepeneurial firm's position in the value chain?
2. What is the purpose of the business model?
3. Why do many business models fail?
4. Why do business models change and what are the implications of this for entrepreneurs and their business strategies?

Pandora—There Must Be a Business Model that Works

Imagine being an entrepreneur with a company that launched in 1999 and has been on the brink of disaster every year since then. It takes a lot of faith and persistence to keep going when everyone is betting against you, and Tim Westergren is a fountain of faith and persistence. His company, Pandora, an online radio company, was inspired by his interest in music. As a student at Stanford in the late 1980s, he was fortunate to study under the great jazz musician Stan Getz and came away with the firm belief that he wanted to find a way to make money from music.

Westergren began in a fairly traditional way by composing scores for independent films. The challenge he always faced was that directors struggled to find the right words to describe the kind of music they were looking for in the movie. That made it difficult for composers to come up with the exact mix of melody, rhythm, and tone to match the situation. He had also become aware of the plight of many independent artists who couldn't get distribution from the major record labels so they didn't have an easy way to be heard by the masses.

Like everyone else during the dot-com era, by the time 1999 came around, Westergren was ready to start a company. With two friends, Jon Kraft and Will Glaser, he launched Savage Beast Technologies to support and promote his Music Genome Project in which he had identified 600 qualities of a piece of music. Glaser, the software engineer, designed an algorithm that included 400 "genes" for each musical genre—pop, classical, hip-hop, jazz, and so forth. Then each piece of music in his database was analyzed against this algorithm to produce the song's unique DNA.

Having a great technology that can do interesting things is one thing—making money from it is quite another. Westergren's first business model for the Music Genome Project was tested in 2000 when he raised $1.5 million to launch a site that recommended music to users based on their interests. Timing is everything for entrepreneurs and, unfortunately, two weeks following the launch, the stock market crashed and he began a cycle of one business model after the other over several years. Westergren attempted to license the genome as a "recommendation engine," but only succeeded in doing a deal with Barnes & Noble.com, which eventually fell apart. The next business model involved installing the software into kiosks that would reside at music retailers and near the end of 2002, he had deals with AOL Music, and Best Buy to beta test the kiosks. At that time, the company was in bad financial shape and Kraft had left to join another company; so in 2004, Westergren went out again to seek capital—this time $8 million from Walden Venture Capital. It was the first time, he had been able to pay his employees in a long time. However, in 2005 when deals with Borders and Best Buy collapsed, Westergren once again was faced with reinventing the company.

With no more business-to-business models on the horizon, Westergren turned to the consumer market and decided to try the online radio concept with a new company he called Pandora. He would offer personalized radio stations to users for an annual subscription fee of $36. Because actual musicians did the expert selection of music in the background, the model had little chance to scale to a size that would attract more venture capital. Not only that, but e soon found that his customers had figured out how

(continued)

(continued)

to never have to pay for the music. Pandora provided customers with 10 hours of free music before they had to subscribe. Savvy customers quickly learned that by changing their email address, they could continue to receive free music on a trial basis. Frustrated, Westergren gave up on subcriptions and went to an advertising model. That worked for about a year when the Copyright Royalty Board decided to change the way Internet radio stations are charged by charging them a per listener, per song rate plus $500 a year per individual station. That meant that Pandora's costs would triple and the business model would ultimately collapse.

In 2007, while Westergren waited to hear whether the Copyright Royalty Board would concede a bit on the new rates due to pressure from online radio stations, he undertook his biggest launch to date with yet another business model—mobile products that enable listeners to access their personal radio stations from their phones. Will this be the business model that gives Pandora sustainability?

Sources: Clifford, S. (October 2007). "Pandora's Long Strange Trip," *Inc Magazine;* Weisman, R. (May 9, 2005). "Start-up Composes a Music Genome," *The Boston Globe,* www.boston.com; (February 25, 2003). "America Online Chooses Savage Beast Technologies to Provide Integrated Music Recommendation Across AOL Music's Leading Offerings," *Business Wire.com,* accessed September 19, 2008.

Endnotes

1. Shafer, S.M., Smith, H.J., & Linder, J.C. (2005). "The Power of Business Models," *Business Horizons* 48: 199–207.
2. Chesbrough, H., & Rosenbloom, R.S. (2002). "The Role of the Business Model in Capturing Value from Innovation: Evidence from Xerox Corporation's Technology Spin-off Companies," *Industrial and Corporate Change* 11(3): 529–555.
3. Skarzynski, P., & Gibson, R. (March 18, 2008). "Innovating Across the Business Model," Chapter 5 in *Innovation to the Core: A Blueprint for Transforming the Way Your Company Innovates* (Boston, MA: Harvard Business School Press).
4. Tucker, R.B. (May–June 2001). "Strategy Innovation Takes Imagination," *The Journal of Business Strategy* 22(3): 23–27.
5. Boer, F.P. (1999). *The Valuation of Technology* (New York: John Wiley & Sons), p. 266.
6. Shane, S. (1999). "Three Dimensional Printing," A Case Study Prepared at the Darden Graduate School of Management, University of Virginia.
7. Hamermesh, R.G., Marshall, P.W., & Pirmohamed, T. (January 22, 2002). "Note on Business Model Analysis for the Entrepreneur," Product Number: 9–802–048, *Harvard Business School,* 9.
8. Linder, J., & Cantrell, S. (2001). "What Makes a Good Business Model Anyway? Can Yours Stand the Test of Change?" *Outlook: Point of View,* Accenture. www. accenture.com.
9. Shafer, S.M., Smith, H.J., & Linder, J.C. (2005). "The Power of Business Models," *Business Horizons* 48: 199–207.
10. Magretta, J. (May 2002). "Why Business Models Matter," *Harvard Business Review* (Boston, MA: Harvard Business School Publishing), p. 5.
11. Elgin, B., & Grover, R. (June 2, 2003). "Yahoo! Act Two," *Business Week* 3835: 70–76.

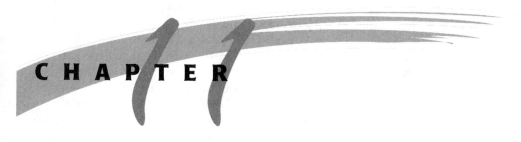

CHAPTER 11

FUNDING THE TECHNOLOGY START-UP

One of the biggest challenges to starting a new technology venture is building a resource base that will enable the company to survive and grow over the long term.[1] Technology start-ups are dynamic organizations characterized more often than not by inexperienced management, immature systems and controls, and inconsistent quality. These perils and many others constitute what researchers have called the "liability of newness," and it is compounded by the fact that new technology ventures often require far more resources early in the commercialization process and face more complex problems than nontechnology ventures.[2]

Resources are broadly defined as physical assets, intellectual property, human capital, or financial capital, and research suggests that a unique bundle of resources can produce a significant competitive advantage for a new venture.[3] Entrepreneurs may seek resource partners from any part of the value chain—suppliers, distributors, customers, and investors. Suppliers provide entrepreneurs with credit lines that help to ensure the start-up venture's cash flow, and they may also partner with the new venture in the design and development of a new product. Distributors help entrepreneurs avoid the added expense of warehousing and distribution. Customers may want a new product enough to pay a deposit to cover the costs to produce it, and investors supply vital funding to help the company grow. Finally, entrepreneurs can outsource capabilities they don't have in-house to other companies rather than incur the cost of developing those capabilities.

Resource partners are very aware of the risks involved in high-tech start-ups. For this reason, a partner will often not want to be the first to make a commitment to the new venture; consequently, the challenge for the entrepreneur becomes one of optimal sequencing; that is, which potential partner should the entrepreneur approach first to ensure that he or she can get the second partner, and so on. This situation often requires that the entrepreneur achieve at least a conditional commitment from the first partner in order to leverage that relationship to entice the second partner to come on board. Unfortunately, resource partners are frequently chosen based on their willingness to be the first to invest in the company; however, this approach does not maximize the value of the new venture. Any resource decision involves trade-offs of efficiency, urgency, and bargaining power. Entrepreneurs will not always make the best decision and choose the partner that provides the greatest value. Instead, they will often accept a less efficient partner in exchange for retaining more of the equity in their company.[4]

The retain-as-much-equity-as-possible approach works if the company has the luxury of growing slowly; but in today's volatile marketplace, this is a luxury that most high-tech ventures do not enjoy. Ideally, an entrepreneur moves sequentially from one partner to the next, and partners make commitments conditional on the other partners' acceptance. If no partner is willing to be the first to commit, the entrepreneur may end up shuttling back and forth between partners in an attempt to achieve an agreement until eventually the window of opportunity disappears.

One of the primary reasons that high-tech entrepreneurs have difficulty getting that first commitment is that they often are unable to adequately express the value proposition to interested parties. Because their companies are new and have little clout, they may even find it difficult to gain the attention of resource providers.[5] Furthermore, without external validation through partnerships or boards of directors, they often cannot convince potential funding sources of the value of their technology.

This chapter looks at the financing of a start-up technology venture and the various sources of funding available at the seed and early start-up stages. Chapter 12 will consider funding for growth.

RISKS AND STAGES OF FUNDING

For purposes of discussion, seed capital is that funding that usually enables the entrepreneur to build a prototype and prove the technology and the business concept. Start-up capital, by contrast, is used to launch a new company, and growth capital is typically capital that is obtained from angel investment networks and venture capital firms. Angel investors are discussed later in the chapter, and venture capital is the subject of Chapter 12. Nothing affects the ability of a high-tech venture to obtain seed and start-up capital more than information asymmetry. When entrepreneurs possess more information about their ventures than potential investors do, conflicts arise that can affect the willingness of investors and lenders to deal with the new venture unless they are able to closely monitor the business and advise the entrepreneur.[6] At no time in the life of a business is information asymmetry greater than at the seed stage of a high-tech venture. At this early stage, the technology has yet to be proven; therefore, it is difficult to assess the market for the technology. In fact, for a radical innovation, the market may not yet exist, but must be created. The risk of the unknown at this stage is intolerable for most investors, which explains why so much stage product development is funded by government grants. The staged development of many high-tech companies presents additional risks for investors because lack of sufficient financing at any stage of the new venture could cause it to fail. Biotech ventures are especially subject to this risk because they typically have far longer development periods that may last as long as 10 to 15 years. The unique challenges of biotech ventures are discussed later in the chapter.

Every technology venture faces several risk points. The type of risk determines the type of investor the company can realistically expect to attract and the amount of equity it will have to give up for that investment. Figure 11-1 depicts the various categories of risks facing an entrepreneurial venture from pre-start-up to initial public offering (IPO). It also includes the types of equity investors that may be interested in the venture at each point.

The seed capital stage occurs during pre-start-up and generally involves funding for product development and preparation for the business launch. In this stage, the risks are related to the technical feasibility of the technology and the risk that an effective and efficient means of manufacturing will not be found. The focus of the entrepreneur is on product development and testing in addition to feasibility analysis of the business concept to insure that the technology is meeting

FIGURE 11-1   Risk Points and Associated Funding Types

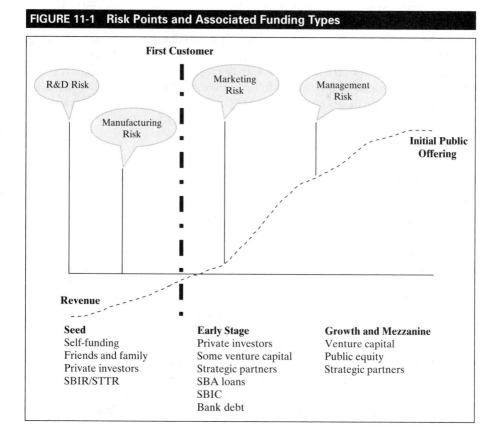

Seed	Early Stage	Growth and Mezzanine
Self-funding	Private investors	Venture capital
Friends and family	Some venture capital	Public equity
Private investors	Strategic partners	Strategic partners
SBIR/STTR	SBA loans	
	SBIC	
	Bank debt	

a real customer need and that there is sufficient demand to eventually sustain the business. In general, this is the riskiest stage for investors because the technology and business concept have not been proven in the market, so investment capital will be difficult to secure. Most entrepreneurs rely on grant money to fund product development or friendly money from people who believe in what the entrepreneur is attempting to do.

Early stage or start-up funding is needed when the company plans to secure its first customer and is officially in business. When this milestone occurs, the focus of the entrepreneur shifts to the market and the risks associated with entering the market and capturing enough customers to create critical mass for product acceptance. If the first customer is secured, the entrepreneur will have reduced significant risk for investors, so angel investor groups (bands of private investors) will become a funding source as will a limited number of venture capital firms that focus on early stage start-ups.

During the growth and mezzanine funding stage, the entrepreneur's focus shifts again, this time to management issues. The need to professionally manage the growth of the company and incorporate systems and controls to handle growth becomes critical. It is often necessary to bring in a professional management team with experience in growing a technology company to take a leadership role. This is the stage that most venture capital firms prefer for investment because all the issues of the market have generally been resolved and now funding can go toward growth. Often when a company is preparing for an IPO, it will require mezzanine financing to fund that very expensive process. Mezzanine financing is a combination of debt and equity; the investor provides a loan with the rights to convert to an equity stake if the loan is not repaid on time and in full. It should be noted that not all technology companies culminate their journey with an IPO. In fact, only a very small number do for a variety of reasons that will be discussed in Chapter 12.

THE COST OF RAISING CAPITAL

The cost of raising capital at start-up or for growth is high, both in terms of human and financial capital. Because the process is stressful and pulls the entrepreneur and company management away from the daily activities of the business at a time when they are most needed, many entrepreneurs decide to start and grow slowly, taking advantage of internal cash flows. However, it is rare that a high-tech company can survive and grow without accessing some outside capital in the form of debt or equity along the way. With that in mind, it is important to understand what is involved in raising capital so that expectations are not set unreasonably high.

Entrepreneurs need to set aside enough time to raise capital and not wait until their company actually needs it to begin the process. It is realistic to expect to spend several months locating the proper financing, to wait a few more months for due diligence to be completed, and then to wait up to six more months to actually receive the money. Moreover, in many cases, the first financing source tapped will not end up closing the deal, even after months of courting and negotiations, so it is vital to have backups in place so that the process will not have to start again from scratch.

If the entrepreneur is seeking a second round of funding, new investors often will want to buy out the first-round investors, who are typically friends and family, because they do not want to deal with them and believe that they do not contribute anything significant to the company. This can be a very awkward time for entrepreneurs, who are caught between a rock and a hard place, wanting to keep their first-round funders but knowing that the investor can easily walk to another deal if they do not acquiesce.

Some costs associated with raising money must be paid up front by the entrepreneur. These costs include those involved in the preparation of financial statements, the business plan, and a prospectus or offering document, as well as fees for legal advice and the expenses of marketing the offering to potential investors. In addition to these upfront costs are the back-end costs of selling securities, which include investment banking fees, legal fees, marketing costs, brokerage fees, and various other fees charged by state and federal authorities. The total cost of raising equity capital can be as high as 25 percent of the total amount raised. Add to that the interest or return on investment paid to the funding source, and it is easy to see why it costs money to raise money.

BOOTSTRAPPING THE START-UP

Most entrepreneurs attempt to bootstrap the start-up of their ventures. Bootstrapping refers to the various ways in which entrepreneurs can use as few resources as possible in the earliest stages of their businesses. When they do need to acquire particular assets, they often use other people's resources through purchasing, borrowing, partnering, or leasing.[7] This approach works well for many types of businesses; but, in general, technology businesses do require a fair amount of resources, even before launch, for patents, product development, prototyping, and testing. In general, the personal resources of the entrepreneur will need to be tapped first before attempting to access third party capital. Those resources are discussed further in the next section.

The rules for bootstrapping are simple.

- Get into business in some manner quickly to get traction and conduct a minimal proof of concept. This could involve putting up a Web site to gauge interest, or putting initial versions of the technology in the hands of early adopters to insure that the technology is meeting a real need. Obviously, with technologies that require a long period of product development, this will not be a viable option.

- Hire as few employees as possible because employees are the single greatest expense of the business. Using independent contractors or partnering with other companies will be less expensive and generally less stressful on the entrepreneur. Using student interns has been a very effective to get help and also test a potential employee.

- Lease or share as much as possible. Eventually, even the smartest bootstrapper will need to acquire equipment, facilities, and furnishings; but, by judiciously seeking creative ways to acquire these resources, expenses can be kept at a minimum.

- Use other people's resources. Suppliers will often give favorable terms if they understand the benefit to them of dealing with the entrepreneur. Some companies have been successful at getting customers to pay half up-front. This was the strategy of Nordic Trak, the fitness company that had customers pay the full amount when they ordered the company's first product. This is especially helpful when the cost of producing the technology is relatively high.

The bottom line is entrepreneurs need to conserve resources and put them where they will generate revenues for the company.

GOVERNMENT FUNDING SOURCES

For start-up technology ventures, particularly those in the product development stage, the government and its agencies have long been a lucrative source of funding. Here we review some of the major sources of government funding available to new technology ventures to help them develop and commercialize their technologies.

SMALL BUSINESS INNOVATION RESEARCH GRANTS

Small Business Innovation Research (SBIR) grants are competitive awards administered by the Small Business Administration (SBA). They are designed to encourage the transfer and commercialization of technologies of U.S. companies with fewer than 500 employees and at least 51 percent owned by a U.S. citizen. The government contracts with businesses to find technology solutions for problems it has identified and it is then able to license that technology free for four years. For example, Savi Technology Company was awarded a Department of Defense contract to develop a system for tracking equipment and supplies being shipped to U.S. forces during the Persian Gulf War. At the end of the war, Savi was acquired by Texas Instruments, which is now free to market the technology to companies such as FedEx and Airborne Express.[8]

All federal agencies with R&D budgets that exceed $100 million must allocate a portion of their budgets to technology-based small businesses. Eleven federal agencies participate in the SBIR program: Agriculture, Commerce, Defense, Education, Energy, Health and Human Services, Transportation, EPA, NASA, NSF, and the Nuclear Regulatory Commission.

The award process consists of three phases:

Phase I: This phase provides funds up to $100,000 to evaluate the technical merit and commercial feasibility of the technology.

Phase II: This phase is by invitation only after a successful Phase I award and continues the evaluation of commercial feasibility. It provides funds up to about $750,000 for no more than two years.

Phase III: This phase is the commercialization phase and does not include SBIR funds. At this point, the company is required to seek other sources of funding, such as private investors and venture capital.

A study of 1,435 firms participating in SBIR programs over a 10-year period found that SBIR awardees enjoyed greater employment and sales growth than nonawardees.[9] They also grew significantly over the period and were more likely to attract venture capital. This result was particularly evident in regions with venture capital activity and in high-tech industries. Some well-known companies began their careers with funding from federal programs, including Apple Computer, Chiron, Compaq, Federal Express, and Intel, to name a few.

SMALL BUSINESS TECHNOLOGY TRANSFER RESEARCH PROGRAM

The SBA also administers the Small Business Technology Transfer Research (STTR) program, which is designed to promote joint research between nonprofit research institutes and small high-tech companies in the United States with fewer than 500 employees. The small company must submit the request and perform at least 40 percent of the work. The research institute must contribute at least 30 percent of the work. Like the SBIR program, the STTR has three phases.

SMALL BUSINESS INVESTMENT COMPANY PROGRAM

The SBA also backs the Small Business Investment Company (SBIC) program, which provides venture capital to small businesses. SBICs are private venture capital firms licensed by the SBA. Funds are raised through the sale of securities and debentures to a variety of sophisticated investors such as venture capitalists, corporate pension funds, banks, and individuals. The SBIC functions as a financier to small businesses and can provide long-term loans with a minimum of 5 years independently or in conjunction with a public or private lender. It can also provide equity capital by purchasing the small business's securities. It may not, however, become a general partner in a small business or be liable in any way for the obligations of the business. To qualify, companies must have a net worth under $18 million and average after-tax earnings of less than $6 million during the two years preceding the application. Furthermore, at least 51 percent of the company's assets and employees must be located in the United States.

THE SMALL BUSINESS ADMINISTRATION

The SBA loan guarantee program encourages banks to lend to businesses at favorable rates even in times when money is tight. It also provides for longer terms, which helps a young business with its cash flow. The SBA partners with commercial banks and guarantees 75 percent of the business loan should the entrepreneur default. Having an SBA guarantee makes it easier for the entrepreneur to secure a loan, but entrepreneurs should be aware that the documentation and paperwork are extensive and interest rates are no more favorable than conventional loan rates.

The SBA also offers a micro loan program for amounts up to $35,000, with the average loan being about $13,000. Rather than using commercial banks, the SBA partners with nonprofit community development coporations. Entrepreneurs who request this type of loan are required to participate in business training and technical assistance.

SEED CAPITAL

The most risky stage of financing is the seed capital stage, that is, when the company is still in product development. The reason for this high risk relates to the risk/reward curve. Most investors want to minimize their risk and maximize their reward for investing in a technology venture. The highest risk is certainly during the development of the technology, whereas the lowest risk is when the company is established and customers are purchasing the technology.

Because of the high risk involved, funding at this stage usually comes from friends, family, and those who believe in the business opportunity. For a new venture to make it past this stage and be in a position to access a wider variety of financing sources, it needs to quickly achieve an operating mode and launch products and services that will provide rapid cash flow and an early break-even point. At the seed stage, overhead must be kept to a minimum, and the entrepreneur should not bring expensive management talent on board. If the company will eventually need outside capital from angel investors or venture capitalists, it is best to reduce as much of the perceived risk as early as possible by proving the technology and the market. These actions will put the venture in a stronger bargaining position with investors.

FRIENDLY MONEY

Because first-time entrepreneurs often have little experience, no collateral, and few resources, they tend to resort to friends and family who believe in them to secure start-up capital. Although it may be easier to obtain this type of funding, in the long run it may be the most expensive money ever obtained; as some have said, "you pay for it the rest of your life." To help ensure a successful experience for the company and its friendly investors, the following guidelines should be considered

- If a friendly investor says no to the offer, do not persist, particularly if the relationship is important.
- Provide full disclosure. An entrepreneur must be completely honest with friends and family and not oversell the business concept because if the company cannot perform to their expectations, it may damage those relationships. All risks should be disclosed so that friendly investors can make informed decisions.
- Do not take more money than a friendly investor can afford to lose. In other words, if the business should fail, the investor will suffer a loss but will still be financially whole.

- Put all financial agreements in writing. Even though these investors may be friends and family, this transaction is a business deal and should be structured as such to protect all the parties involved.

- Know the investors and how they will act. Understand whether a particular investor will be a silent investor or an active investor who is on the phone daily to learn the status of their investment.

It is also important to remember that friendly money means just that—people the entrepreneur knows well. If the entrepreneur seeks money from strangers, a formal private placement memorandum and prospectus will be required. This document spells out all the risks to the investor and assures that the investor meets the state's "blue sky" laws to be a qualified investor. Private offerings are discussed in Chapter 12.

DEBT FINANCING

Commercial banks have strict lending policies that prevent them from taking risks; consequently, start-up companies are usually not good candidates for this type of financing. Even if an entrepreneur cannot secure a bank loan, it's still wise to begin to create a banking relationship so that later on, when the company has a bit of a track record, it will be easier for the entrepreneur to get a positive response to a loan request. Commercial finance companies, also called "hard asset" lenders, will often go where banks will not, but entrepreneurs should be aware that the cost of these loans is significantly higher than commercial bank loans.

Many entrepreneurs have funded the start-up of their businesses with credit cards, especially in industries other than biotech. Credit card funding is expensive, but when there are no other choices, it may be better than not starting the business at all. Today, credit card companies such as Visa and American Express offer unsecured credit lines to small businesses, and the cap on these can often be increased once the entrepreneur has demonstrated the ability to pay down the credit line. Entrepreneurs should know that debt financing of any type is generally less expensive than equity because no ownership in the company is forfeited.

EQUITY ARRANGEMENTS

Exchanging equity for cash is a common arrangement for seed stage companies using friendly money, but entrepreneurs also trade equity for other things as well, such as professional services, management expertise, and so forth. When a new company is starving for cash, it is tempting to give equity instead of paying someone, but this is not often wise for a number of reasons. People who are hired to do a job can be let go, but it's much more difficult to rid the company of an unwanted shareholder. Therefore, it's important to have a probationary period to see if this person is compatible with the entrepreneur and the culture of the company. Furthermore, equity is most expensive in the earliest stages of the company when the risk is the highest. Later, when the entrepreneur has created significant value in the company, he or she will not have to give up as much equity for the same ownership stake in the company.

STRATEGIC PARTNERSHIPS AND OTHER INTERMEDIARIES

For entrepreneurs who do not want to or cannot take advantage of debt and equity sources of capital, taking on a strategic partner can provide an infusion of capital or in-kind expertise and capability. Although cash from strategic partners is generally in smaller amounts than cash from other sources, it can be the cement to a relationship that carries with it long-term benefits for the new company. If the new company's activities take the entrepreneur abroad, strategic partnerships are often the only choice when a banker is nervous about funding high-risk activities. An additional benefit of an overseas strategic partner is that they can serve as a liaison to international bankers and help collect bills from foreign customers.

When two companies form a relationship, there are reciprocal benefits and risks. For example, the failure of a small business might damage the larger partner's reputation. By contrast, the smaller company generally benefits from the association with the larger firm. If a prominent company associates with and transacts with a start-up company, it effectively puts its stamp of approval on the smaller company. If a small firm gains a partnership with a large, prominent firm, it can be assumed that the large firm believes that the smaller firm is reliable. Consequently, when a small technology start-up manages to gain a prominent partner in a larger firm, the small company gains a more prominent reputation and a higher perceived level of quality and reliability by association.[10]

One type of alliance that is of particular interest in the seed capital stage is an R&D partnership where a high-tech venture can share the risk of R&D with a more established company, government laboratory, or government agency. With government entities, these partnerships take the form of cooperative agreements where the federal government works with state or local governments or universities to support or stimulate research. They may also be in the form of a cooperative R&D agreement where a federal laboratory and a nonfederal party, such as a high-tech venture, agree to share personnel, services, facilities, or equipment to conduct joint research in a particular area or an agreement whereby the company pays for the right to use government facilities, such as laboratories.

START-UP FUNDING

Once a new venture has completed product development and confirmed the feasibility of its business concept, it is in a stronger position to tap into private investors and some venture capital firms to launch the venture. Investors generally consider four broad risk factors when evaluating a new venture opportunity. The first factor is the degree of uncertainty. New ventures are fraught with ambiguity and uncertainty because there are so many unknowns and the information that the entrepreneurs gather is generally imperfect. Consequently, it is difficult to predict the venture's future. This uncertainty compels investors to carefully consider such an investment, and, if they do decide to invest, they may invest in stages to mitigate some of the risk. The second factor is asymmetric information. In the earliest stages of a new venture, the entrepreneur knows far more about the venture and its potential than the investor. Therefore, it is possible that the entrepreneur might make a decision that adversely affects the investment, and the investor will not be able to immediately observe the effects. This situation puts the investor at risk because they have to make decisions without having critical information. The third characteristic of high-tech start-ups is that their asset base is principally intangible assets—intellectual property, know-how, and so forth. By contrast, firms that have the bulk of their assets in tangible equipment such as buildings, land, and inventory are easier to value and track; investors feel more comfortable investing in these types of firms. When intangible assets are predominant, investors incur a larger risk because these assets are difficult to value and protect. Finally, the markets for high technology also affect a company's ability to obtain outside capital. The supply of capital varies with market conditions and is often erratic.

ANGEL INVESTORS AND NETWORKS

The most common first-round funding after friendly money is angel capital. Angels are private investors, and they make up a significant portion of the informal risk-capital market. Although venture capitalists receive all the media attention, angel investors fund the vast majority of all start-ups. Their funding makes it possible for high-tech companies to move to the stage where they can attract venture capital funding and eventually become publicly traded companies. Angel investors typically fund ventures for $500,000 or less as individuals, although in the past few years when many professional venture capital firms have focused on large investments, angel investors have banded together to close the gap in the range up to a million dollars or more.

The primary reason that entrepreneurs often know very little about angel investors is that they are, for the most part, a low-profile group. With the exception of networks of angels such as the Tech Coast Angeles in Los Angeles, they are very private individuals who have typically been successful entrepreneurs in their own right or are professionals such as physicians and lawyers who want to participate in a start-up without being involved on a daily basis. Angels tend to invest in people first and technology second. Therefore, they must feel confident that the people in whom they are investing are trustworthy, have integrity and experience, and can successfully execute the business concept.

Angel investors are a heterogeneous group and they typically have other business activities besides their investments.[11] Like venture capitalists, they tend to have problems identifying sound potential investments and are subject to the same risks of information asymmetry and moral hazard that venture capitalists are. Moral hazard is the risk that one of the parties to the investment deal has not acted in good faith, for example, provided misleading financial information. One way that angels seek to mitigate these risks is by becoming more involved in the activities of the business in which they invest. However, although they want to be involved in the business, they do not generally take a controlling interest in the way that many venture capitalists do. Angels typically look for investments in industries with which they are familiar, and they place a lot of importance on knowing the management team. The candidate company needs to have substantial growth potential; and although the returns that angels require are not as enormous as those of venture capitalists, on average, they seek annual returns in excess of 20 percent.

Similar to venture capitalists, angels need a way to exit the business, either through a sale, a merger, or another round of financing; although unlike venture capitalists, angels tend to hold their investments longer and cash out through a buyout rather than an IPO. A recent study of 539 North American angel investors by the Kauffman Foundation found that since 2004, they had experienced 1,137 exits through acquisition or IPO and reported an average return of 2.6 times their initial investment in 3.5 years. This equates to an internal rate of return of 27 percent, generally in seed or start-up stage ventures.[12] Despite those results, or perhaps because of them, more angel investors are investing in fewer ventures, according to the University of New Hampshire's Center for Venture Research. In addition, the size of the deals is also declining; and in what appears to be a trend, most of the funding is going to post seed stage investments.[13]

Angels bring a mixed bag of emotions to any investment. Because they are usually older than the entrepreneurs in whom they invest and have been successful business people themselves, angels often want to mentor the entrepreneur. By investing in the young entrepreneur's business, the angel gets to relive the excitement of building a business without having to deal with the day-to-day struggles.

The characteristics of a business that an angel is *not* likely to invest in are listed in Table 11-1. If the entrepreneur's business possesses any of these characteristics, the business concept should be reconsidered to make it more attractive to a private investor should one be needed.

In general, the angel investment process has three stages. The first stage is the screening of new venture opportunities, most of which end up being rejected

TABLE 11-1 An Unlikely Angel Investment

Characteristics Not Favorable to Private Investment by an Angel

A "me-too" type of product	A poorly defined vision for the company
No intellectual property	No management team, a solo entrepreneur
Business location more than 100 miles away	Weak management team with no experience
Mature or fading industry	Exit time more than 7 years away
Return on investment less than 15 percent	Unfamiliar business or industry
Not enough market research with customer	Minority position with no voting rights
Weak competitive analysis	Too many coinvestors

because they do not fit with the angel investor's profile of desired companies. Once an opportunity is identified, however, the second stage begins and the investor will perform a thorough examination of the business plan, the business itself, and the entrepreneur. If the investor decides to proceed, the final stage entails negotiation between the parties to determine the terms and conditions of the investment. Many angel groups will also mentor investment candidates to prepare them for the investment and to achieve a higher valuation. The best way to find angel investors and angel networks is through professional advisors such as attorneys, accountants, consultants, professors, and bankers. Angel investors prefer to receive business plans through people they know, so cold calling a private investor is probably not the best tactic.

Of course angel investors will demand an equity stake in the company, but there are some ways to structure the deal more favorably for the entrepreneur. One approach that not only attracts investors but is beneficial to the entrepreneur as well is the clawback technique. With this technique, the deal begins with terms that give the equity investor a certain percentage of stock in exchange for a specific amount of capital. The terms then change depending on how the company performs relative to specified milestones. If performance is good or exceeds the milestones, the entrepreneur regains some of the equity given in the beginning. This approach works well in uncertain times.[14]

FUNDING BIOTECHNOLOGY

Biotechnology companies face unique issues when seeking start-up funding for a variety of reasons:

- It takes 7 to 9 years to bring a new drug to market at a cost of hundreds of millions of dollars; therefore, investing in biotech is definitely a long-term proposition. This means that the venture team is constantly in fund-raising mode, which can detract from its research efforts.

- The technology is typically in the earliest stages of development and has not been proven.

- Most biotechnology is licensed from universities and research institutes and not owned by the company.

- It is very difficult to calculate the value of biotech firms as it is measured by intangibles such as their patent portfolio and the credibility of their scientific team.

SEED STAGE

In general, scientists start biotech companies very early in the development stage of their scientific discovery. At this stage, government grants or major corporations in the industry have funded the basic research. Additional money is required to prove the technology and consider its commercial applications.

Therefore, biotech entrepreneurs seek seed capital from angels and venture capitalists based on the strength of the technology and initial market research. Giving up equity at the seed stage is costly, amounting to as much as 49 percent or more of the company, depending on how much risk to the investor has been reduced. With the exception of about 20 percent of the equity, which is retained in a pool to attract professional management, the founders control the remaining equity, at least until the second stage of funding. The team's goal is to create sufficient value in the company before the next round of funding to secure enough capital to take the company through the first phase of Food and Drug Administration (FDA) approval.[15]

FIRST-ROUND FUNDING: FDA PHASE I TESTING

Phase I FDA testing is designed to assess the safety of the drug, procedure, or other biotechnology and lasts about 18 months. The amount of money required to go through this phase depends on the quality of the seed phase results, but is generally substantially higher than that required in the seed stage, in the range of $15 to $20 million. Value is also added at this stage through the acquisition of intellectual property in the form of patents and know-how.

SECOND-ROUND FUNDING: THE BUSINESS MODEL

Once the company has established the scientific value of the technology, it is time to develop the business model. At this point, the entrepreneurs have access to a wider variety of financing alternatives. Two basic business models are prevalent in biotechnology: the Fully Integrated Pharmaceutical Company (FIPCO) and the licensing model.[16]

THE FIPCO MODEL

The FIPCO model is essentially a start-up venture that takes the technology from discovery to market without using any outside partners. This model is highly capital intensive and has fallen into disfavor in recent years given the speed with which most companies must develop their products and the existence of major pharmaceutical companies that make niche entry difficult. One company that has successfully implemented this model is Pennsylvania-based Centocor, a pioneer in immunology. The FIPCO model necessitates an IPO to secure enough funding to build manufacturing capabilities and develop marketing and distribution strength. Unfortunately, the amount of money raised in the IPO is rarely enough to sustain the company through FDA Phase III testing and market launch. A recent study found that the out-of-pocket cost of taking an approved drug from discovery to market was $540 million in 2001 and projected to be $970 million by 2013. The capitalized cost (expenses incurred in developing and financing the drug) was projected to be $1.9 billion by that time.[17] Recent pricings of IPOs indicate that the average value of an IPO ranged from $190 million to $309 million, so the news is not encouraging for entrepreneurs desiring to follow the FIPCO model.[18] IPOs are discussed more fully in Chapter 12.

Nevertheless, with a successful IPO, biotech entrepreneurs now have access to a range of financial options not previously available to them. They can do a secondary IPO to raise additional capital from the market, although this will dilute their outstanding shares. They can also consider convertible bonds, a debt instrument that has become a common method for raising capital in publicly traded biotech companies. The use of bonds is more feasible in the late stages of Phase III testing where FDA approval is imminent. Entrepreneurs should be aware that the recurring interest payments on the bonds could be a drain on the company's cash flow. This approach is far more advantageous to the investor than to the company because the investor can choose to convert the debt to equity at their option.

THE LICENSING MODEL

Under the licensing model, the scientists start a company that focuses on the development and testing of the technology, and then that company licenses the development of applications, clinical trials, or the applications themselves to large pharmaceutical or biotech companies that have existing manufacturing, marketing, and distribution channels. This model requires the least amount of capital to implement, but it has few financing options associated with it. In general, the new company enters into a licensing agreement with a large pharmaceutical company and receives a negotiated royalty on sales. Alternatively, the large pharmaceutical company may choose to purchase the small R&D start-up to diversify its portfolio. Yet another approach is for the small biotech firm to outsource the manufacturing and distribution of its technology to a large biotech firm in exchange for retaining a share of the revenues generated.

The launch stage of a new company presents many challenges for entrepreneurs seeking funding. Creative thinking and careful planning will be needed to insure the business has the resources it needs to be successful.

Summary

Finding and developing the resources needed to start a new technology venture is a challenging task because new technology ventures typically require far more resources and face more complex problems than traditional ventures. Furthermore, resource providers are aware of these risks and often find it difficult to commit valuable resources at the earliest stages of a new venture. Before the launch of a new venture, seed capital is required to finish product development, test the business concept, and prepare for product launch. This capital is typically in the form of friendly money and government grants. Once the business is operational, early stage funding is needed to launch the business. Friendly money and private investors, as well as strategic partners, come into play. In the later stages of the venture, the company has access to venture capital and public equity. Biotechnology firms represent a unique scenario in technology commercialization. Many biotech companies license their technology to large pharmaceutical firms as it is much more difficult and costly to start such a venture. In the pharmaceutical and software industries, corporate venturing is another source of equity financing for technology start-ups.

Discussion Questions

1. Suppose you want to launch a radical innovation. You have a working proto-type and have begun to test the early adopter market. It will take a lot of capital to "cross the chasm" to mainstream adoption. What would your finan-cial strategy be?
2. Compare the roles and goals of angel investors with those of venture capitalists.
3. What are the unique issues related to biotech start-ups that make them differ-ent from other high-tech ventures in the start-up stage?
4. What role does the government play in the commercialization of new technology?
5. How can strategic partners be used to speed up the process of innovation and commercialization?

CASE STUDY

Alibaba—From Apartment to Stock Exchange

Three events changed the path of Jack Ma's life. First, in 1977, as a young boy in the city of Hangzhou, about 100 miles southwest of Shanghai, China, Ma used to bicycle to the West Lake District where international tourists and business people stayed. There he would offer to serve as a guide so he could practice his English and learn what was going on in the world from an outsider's perspective. The second event proved to him that what he was learning about the world in China was very different from the way the world actually was. In 1979, he met an Australian family and continued to correspond with them when they returned to their country. Then in 1985, when he traveled to Australia, he discovered how underdeveloped his home country of China really was. From that point on, he knew he could never be isolated from the rest of the world.

Upon graduating from his city's "worst university," Ma began teaching English, but he knew that this was not what he really wanted to do. Fortunately, the third event came along and once again changed his path. In 1995, Ma received an opportunity to travel to Seattle, Washington, as part of a trade delegation. It was there that he learned about the Internet and discovered that he could find nothing about China on it. This was the inspiration for his first venture—China Pages. He borrowed $2,000 to start the company but soon realized that he really knew nothing about what he was doing. A partnership with China Telecom produced an investment of $185,000 in the fledgling company, but it also put the telecom company in the driver's seat. Ma eventually resigned out of frustration.

His real dream was to have his own e-commerce company. By 1999, he had gath-ered together 18 friends who put in a total of $60,000 to start Alibaba, an online B2B company that would focus on helping small and medium-sized companies make money. They did not skate easily through the dot-com bust in 2001. Like many other Internet companies, they raised significant funds from Goldman Sachs and Softbank Corpora-tion, but they also expanded too quickly and ended up in 2002 laying off people and

(continued)

(*continued*)

barely able to survive. Alibaba needed a way to create revenues and they did that by building a product that would connect Chinese exporters with U.S. buyers. It worked. Jack Ma had found the pain in the market and that realization became his mantra going forward: "don't complain about problems. Build solutions for them." So when people complained about Chinese businesses using pirated software, he immediately set out to create Alisoft, an inexpensive software for small businesses. Alibaba B2B became a very profitable company within the Alibaba Group and its income derives from membership services and renewals. Taobao is their very successful version of e-Bay and Alipay mimics Paypal.

In 2005, Yahoo became a strategic partner and invested $1 billion in Alibaba for a 39 percent equity stake. Alibaba now manages Yahoo's Chinese operations. In 2008, with Microsoft attempting to acquire Yahoo, Alibaba was planning to exercise a clause in its Yahoo agreement that might permit it to buy back Yahoo's stake in its company and thereby increase Chinese control of the company.

Sources: Fannin, R. (January 2008). "How I Did It: Jack Ma, Alibaba.com," *Inc. Magazine.* www.inc.com; Bmpc "Interview with Alibaba.com's Chairman, Jack Ma," www.alibaba.com, accessed September 19, 2008; Dean, J. (February 16, 2008). "Microsoft's Yahoo Bid Ruffles China's Alibaba," *Wall Street Journal,* p. A2; (May 7, 2006). "On the Record: Jack Ma," *SFGATE,* San Francisco Chronicle, F1, www.sfgate.com, accessed September 20, 2008.

Endnotes

1. Brush, C.G., Greene, P.G., Hart, M.M., & Haller, H.S. (February 2001). "From Initial Idea to Unique Advantage: The Entrepreneurial Challenge of Constructing a Resource Base," *The Academy of Management Executive* 15(1): 64–78.
2. Aldrich, H.E., & Fiol, C.M. (1993). "Fools Rush In? The Institutional Context of Industry Creation," *Academy of Management Review* 19: 645–670.
3. Collis, D., & Montgomery, C. (July–August 1995). "Competing on Resources: Strategy in the 1990s," *Harvard Business Review,* 118–128.
4. Hellmann, T. (2000). "Entrepreneurship and The Process of Obtaining Resource Commitments," Working Paper, Graduate School Of Business, Stanford University, Palo Alto, CA.
5. Ibid., p. 18.
6. Brierley, P. (2001). "The Financing of Technology-Based Small Firms: A Review of The Literature," *Bank of England Quarterly Bulletin* 41(1): 64–83.
7. Bhide, A. (1992). "Bootstrapping Finance: The Art of Start-Ups." *Harvard Business Review* 70(6): 109–117.
8. Weaver, P. (July–August 2001). "SBA: More Than Loans," *Business Advisor,* pp. 29–42. www.business.gov/.
9. Lerner, J. (July 1999). "The Government as Venture Capitalist: The Long-Run Impact of the SBIR Program," *The Journal of Business* 72(3): 285.
10. Stuart, T.E. (1998). "Network Positions and Propensities to Collaborate: An Investigation of Strategic Alliance Formation in a High Technology Industry," *Administrative Science Quarterly* 43: 668–698.

11. Benjamin, G., & Sandles, W. (1998). "Angel Investors: Cutting the Waters for Private Equity," *Journal of Private Equity* 1(3): 41–59.
12. Wiltbank, R., & Boeker, W. (November 2007). "Returns to Angel Investors in Groups," Ewing Marion Kauffman Foundation report.
13. Loten, A. (September 25, 2007). "As Angel Investor Ranks Swell, Focus Shifts to Later-Stage Companies," *Inc Magazine,* www.inc.com.
14. DeGeeter, M.J. (2004). *Technology Commercialization Manual: Strategy, Tactics, and Economics for Business Success* (Champaign, IL: Med-Launch, Inc.), p. 546.
15. Robbins-Roth, C. (March 2000). *From Alchemy to IPO* (Cambridge, MA: Perseus Publishing), p. 117.
16. Laney, B. (December 5, 2000). "Funding Strategies for Biotechnology Start-Ups," Unpublished Paper, University of Southern California, San Diego.
17. DiMasi, J.A., Hansen, R.W., & Grabowski, H.G. (October 2003). "The Price of Innovation: New Estimates of Drug Development Costs," *Journal of Health Economics*, 22: 151–185 (Elsevier Science).
18. Hoovers IPO Scorecard, Fourth Quarter 2005, Third Quarter 2007, Fourth Quarter 2007, http://premium.hoovers.com/global/ipoc/index.xhtml?pageid=4546

CHAPTER 12

FUNDING GROWTH

Rapid growth is an exciting time in the life of a technology venture, but it can be exhilarating and frightening at the same time. It's frightening because if a new technology achieves mass market acceptance, demand generally outstrips supply and huge amounts of capital are needed to support rapid growth at double and even triple digit rates. It's exhilarating because if a company has achieved its start-up targets and acquired a critical mass of customers, new sources of capital will be available to support that level of growth.

Many factors affect a firm's ability to grow. Chief among them are external, internal, and investment factors. Research suggests that industry population density and market forces are external forces that dictate how a firm grows.[1] Internal forces such as capabilities, culture, or strategy also play a critical role.[2] Finally, venture capital (VC) investments, and the timing of those investments, also contribute to the ability of the firm to grow.[3] VC is simply a pool of professionally managed investment funds. Firms that use VCs in their funding strategy are fundamentally different from start-ups using traditional financing methods in that venture-backed firms tend to be more innovative in their strategic orientation and experience faster time-to-market due in large part to the fact that investors require rapid scale-up to a liquidity event—a sale or IPO that will provide a significant return on their investment.[4] Moreover, VC firms devote significant time, energy, and resources to identifying excellent technology opportunities, so once a promising start-up is identified, the VC firm provides substantial capital and management support, which enhances the probability that the start-up will be successful.

This chapter explores the primary sources of growth capital—VC, private offerings, and public offerings—but begins with a discussion of financial strategy for growth.

FINANCIAL STRATEGY FOR GROWTH

In a perfect world, it would be easy to identify successful companies, and investors, therefore, would not lose money from their investments. However, reality is far from perfect. It is actually very difficult to evaluate the potential of a business in the growth stage (or any other stage for that matter). For this reason, and many others, it is critically important that a technology venture have a financial plan that looks ahead at least five years. If the company's projections forecast that it will reach $50 million in revenues by the fifth year, for example, it is necessary to know how the entrepreneur intends to accomplish that projection. Too many entrepreneurs focus on short-term goals—how much money is needed to launch and make it through the first year—and then find themselves in trouble when additional capital is needed to extend their growth beyond the first year. If the period between 1997 and 2001 with its dot-com bust and technology crash taught entrepreneurs anything, it was that rapid growth too soon in the venture's life with no systems and controls in place can send the business into a tailspin from which it may not recover.

An effective financial plan incorporates the milestones from the entrepreneur's growth plan: first customers (the primary target market), multiple customer segments (secondary markets), and multiple products. Each stage has different requirements for people, equipment, product development, and marketing. The plan also addresses what must happen at each stage and the amount of money and time needed to achieve each milestone. Growing the business more slowly in the earliest stages permits the company to prepare for rapid growth when the company and the market are ready. Some of the questions that should be answered in the financing plan are found in Table 12-1.

VC FUNDING

VC funding is typically a pool of professionally managed funds contributed by individuals and institutions. As a rule, the fund managers are paid a management fee for assuming the role of general partner as well as a percentage of the gain from any

---

TABLE 12-1 Financial Strategy Questions

1. Where will the company be in 5 years? Size? Revenues? Markets?
2. Should the company aim to become a public company or remain private? Why?
3. Does the company have a compelling need for significant capital for a specific purpose at each milestone?
4. How many milestones of value creation will be achieved during the 5-year period?
5. How many rounds of funding will it take to reach the 5-year goal?
6. What sources of funding are most appropriate for this type of business and at which milestones?
7. Which financial instruments are appropriate at which milestones?
8. What is the least amount of money required at each milestone?

of the fund's investments. In exchange for an equity stake (ownership position), VC firms generally invest in companies with excellent management teams and large markets that enable growth to a minimum of $50 million with pretax profits of 20 percent of revenues within about 5–7 years. A company of this size has the potential for an IPO, which is a liquidity event that VCs need to recoup their investment plus realize a gain. VCs are generally looking for at least 10 times their initial investment over five years, an annual rate that equates to a return of 58 percent.[5] The amount invested depends on the size of the fund. Today, the median fund size has grown to about $200 million.[6] This means that VCs with large funds have to find bigger deals to get the returns on investment they require. The minority of VC funds are under $100 million, but they can do deals as low as $2 million. Traditionally VCs have invested primarily in technology companies; but with increasing pressure to find great investments many VC firms have expanded their scope of investments to include other types of businesses that offer the potential for rapid growth, such as distribution and consumer products. Many VC firms are also looking for international deals.

Many entrepreneurs consider themselves successful (and their businesses successful) if they have managed to raise VC funding, even if the company is not profitable. While it is true that venture-backed start-ups have a lot of help in becoming successful, the reality is that if an entrepreneur takes VC funding too early when there is still a significant amount of risk in the venture, that entrepreneur is essentially selling his or her company to the VC because the VCs will design the deal so they can control the business.

VC firms generally have four fundamental principles under which they operate:[7]

1. **The VC firm gets paid first.**   Whether by means of a liquidity event or the liquidation of the company in the event of failure, the VC firm will get paid ahead of the entrepreneur and any early-stage friendly money.

2. **Participation in the upside of the venture.**   The VC firm will benefit from the appreciation in value of the venture over and above the original investment.

3. **Control over critical events.**   The VCs will want to have decision rights in matters that vitally affect the business, such as the decision to do an IPO.

4. **Creation of a path to liquidity.**   There must be a way for the VC firm to cash out of the venture.

VC SCREENING PROCESS

Technology start-ups are dynamic organizations characterized by little experience, lack of commitment on the part of employees, immature systems and controls, and inconsistent quality, which limits their chances of survival.[8] They often require far more resources early on and face more complex problems than traditional ventures. For these reasons, they usually need major outside funding. Despite the negatives, however, they are attractive investments to VCs because their ability to scale to a large company size provides an opportunity for higher returns for the investor.[9] But technology ventures must be carefully screened.

Traditionally, VCs conduct comprehensive and in-depth due diligence on any venture under consideration for investment. It is well known that the experience and integrity of the entrepreneur are as important as the technology and the market. In general, VCs look for an optimal combination of a great management team and reasonable technology/market factors. In their investigation of European and U.S. venture capitalists, Muzyka and Birley found that the top five most important factors that would lead a venture capitalist to invest in a technology venture were related to the management team.[10] The second major group of factors was related to the market. The top five factors were as follows:

1. Leadership potential of the lead entrepreneur.
2. Leadership potential of the management team.
3. Industry expertise of the management team.
4. Track record of the lead entrepreneur.
5. Track record of the management team.

One area of strong consensus in the literature is that because of in-depth due diligence and high hurdle rates for return on investment, VCs reject approximately 95 percent of all applications submitted to them. One of the biggest reasons for rejecting an application is the level of uncertainty in the venture. Uncertainty creates risk and an inability to predict the future with any degree of confidence. VCs grapple with the risks and uncertainty associated with the technology (Will it work? Can it be manufactured?), the business model (Can it be produced at a price that customers will pay and a cost that enables a profit?), and market risks (Are there sufficient customers? Can they be reached?), among many other risks. It is no surprise then that VCs carefully consider an investment at this early stage, and when they do decide to invest, they invest in stages to mitigate some of the risk.

Another area of concern for investors is that the asset base in technology companies resides mainly in intangible assets—intellectual property, know-how, and so forth. Many VCs feel more comfortable investing in ventures that have the bulk of their assets in tangibles—equipment, buildings, land, and inventory—that are easier to value and track. Where intangible assets are predominant, investors incur a greater risk because intangible assets are difficult to value and protect but they balance that risk against the competitive advantage that intellectual property provides the company in the market.

Although every venture fund is different, most VC firms follow a three-step evaluation process of due diligence, risk and return analysis, and control rights assessment when evaluating a technology venture. The valuation of the company is also important and that topic will be taken up in Chapter 13.

Due Diligence

For the potential investor, due diligence is complicated by the fact that new ventures do not have track records or evidence of previous success. This is why most VCs investigate a venture's founders and management team so carefully. The VC firm conducts background and credit checks, looks at previous ventures in which the founders have been involved, and tries to determine their integrity and how easy it will be to get along with them. Recall from Chapter 1 that scientists and engineers often believe they are the best people to run the company. In some cases, that may be true, but, more often than not, the venture will need professional management skills. If the VCs sense that the technology founders will not be willing to step aside in favor of professional management, they will likely walk from the deal.

Estimating the market potential for the venture is another task that takes place during the diligence process. For breakthrough innovations, this is a difficult task, as it is difficult to find information from public sources; thus, the VC firm must rely on the new venture's business plan and portfolio of contacts in the industry, neither of which are always reliable.[11]

RISK AND RETURN ASSESSMENT

The rate of return VCs expect from an investment is directly related to the degree of risk they are taking in making the investment.[12] In general, the required return is a function of the difference between the expected stock market return and the current risk-free interest rate. The type of company and the stage of growth also contribute to the evaluation of risk and reward. The younger the company, the greater the risk and the greater the return required by the VC firm.

Although the returns on investments in early-stage ventures seem astronomical, the reality is that seed and start-up stages are the most risky; therefore, VCs charge more to make up for the 9 ventures out of 10 that do provide supernormal returns. Entrepreneurs may appear to be in a weak position with VCs, but this is only true if the entrepreneur is unprepared and at a point of financial desperation. Although VCs see hundreds of deals every month, they rarely see great deals, so if a great concept is presented, it will get their attention.

Any investment deal has four components that determine its value to the VC: (1) the amount of money to be invested, (2) the timing and use of those monies, (3) the return on investment, and (4) the risk level of the investment. Typically, VCs seek both equity and debt from a venture. Equity provides an ownership interest in the business and debt provides an immediate payback in the form of interest payments. Redeemable preferred stock or debentures (a debt instrument that converts to common stock) are attractive because if the company does well, they can be converted to common stock. On the other hand, if the company fails, the holders of these instruments will be the first to be repaid from the remains of the liquidation. If this strategy is successful, the VC can receive the entire investment back plus interest and still enjoy capital appreciation in the value of the business as a shareholder.

Alternatively, VCs may demand participating preferred stock, which entitles them to participate in dividends with the common stockholders after receiving the preferred dividend rate. They will also want a liquidation preference that entitles them to receive a specified amount multiplied by the purchase price plus all dividends accrued but unpaid, whether or not they were declared. In other words, the VCs want to have their cake and eat it too! It is easy to see why the terms of a VC agreement can be so onerous. Consider the following scenario:

A 2-year-old technology company received a $20 million second round of financing from a venture capital firm to take the company to an IPO in 5 years. Unfortunately, well into the fifth year, the company was still behind in having a marketable application of its technology ready. A compatible company in the same industry saw an opportunity to purchase the struggling venture for $30 million and made an offer. The founders were excited as they prepared to accept the deal. The excitement was short-lived, however, when their attorney informed them that the VCs were entitled to a two-times-purchase-price return on their preferred stock, which equaled $40 million. The founders would, therefore, receive nothing from the sale of the business. Shocked, they were ready to reject the sale, when their attorney further reminded them that the VCs held redeemable preferred stock, which meant that they could require the company to buy them out of the investment; in fact, they were demanding the sale of the company so they could be cashed out.

Unfortunately, this situation is not uncommon. Too many entrepreneurs readily accept investments from VCs without understanding the future ramifications.

VCs protect their investments in others ways as well. They will frequently require an antidilution provision to ensure that the selling of stock at a later date will not decrease the economic value of their investment. To overcome having paid too much for an equity stake in the company, the VCs will require a forfeiture provision, which means that if the company does not achieve its projected performance goals, the founders may have to forfeit some of their stock as a penalty to the VC firm. This, of course, increases the VC firm's equity stake in the company. The entrepreneur can attempt to mitigate this situation by requesting stock bonuses as a reward for meeting or exceeding performance projections.

CONTROL RIGHTS

Venture capitalists often overcome the fact that a company in which they are investing may not yet have a product or revenues by exercising control rights. Control rights refer to the allocation of control over the company and its decisions and how that control is divided between the venture capitalists and the entrepreneurs. Control rights typically have three characteristics: (1) VCs normally exercise a disproportionately large share of control over the entrepreneurs,[13] (2) control rights are not static, they are changed and refined over time,[14] and (3) where significant asymmetric information exists, greater control rights are assigned to the VC.[15]

Kaplan and Stromberg conducted a study of 200 VC investments in 118 high-tech U.S. companies by 14 VC firms over the period 1987–1999.[16] Convertible preferred stock was present in 189 out of 200 financing rounds. With convertible preferred stock in early-stage situations, if the company performs poorly, the VCs take control. As the company's performance improves, the entrepreneur gains more control. If the company performs with a return of more than 30 percent per year over the 4-year period leading to an IPO, the VCs relinquish their control and liquidation rights, but retain their cash flow rights.

The term sheet is also a way to control the new venture because it typically puts a number of requirements on the entrepreneur. These requirements may include audited financial statements, noncompete clauses, stock vesting agreements for employees, limitations on the stock option pool, and limitations on salaries. The term sheet is typically one to two pages and summarizes the structure of the deal with the VC firm. It deals with such issues as the number of preferred shares, the price of the shares, the resulting equity distribution between the founders and the venture capitalists, the vesting period, dividend and liquidation terms, redemption rights, and conversion rights, to name a few.

TIMING OF FUNDING

To reduce their risk, VCs stage the investment and tie funding to achievement milestones. If the entrepreneur achieves the first milestone, which is usually tied to profit and/or revenues, the VC firm will release the next stage of funding. If, on the other hand, the entrepreneur fails to reach the milestone as scheduled, the VC firm may decide to pull out of the investment and write off the first stage. Another way that VCs reduce risk is to enter the investment with another VC firm. In fact, some VCs will not invest in a new venture until another VC has come on board. Funding is timed to support the potential of the venture and help it achieve a consistent pattern of growth without any stops and starts. In other words, funding should never halt the growth of the company, particularly when speed is critical to a competitive advantage.[17] This means that planning for capital acquisition is essential so that the required funding is available when needed. However, in reality funding does not always happen quite that easily. One reason is that VCs use their funding to exercise control and create incentives, which may or may not be aligned with a consistent growth path.[18] Furthermore, entrepreneurs often underestimate their growth funding requirements, and growth is therefore slowed by their inability to hire and support increased production. Overestimating the magnitude and timing of revenues and underestimating their costs can definitely cause cash flow problems.[19]

THE AFTERMATH

Once the entrepreneur receives VC funding, the real work begins. Although each VC firm has its own particular needs, there are some commonalities among them. The VC firm will appoint one person from the firm to act as the lead investor, but often several of the investors in the group will want to be involved in some manner. They will likely expect regular board meetings and impose formal financial reporting requirements. The way that the management team handles the investment capital will largely determine if they will receive additional funding at the next milestone.

THE PRIVATE OFFERING

The purpose of a private offering is to sell securities in the company to potential investors. Securities consist of common and preferred stock, notes, bonds, debentures, voting trust certificates, certificates of deposit, warrants, options, subscription rights, limited partnership shares, and undivided oil or gas interests. Most early-stage funding, approximately 80 percent, is accomplished through private offerings that are exempt from federal and state securities laws.

A private offering is a less costly, less time-consuming process than a public offering. In fact, today, many states offer standard forms and offering documents that make it easy for the entrepreneur to complete them. An entrepreneur undertaking a private offering does not need to have the long track record, assets, or significant credit references needed for bank financing, nor does it have to file with the Securities and Exchange Commission (SEC) as entrepreneurs seeking public offerings are required to do. The venture does have to qualify under the blue sky laws (securities laws) of its state, which are designed to protect investors against fraud.

The SEC's Regulation D rules provide guidelines for a private placement memorandum, which is the equivalent of an initial registration statement that is filed for a public offering. It contains the same information as a prospectus, but the SEC does not review it. The various rules under Regulation D provide for offerings up to a maximum of $5 million with limitations on the number of nonaccredited investors, which are those investors who do not have a net worth of at least $1 million and earned less than $200,000 in the previous two years. In all cases, the company cannot advertise the offering and there are no SEC reporting requirements unless the company has 500 or more shareholders and $3 million in total assets.

SMALL CORPORATE OFFERING REGISTRATION

Many states have adopted the Small Corporate Offering (SCOR U-7) to make the registration process simpler by providing fill-in-the-blank questions to acquire the company's information. SCOR permits the entrepreneur to sell securities to an unlimited number of investors and is a hybrid of a public offering and a private offering. With SCOR U-7, a company can raise up to $1 million by selling common stock at a share price of more than $1 per share directly to the public for at least $5 per share. One major benefit of this is that unless a state specifically prohibits it, the offering can be sold to anyone in amounts as small as $1,000. Moreover, in some states, SCOR companies can trade their common stock on NASDAQ's electronic over-the-counter bulletin board. Entrepreneurs often use this approach to raise money with Internet direct public offerings (DPOs). SCOR permits a variety of securities to be sold, including preferred and common stock, convertible debentures, and debt securities with warrants.

Entrepreneurs should understand that just because a company can raise early-stage capital by selling to the public that does not mean that there is a public market for the stock. Proceeds of a successful offering must be placed in an escrow account until a minimum amount has been raised that will enable the company to meet its offering goals and remain in business for at least 12 months after the offering. When using this or any other type of offering, it is important to consult with an attorney who will make sure that the company follows all the rules and does not leave itself open to a lawsuit.

DIRECT PUBLIC OFFERING: REGULATION A

Under Regulation A of the SEC, a company may do a DPO, but, unlike SCOR, Regulation A permits an offering of up to $5 million over a period of 12 months. To qualify for a DPO, the company should be able to demonstrate several years of profit under the same management, 3 years of audited financial statements, a compelling business story, a strong and loyal customer base that might be induced to invest, and advisors to help with the management of the DPO.

With a Regulation A offering, the company does not have to file a registration statement with the SEC, but it does need to comply with the antifraud and personal liability provisions of the SEC Act of 1933. The disclosures are the same as those for filing a registration statement for a public offering and include a prospectus that identifies the risk factors, financials, use of proceeds, background of the officers and directors, and the goals of the business. Regulation A does not exempt a company from complying with state securities laws, which can be severe.

THE INITIAL PUBLIC OFFERING

An IPO is the first sale of stock by a private company to the public. It differs from the private offering in that it must be registered with the SEC and follow very strict rules and a process that are described later in this section. For high-tech companies and their investors, the lure of the IPO is real. Despite the cyclical and somewhat unpredictable nature of the IPO market, most high-tech and Internet entrepreneurs and their investors see an IPO in their company's future because it is arguably the best way to create wealth. There are many other reasons an entrepreneur would consider an IPO. Once the company is public, it is easy to raise additional cash by doing a secondary offering in the public markets. Public companies can have an unlimited number of investors and enjoy more public exposure both during and after the offering. Jeff Bezos, CEO of Amazon.com, claims that Amazon.com went public not just to raise capital, but also to increase public awareness for the company. Akamai, the Internet content company, also chose an IPO to attract customer and business partner attention.[20] Public companies seem to achieve great credibility almost overnight, making lenders, employees, and customers more likely to do business with them.

For all the positives of a public offering, there are significant negatives that should be weighed as well. A public company is just that—public, which means that financial statements, annual reports, and other documents are available to the public, including competitors. The SEC reporting requirements are onerous and typically require a staff to manage them. Today public companies are subject to the strict disclosure rules under Sarbanes-Oxley, which was passed to respond to the corporate accounting scandals that began with Enron.[21] The cost of compliance with these rules is extremely high, averaging about $3 million annually for large companies.[22] Ownership is more likely to be diluted (reduced) from the sale of stock to raise capital. Entrepreneurs with private companies can focus on long-term goals while sacrificing short-term profits, but public companies are under a great deal of pressure to perform in the short term. The entrepreneur's original vision for the company may get lost in the morass of quarterly and annual reports. Still, for many high-tech companies, a public offering is the only realistic way to raise sufficient growth capital. Perhaps the most challenging negative of a public offering is that the entrepreneur must now satisfy shareholders first and foremost.

Undertaking an IPO requires that the company have a compelling need to raise a significant amount of capital for a specific purpose. That purpose must be clear to everyone involved with the company. The company must also start acting like a public company well before the IPO process; that is, it must begin to manage the expectations of its investors and improve its ability to accurately forecast earnings on a quarterly basis. It must also develop methods for communicating regularly with stakeholders.

Timing the IPO is perhaps one of the most difficult tasks to accomplish because some years, or portions of years, are more favorable to IPOs than others. The value of the stock at the time of the IPO is certainly critical to making the decision to go forward with the offering.[23] Entrepreneurs should learn from the case of Vonage, the VoIP company that launched its IPO on May 24, 2006. Seven days later, the stock had lost approximately 30 percent of its value, which then precipitated a class action lawsuit by its shareholders.[24]

Today many entrepreneurs with companies holding smaller valutions of $10 to $60 million look to European and Asian markets, which have less stringent capitalization and reporting requirements, so it's much easier to go public. European and Asian investors are often looking for early-stage companies that exhibit huge growth potential.

THE IPO PROCESS

The IPO process is time consuming and lengthy, with no guarantee that it will be completed. Many a company has reached the end of the road show, which is designed to sign up institutional investors, only to find itself undersold or sold at a price much below the projected offering price. Before starting the IPO process, it is wise to consult with several people who have gone through the process. By doing so, entrepreneurs can enter the process with full knowledge of what lies ahead. Part of preparing the company for an IPO is developing audited financial statements, putting appropriate accounting systems and controls in place to meet the requirements of Sarbanes-Oxley, bringing on board any needed professional management, and securing the board of directors for the public company.

The various steps of the IPO process are depicted in Figure 12-1. The process starts with selecting an investment bank, the firm that underwrites the IPO, sells the securities, and essentially guides the company through the IPO process. This is arguably one of the most critical tasks the entrepreneur will assume because a mediocre investment banker can not only cause problems during the IPO but

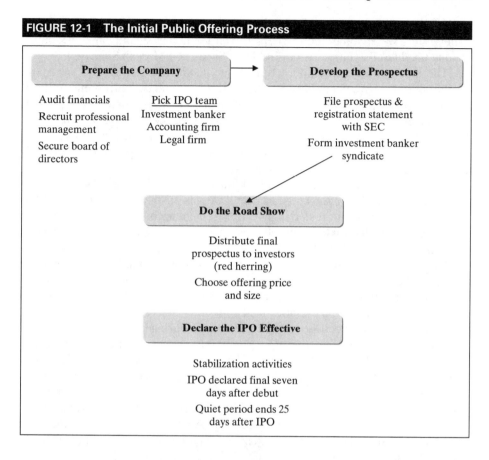

FIGURE 12-1   The Initial Public Offering Process

once the company is public, a poor underwriter may not successfully create a market for the stock or develop any analyst coverage, which means that few if any analysts will write about the company. If that happens, the entrepreneur will have the worst of all worlds—a public company with all the onerous SEC reporting requirements but none of the advantages of having a stock that generates interest and becomes a source of growth capital.[25] It is important to select the investment bank as early as possible because it will be the major contact with all the financial interests involved in the IPO.

A very young company that is seeking a public offering before it has achieved at least $50 million in sales will likely have a difficult time attracting one of the major investment banking houses because they will find it challenging to sell the entrepreneur's company to their major institutional investors. The one exception may be an Internet venture that is attracting a lot of unique users and offers an innovative value proposition. Consequently, entrepreneurs with smaller companies should consider contacts they might have in the investment banking community or investigate the numerous regional or boutique investment banking firms that often serve small- to mid-market companies. They should also study the post IPO performance during the first 12 months of recent IPOs and determine who the lead underwriters were. Some underwriters known for taking small companies public include Credit Suisse First Boston, Goldman Sachs, and Morgan Stanley.

The underwriter draws up a letter of intent, which spells out the terms and conditions of the agreement between the underwriter and the entrepreneur. It will detail a range of prices for the stock, which is merely an estimate of the price at which the underwriter believes the stock will be sold. These actions also initiate a "quiet period" that extends to 25 days after the IPO during which information not included in the registration statement cannot be disclosed to potential shareholders or the public.

A registration statement is filed with the SEC. This document is referred to as a "red herring" or prospectus because it details all the potential risks of the investment to anyone interested in investing. It includes biographical material on the officers and directors, the number of shares owned by all insiders (people who work for the company), complete financial statements, use of proceeds, and any legal issues related to the company. The prospectus is valid for 9 months, after which any changes must occur through an official amendment. Following the registration, the underwriter places an advertisement, called a *tombstone,* in the financial press announcing the offering.

One of the major decisions that must be made during the process is on which stock exchange to list the offering. In general, smaller companies list on the American Stock Exchange (AMEX), the National Association of Securities Dealers Automated Quotation (NASDAQ), or one of the regional exchanges. The New York Stock Exchange (NYSE), home to over 80 percent of American securities, has more stringent listing requirements. The NASDAQ operates differently than the other exchanges. The NYSE and AMEX are auction markets with securities traded on the floor of the exchange, enabling investors to trade directly with each other. In contrast, the NASDAQ is an electronic exchange that trades on the National Market System through a system of broker-dealers from respected securities firms who compete for orders. Most high-tech companies that are still growing are listed on the NASDAQ.

The culmination of all the preparatory work for the IPO comes with the "road show," a 3–4 week whirlwind tour of all the major institutional investors. The purpose of the trip is to make sure that once the registration statement has met all the SEC requirements and the final price of the stock is determined, it can sell in a day. It is also designed to introduce the management team to analysts, brokers, potential investors, and others. How the team responds to questions about its products, business, and competition will determine the ultimate success of the offering. It is no wonder then that the management team spends many hours preparing its road show presentation and practices fielding questions.

The day before the offering and after the market closes, the firm and the lead underwriter meet to determine the offering price and the number of shares to be sold. In general, the going-out price is typically undervalued so that the company shows an upsurge in stock price immediately after the offering hits the market, generally about 15 percent. In the case of technology companies, highly anticipated IPOs can generate much higher prices. If the entrepreneur is unhappy with the price the underwriter proposes the night before the offering, the only choice is to cancel the offering. Of course, the entrepreneur still incurs the expenses to date, which can be substantial.

If the IPO goes forward, a final prospectus is printed and the stock opens for trade. The transaction closes three days later when the stock is delivered and the underwriter places the net proceeds from the IPO into the firm's account. The IPO is declared effective approximately seven days after the offering and the quiet period ends 25 days after the IPO, enabling the underwriters to begin providing earnings estimates on the company. It is the underwriter's job to stabilize the market and support the stock by buying shares aggressively if necessary for a short period of time after trading has begun.

Growth is a journey, not a destination, and the means used to fund that growth are critical to the long-term sustainability of the company. Entrepreneurs need to plan for growth long before it happens so that they can gather the necessary resources and put in place the systems needed to support effective growth.

Summary

Growth is a very exciting time in the life of a new venture, but it also strains the venture's resources because growth requires large amounts of capital. Entrepreneurs raise capital by securing debt or selling equity stakes in their companies. When the returns on the business exceed the cost of borrowing money, debt is a wise choice, but selling shares of stock in the company is the most common way that entrepreneurs raise capital to grow the business. Raising capital requires a well-thought-out plan that identifies milestones and their associated triggers. The plan also details how those milestones will be reached and how much funding each will require. VC funds less than one percent of all ventures, but it is an important funding source for technology ventures attempting to grow. The private offering is a less costly way to sell securities in the company to potential investors without being subject to the strict rules of a public offering. Many technology companies plan for an IPO in their future. Going public gives the venture more clout in the market and makes it easier to raise additional money, however, the SEC reporting requirements are onerous, the entrepreneur's ownership is likely to be diluted, and the entrepreneur may have to forego a long-held vision to satisfy stockholders in the short term.

Discussion Questions

1. When growing a company, why would an entrepreneur choose debt over equity?
2. What elements should an effective financing strategy contain?
3. What is meant by control rights and how do venture capitalists exercise them?
4. What effect does the timing of funding have on a growing venture's success? Why?
5. What important tasks must take place prior to undertaking an IPO?

From Riches to Rags and Back? When Going Public May Not Be the Right Path

In January 1998, 33-year-old Doug Mellinger was on top of the world. Touted as "the next Bill Gates," Mellinger's software programming business, PRT Group, had just completed a successful public offering, and the stock was rising. His own stake in the company was worth $44 million; his family's stake had grown to $112 million. Life was good for this entrepreneur. However, in the space of only a year and a half, the company headed into a tailspin, and Mellinger found himself out on the streets having lost his job as CEO. How could something like this happen in only 19 months?

In the early 1990s, PRT was a small software company that provided on-site software engineers to clients. It was a difficult business; software engineers were in short supply and immigration laws prevented companies such as Mellinger's from importing talent in sufficient quantities from places such as India. For a time, Mellinger tried operating offshore, but most of the countries he investigated were too far away, had inadequate labor, or other problems. Moreover, his clients were not comfortable with the concept of his company operating out of another country. Finally, in 1994, he conceived the idea of creating his own perfect country on the island of Barbados in the Caribbean. He built a village, imported programmers, secured capital, created an infrastructure, and found customers. His goal was to create an environment where programmers were completely taken care of while they spent their days writing code. In essence, Mellinger gave his programmers a turnkey life.

Within a short amount of time, Mellinger had imported 350 employees from 16 countries. Huge companies such as J.P. Morgan and Chase Manhattan were so enthralled with the concept that they gave PRT their business and contributed $12 million to the business's construction needs. Mellinger began creating partnerships with the local government with plans to improve schools and take a nontech country into the technological age. It was a grand vision to solve a real problem.

Riding the crest of a wave of popularity with a great story to tell, Mellinger decided in 1997 that it was time to do a public offering to raise more growth capital. Mellinger was unprepared for the amount of time it would take to do the offering. For 5 months, he sat in meetings with attorneys, investment bankers, and potential investors as they prepared for the offering date. On November 20, 1997, PRT Group went public at $13 a share (NASDAQ: PRTG). By the end of the first day of trading, it listed at $13.25. By February 26, 1998, the stock hit what was to be its high point at $21.63, producing $156 million for Mellinger and his family. PRT was projecting that it would double its revenues in 1998 to $120 million, so Mellinger expanded PRT's programming capability to meet the projected demand. Unfortunately, that demand never materialized, and when several projects dissolved in early 1998, PRT was left with high overhead. Ironically, in 1997, when PRT did not have sufficient programmers to handle the demand, it told its salespeople to slow the pace at which they were attracting new customers.

On March 6, 1998, PRT announced that it would post a first quarter loss of $3 million rather than the small profit it had originally projected. The result: PRT stock dropped $9.56 in the first hour of trading. Mellinger learned that the concept of shipping custom programming from Barbados did not catch on as quickly as he had thought it would.

(continued)

(continued)

That, coupled with the fact that custom programming entailed a longer development time and a longer sales cycle, made cash flow a real problem.

The pressure to change the direction of the stock changed the way Mellinger ran the company. Everyone began to panic and reorganization became the norm. By September 1998, a shareholder lawsuit was brought against the company, which caused the stock to slump. By then, the stock was trading at $4 a share.

PRT ended 1998 with revenues of $85 million, $35 million below projections. The company had lost 100 employees. Nearly 70 percent of the sales staff had left within the year. Mellinger became the primary salesperson in the organization, but he could not single-handedly develop the sales volume that PRT needed and his sales staff was never properly trained. In May 1999, PRT hired a new president and COO, displacing Mellinger's brother, and he began auditing the company's processes. Changes began to take place, and it was then that Doug Mellinger realized that he was an entrepreneur, not a manager; he did not have the appropriate skills to run a large company. In late June 1999, the COO, Dan Woodward, became the CEO, and Mellinger was no longer an officer of the corporation.

Since June 30, 1999, analysts and others have attempted to understand how something like this could have happened. Logically, it could be attributed to a poor sales force and too much reliance on the selling ability of Mellinger, as well as too much focus on the production side at the expense of marketing. However, many analysts speculate that it was the decision to become a public company that was PRT's undoing. While still a young company, it had the pressure of short-term performance gains that it could not keep up with.

Epilogue: On May 31, 2000, PRT Group Inc. underwent a brand makeover and became Enherent Corp. with a new logo, website, and refined strategic direction. At the same time, the company announced that it was moving its headquarters to Dallas, Texas. In December, 2005, Douglas Mellinger retired as Vice Chairman of Enherent, but stayed on as a director of the company. He also cofounded Foundation Source, which provides support services for private foundations.

Sources: Form 8-K, United States Securities and Exchange Commission, December, 2005 (May 8, 2001). "U.S. Firm Brings *Fortune* 500 Clients to Barbados," Enherent Corp. press release, Dallas, TX (May 31, 2000). "PRT Group Evolves to Become Enherent Corp." Business Wire, http://findarticles.com/p/articles/mi_m0EIN/is_2000_May_31/ai_62418430, accessed September 19, 2008; Hopkins, M.S. (November 1, 1999). "Paradise Lost," *Inc.*, www.inc.com (September 22, 1999). "PRT Group Inc. Selected as Technology Fast 50 Company by Deloitte & Touche," *Business Wire,* http://findarticles.com/p/articles/mi_m0EIN/is_1999_Sept_22/ai_55824472, accessed September 19, 2008, CT.

Endnotes

1. Hannon, M.T., & Freeman, J. (1989). *Organizational Ecology* (Cambridge, MA: Harvard University Press).
2. Teece, D.J., Pisano, G., & Shuen, A. (1997). "Dynamic Capabilities and Strategic Management," *Strategic Management Journal* 18(7): 509–533.
3. Davila, A., Foster, G., & Gupta, M. (November 2000). "Venture-Capital Financing and the Growth of Start-Up Firms," *Research Paper Series,* Graduate School of Business, Stanford University, Palo Alto, CA.
4. Hellmann, T., & Purl, M. (1999). "The Interaction between Product, Market, and Financing Strategy: The Role of Venture Capital," Working Paper, Stanford University, Palo Alto, CA.

5. Bygrave, W. (2000). "How the Venture Capitalists Work Out the Financial Odds," In S. Birley, & D.F. Muzyka (Eds.), *Financial Times: Mastering Entrepreneurship* (London: Pearson Education), pp. 105–109.

6. Cutland, L. (November 10, 2006). "VC Funds Find Size Matters," *Silicon Valley/San Jose Business Journal,* http://sanjose.bizjournals.com.

7. Weirick, B. (November 7, 2001). "Introduction to Venture Capital," Presentation at the University of Southern California, San Diego, CA.

8. Carroll, G.R., & Hannan, M.T. (2000). *The Demography of Corporations and Industries* (Princeton, NJ: Princeton University Press).

9. Davila, A., Foster, G., & Gupta, M. (November 2000). "Venture-Capital Financing and the Growth of Start-Up Firms," Working Paper, Graduate School of Business, Stanford University, Palo Alto, CA.

10. Muzyka D., & Birley, S. (2000). "What Venture Capitalists Look For," In S. Birley, & D.F. Muzyka (Eds.), *Financial Times: Mastering Entrepreneurship* (London: Pearson Education, 2000), pp. 103–105.

11. Steir, L. (1995). "Venture Capitalists Relationships in the Deal Structuring and Post-Investment Stages of New Firm Creation," *Journal of Management Studies* 32(2): 337–357.

12. Wright, M., & Robbie, K. (1996). "Venture Capitalists, Unquoted Equity Investment Appraisal and the Role of Accounting Information," *Accounting and Business Research* 26(20): 153–168.

13. Gompers, P.A. (1997). "Ownership and Control in Entrepreneurial Firms: An Examination of Convertible Securities in Venture Capital Investments," Working Paper, Harvard University, Cambridge, MA; Black, B.S., & Gilson, R.J. (1998). "Venture Capital and the Structure of Capital Markets: Banks Versus Stock Markets," *Journal of Financial Economics* 47: 243–277.

14. Kaplan, S.N., & Stromberg, P. (1999). "Financial Contracting Theory Meets the Real World: An Empirical Analysis of Venture Capital Projects," Working Paper, University of Chicago, Chicago, IL.

15. Kirilenko, A.A. (2001). "Valuation and Control in Venture Finance," *The Journal of Finance* 56(2): 565–588.

16. Kaplan, & Stromberg, *op. cit.*

17. Saloner, G., Shepard, A., & Podolny, J. (2000). *Strategic Management* (New York: Wiley).

18. Davila et al., *op. cit.*, p. 11.

19. Zacharakis, A.L., & Meyer, G.D. (2000). "The Potential of Actuarial Decision Models: Can They Improve the Venture Capital Investment Decision?" *Journal of Business Venturing* 15: 323–346.

20. Song, J.H. (July 2001). "Maximizing the Financial and Product Market Values of the IPO Opportunity," *Business Horizons* 44(4): 39.

21. Feldman, A. (September 2005). "Five Ways That Smart Companies Comply," *Inc. Magazine,* www.inc.com, accessed September 19, 2008.

22. SmartPros Editorial Staff (May 19, 2004). "Public and Private Cos. Reveal True Cost of SOX Compliance," smartpros.com, accessed September 19, 2008.

23. Baker, M., & Wurgler, J. (November 2000). "Market Timing and Capital Structure," Harvard School of Business, Working Paper. http://som.yale.edu/finance.center/pdf/capitalstructure.pdf.

24. Ibid.

25. Andresky Fraser, J., & Barker, E. (June 2002). "The Road to Wall Street," *Inc. Magazine,* www.inc.com.

CHAPTER 13

TECHNOLOGY VALUATION

Anytime a technology is licensed or sold or a technology company seeks funding, is acquired, or merges with another company, a valuation of its assets takes place. Valuation is simply the process by which an investor, lender, or buyer determines the current worth of a company or a particular asset, such as a technology. Entrepreneurs should understand the valuation process because at some point in the development of their technology and their company, they will face a valuation. Some of the events that trigger a valuation include (1) raising seed capital for product development, (2) raising start-up capital to launch a business, (3) raising growth capital to expand the business, (4) selling the technology or the company, (5) going public, or (6) selling the rights to develop, manufacture, and distribute the technology (called licensing). It is important to understand at the outset that valuation is in the eye of the beholder, which means that it is entirely possible that different people can value a business differently depending on their needs and how they view the business relative to those needs. Therefore, most entrepreneurs end up with a range of values that results in a ballpark figure that everyone is happy with.

There are significant challenges related to the valuation of technology assets and they stem from the uncertainty that surrounds new technology and the fact that most technologies also have associated know-how and other intangibles, such as patents, that in themselves are difficult to value.[1] In actual fact, some research has found that the value of a company's intangible assets now exceeds that of its tangible assets by six to seven times, making the valuation process that much more challenging.[2] Another problem with technology valuation is that a given technology considered on its own will not result in the total possible value. To realize its full value, the technology must be linked to other technologies and/or physical assets. In other words, the linkages must be valued.[3] These linkages may include relationships with technologies owned by third parties, such as competitors, suppliers, and customers, and these relationships directly determine the success or failure of the new technology.

Many technology valuation techniques are quantitative and derive from decision theory and financial analysis. Although these techniques work very effectively with more mature technologies, they are less effective from a contextual perspective in large part because of the nature of the forecasts that entrepreneurs provide. Start-up technology ventures have no track record of cash flow or earnings on which to rely so the quality of the forecast numbers for cash or earnings is directly related to the assumptions used to derive them. Given that it is difficult at best for investors to judge the quality of the forecasts that entrepreneurs provide to them, they typically examine the process and assumptions the entrepreneur used to make the forecast to determine if the rationale behind the numbers is valid.[4] Investors normally employ quantitative methods, which will be discussed in a later section.

Qualitative approaches to valuation are also employed, often in conjunction with quantitative methods. Qualitative methods involve developing a deep understanding of the company and its technology. Because they are used to investigate complex issues that can't easily be quantified, qualitative methods are particularly useful for looking at businesses where the interplay of people, technology, and environment can have an enormous effect on the success or failure of a business. Technology road maps, one example of a qualitative method, help to shape decisions about value. Road mapping is simply a framework for brainstorming about the future potential of a technology against a timeline and an identification of enablers and barriers to achievement in the market.[5] The problem with this approach is that despite discovering enormous potential for a technology, it is still unknown whether the company can extract value from it. Technology readiness levels (TRLs), another qualitative method, are used by the U.S. General Accounting Office to determine where in its development a technology lies, which can assist in determining value. Table 13-1 presents an example of a TRL for a software product. Levels 1–3 represent the earliest stages of product development where the risk is highest because of so many uncertainties. Farther up the TRL, the risk is reduced because a prototype has been developed and, therefore, many of the unknowns have been resolved, so the valuation may be higher as a result.

THE DRIVERS OF VALUE

Drivers of value are those things that the entrepreneurial firm does or invests in that result in higher performance in terms of competitive advantage, growth, and savings that might contribute to the overall valuation of the company. Figure 13-1 depicts the primary value drivers that produce performance in these broad areas and have strategic implications for the business. Research has learned that potential profitability and the uniqueness of the innovation are the most important value drivers across three industries: biotech, information technology, and energy

TABLE 13-1   Sample Technology Readiness Levels for Software Development

Level 1: Basic principles observed and reported

Lowest level of software readiness. Basic research begins to be translated into applied R&D.

Level 2: Technology concept and/or application formulated

Invention begins. Once basic principles are observed, practical applications can be postulated. The application is speculative and there is no proof or detailed analysis to support the assumptions.

Level 3: Analytical and experimental critical function and/or characteristic proof of concept

Active R&D is initiated. This includes analytical studies to produce code that validates analytical predictions of separate software elements of the technology.

Level 4: Technology component and/or basic technology subsystem validation in laboratory environment

Basic software components are integrated to establish that they will work together. They are relatively primitive with regard to efficiency and reliability compared to the eventual system. System software architecture development initiated to include interoperability, reliability, maintainability, extensibility, scalability, and security issues.

Level 5: Technology component and/or basic subsystem validation in relevant environment

Reliability of software ensemble increases significantly. The basic software components are integrated with reasonably realistic supporting elements so that it can be tested in a simulated environment. System software architecture established.

Level 6: Technology system/subsystem model or prototype demonstration in a relevant environment

Representative model or prototype system, which is well beyond that of Level 5, is tested in a relevant environment. Represents a major step-up in software demonstrated readiness. Software releases are "Beta" versions and configuration controlled. Software support structure is in development.

Level 7: System prototype demonstration in an operational environment

Represents a major step up from Level 6, requiring the demonstration of an actual system prototype in an operational environment.

Level 8: Actual system completed and qualified through test and demonstration

Software has been proven to work in its final form and under expected conditions. In most cases, this level represents the end of true system development.

Level 9: Technology System proven through successful operations

Application of the software in its final form and under usage conditions, such as those encountered in operational test, evaluation and reliability trials. In almost all case, this is the end of the last "bug fixing" aspects of the system development.

and environmental.[6] Both value drivers are critical to an advantageous market position and market share. Next in importance is the effectiveness of the management team. To the extent that the entrepreneur's team consists of highly regarded people in their fields of expertise—for example, R&D and sales—the venture will

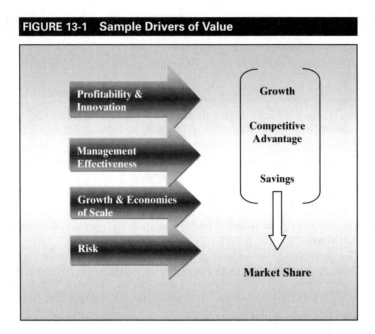

FIGURE 13-1 Sample Drivers of Value

be more attractive to investors and command a higher valuation. The growth potential of the company is another critical value driver and it arises from the competitive positioning of the company, its product portfolio, its market share, and its profitability.[7] Growth is also related to the value created by keeping costs low. As a new company grows, it acquires economies of scale that enable cost-reducing competitive advantages. For example, running a lean operation saves on costs, which can be passed on to customers in the form of lower prices, producing a savings and a competitive advantage for the company.

Risk is also a value driver. Recall that while all technology ventures entail significant risk, the value of the company at any point in time is directly related to the entrepreneur's ability to reduce that risk and demonstrate a sizeable market.[8]

WHEN VALUE IS DISCOUNTED

Just as certain factors serve to enhance the market value of a technology company, other factors cause that value to be discounted. For example, when a company is poorly managed, investors will charge a control premium, which is essentially a discount or penalty they assess against the valuation. They may also discount the valuation of a company based on poor financial leverage, the nature and magnitude of the nonoperating assets, and the opportunity cost of not exploiting other business opportunities at that time.[9] Furthermore, investors will lower the valuation based on lack of marketability of the stock acquired (it can't be resold), the financial stability of the company (it's not sustainable), whether the shares available are a controlling or minority interest (the investor ends up with a minority stake so they have no control), and the size of the underlying assets (the technology and the equity shares are not valuable enough) in the company, among other things.

FINANCIAL MODELS FOR ASSESSING VALUE

Valuation methods are generally categorized into four broad groups: the cost approach, the market method, the income method, and the real option method.[10] Venture capitalists and others approach the valuation process from a variety of points of view in an attempt to converge on the best estimate of value for a technology or a technology company given all the information at hand. In general, all financial valuation methods are based on an analysis of a market at some point in the future under the assumption that the company is a "going concern," that is, still in business.

In general, valuations are based on three assumptions:

1. **Existing use**. The value that comes from present operations, marketing, and financial strategies.
2. **Market value**. The price obtainable in the open market.
3. **Liquidation value**. The actual value of assets when the business closes.

In the case of new ventures, market value is probably the most reliable assumption. However, no matter what type of valuation method is chosen, and several will be discussed, there are a number of factors that should be addressed:

- The economic life of the intellectual property and/or technology, which is how long it can reasonably generate revenue.
- Transfer capability of the technology, which is how easily it can be licensed or sold and whether it requires the transfer of know-how as well.
- Restrictions on commercialization, which may be imposed by the Department of Commerce. For example, technology related to national defense cannot be transferred out of the United States.
- The cost of developing a substitute product, which, if expensive, could be a valuable barrier to competitors.
- A return on investment appropriate to the type of technology.

In the following sections, various financial models for assessing the value of technology and technology companies are discussed.

VALUATIONS BASED ON COST

Cost-based valuations rely on calculating the actual cost of the investment in technology, which includes accounting for inflation and the rate of return an investor might require. This might seem simple enough, but research indicates that there is no correlation between the amount of money spent on researching and developing a new technology and what the actual market value of that technology is. If the technology fails or has no commercial potential, then all of the money spent to develop it is lost and not recoverable in the form of revenues. It simply becomes a loss to the company and is written off on the company's financial statements as such. A cost-based valuation is frequently used as a hurdle rate to judge whether to pursue a particular technology, but it must be coupled with other methods to provide a more accurate total market valuation.

INCOME METHOD: THE PRO FORMA DISCOUNTED CASH FLOW MODEL

The most commonly used tool for valuing technology companies, R&D projects, or securities is the discounted cash flow (DCF) model. This model calculates the present value of the company's projected cash flow for a specified period, typically 3 to 5 years, in other words, what an investor would pay today for this cash flow over the defined period. The period of time is often dependent on when the company expects to do an initial public offering (IPO) or experience some other type of liquidity event where investors are cashed out. The cash flow is based on sales revenues less operating costs and debt repayment (it does not include interest), plus an estimate of the company's terminal value at the end of the period. All this is discounted back to the present using a risk-adjusted, weighted average cost of capital, which is equivalent to an interest rate. The calculation of an internal rate of return (IRR) is also used by investors; however, the two methods produce the same result. The IRR is simply the discount rate that produces a net present value of zero. So, if the IRR on an investment is 20 percent, it means that any discount rate less than 20 percent will be a sound investment (assuming valid premises). DCF is superior to other methods because it is based on a true economic measure of value—cash flow. There are five basic components to the DCF model.

- **Assumptions.** The assumptions are really the critical part of any model because they detail the basis on which the model was constructed. In other words, they explain the rationale behind the numbers. Assumptions should be based on industry practices, current economic conditions, the cost of R&D, working capital requirements, market strategy, and projected revenue based on sales.

- **Forecast period.** In general, investors like to see projections of 3 to 5 years because that is typically the maximum amount of time they will hold an investment. Moreover, projections beyond 5 years are inaccurate at best in a rapidly changing environment, and the impact of DCF. Many technologies take as long as 10 years or more to develop. Nutrasweet, the food sweetener, took nearly the entire 17 years of its patent protection in development. Had a DCF analysis been applied to that long-term investment, the product would have never gone to market; yet it created enormous wealth for the company that created it.

- **Free cash flows.**   Free cash flows are simply the entrepreneur's estimate of the net cash the company generates annually after capital expenditures (plant and equipment) are subtracted. (Operating cash flow minus capital expenditures = free cash flow.)

- **Terminal value.**   This is the "going concern" value that is applied to the company at the end of the forecast period to account for the fact that the business is expected to keep operating and producing cash flows. Without the terminal value, we would be assuming that the business stopped operating at the end of the forecast period. To figure terminal value, income capitalization and market multiple techniques can be used. Under the income capitalization approach, the company's earnings in the last year of the forecast are divided by the discount rate (cost of capital) required to sustain the earnings into the future. The market multiple approach is often used when the company under consideration is planning an IPO or acquisition at the end of the forecast period. With this method, the earnings are multiplied by the appropriate price/earnings (P/E) ratio of similar public companies. Both methods are subject to a lot of uncertainty, and the income capitalization method is particularly affected by the accuracy of the earnings forecasts. A simple way to calculate terminal value is to employ the Gordon Growth Model, which is found by the following formula:

$$\frac{\text{Final Projected Year Cash Flow} \times (1 + \text{Long-Term Cash Flow Growth Rate})}{(\text{Discount Rate} - \text{Long-Term Cash Flow Growth Rate})}$$

The long-term cash flow growth rate is expressed as a percentage.

- **Discount rate.**   One of the most critical components of the DCF model is the discount rate, which determines the net present value of the projected cash flows. In simpler terms, when we calculate the discount rate, we are calculating what these cash flows are worth today. For the investor, the discount rate represents the expected return on investment or weighted average cost of capital, so as the discount rate increases, the present value of the company (what a buyer would pay for it today) decreases. One of the most commonly used tools for producing the discount rate is the Capital Asset Pricing Model (CAPM), which recognizes that investors want to be compensated for the time value of money and the risk inherent in the investment. The CAPM calculates the discount rate based on two factors: (1) the cost of risk-free debt and (2) a risk premium related to the type of business, which assumes that some businesses are more risky than others—in other words their cost of equity. This method typically generates discount rates from 10 to 20 percent. However, it should be noted that most venture capitalists do not use the

CAPM because it produces discount rates much lower than they like to see. Furthermore, it is not likely that any two people will actually arrive at the same value for the same business. See the Venture Capital Methods section for more information on venture capital methods of valuation.

Once all of the needed components are figured, it is possible to arrive at the total expected value of the company, which is the sum of the discounted cash flows and the discounted terminal value minus debt.

$$\text{TEV} = \left(\frac{CF_1}{(1 + r)^1} + \frac{CF_2}{(1 + r)^2} + \cdots \right.$$
$$\left. + \frac{CF_n}{(1 + r)^n} + \frac{TV}{(1 + r)^n} \right) \text{ minus debt}$$

where r = discount rate or weighted average cost of capital (WACC)
   TV = terminal value
   CF = cash flow

For an example of an in-depth DCF model, see Boer's *The Valuation of Technology*.[11]

Use of DCF for very early stage technologies is discouraged because of the high degree of uncertainty, which results in higher discount rates and more inaccuracies in the forecasts due principally to changes in the discount rate over time. The DCF method does not allow for the benefit of waiting to make a decision until more information is available. The next method, real options, does permit more flexibility in timing.

THE REAL OPTIONS MODEL

Given the "irrational exuberance" of the investment community in assigning huge multiples of revenues or projected revenues to new technology companies during the period from 1997 to 2000, and the subsequent devaluation of technology stocks after the dot-com implosion of April 2000, many investors are now looking more seriously at the real options approach to valuing technology because it cuts the risk into stages.[12] Real options are analogous to financial options applied to securities, currencies, and commodities. Financial options are instruments that give the holder the right, but not the obligation, to enter into a future transaction based on some type of security such as debt, bonds, and stock. In other words, the investor purchases the right to buy a particular security at a particular price. If the investor does not exercise the option, he or she only loses the option price. In the case of real options, the options are applied to business situations where decisions are made under changing circumstances.[13] Simply put, real options theory recognizes that R&D, for example, is actually a process designed to reduce risk. At each stage of product development, more information is gained and some of the risk of uncertainty is reduced. The investor purchases from the entrepreneur the right to exercise an option at a fixed price at each stage of product development but does not have

FIGURE 13-2   Figuring Business Value with Real Options

1 Calculate economic value (EV), which consists of
- Cash flow over defined period
- Terminal value at end
- Cost of capital
- EV = FCF/(Cost of capital − Growth rate)

2 Define the business options
- Choices to be made over time

3 Figure the option premium
- This is the cost of the option

4 Calculate the value of the plan
- Calculate the NPV of the underlying security

5 Calculate the total value (TV)
- Apply the Black-Scholes formula using...

- Value of underlying security
- Exercise price
- Time period of option
- Volatility factor
- Risk-free rate

6 Calculate the Total Value (TV)
- TV = EV(Step 1) + Option Value (Step 4) − Option cost (Step 3)

the obligation to do so. Figure 13-2 depicts the basic process behind real options theory. It consists of six steps. We will use a simple example of a small technology company to work through the steps. Assume that Newtech is projected to have an annual free cash flow (FCF) of $100,000, an annual growth rate of 5 percent, and a weighted average cost of capital of 10 percent. The economic value (EV) for the business would then be:[14]

$$EV = \frac{FCF}{[\text{Cost of capital } - \text{ Growth rate}]}$$

$$\frac{\$100,000}{[10\% - 5\%]} = \$2 \text{ million}$$

Next, the option must be considered. Newtech's investors must make a decision about funding the R&D for a new product that the company needs to penetrate a new market. Newtech's entrepreneur would like the investors to invest $50,000 in a feasibility study to determine the best applications of the technology and that study would take about six months. A positive outcome from the study will give the investors the option to invest $150,000 to develop the prototype, a process that will take about a year. Once the product is ready for market, the entrepreneur figures that he can generate $100,000 in cash flow from the product and that the cash flow will grow at an annual rate of 5 percent like his previous product. The $50,000 for the feasibility study can be called an opportunity cost because it represents the investors' commitment not to place that money elsewhere. Once the investors pay the $50,000, the funding of the prototype development becomes an option whose value is calculated in Step 4.

Step 3 involves figuring the option premium, which is simply the cost of the option to the investors. In this case, it is the cost of doing the feasibility study, which is $50,000. Investing the $50,000 gives the investors the option of going forward with product development should the feasibility study be favorable. Now it is important to determine what the value of prototyping will be. The value of the prototype development plan (the *underlying security* in real options terminology) is found in Step 4 by calculating the net present value of the pro forma projections of cash flow that will derive from the new product once it is in the market—the investors' return on investment in implementing the prototype development plan. In our example, the result is already given because this new product is projected to produce the same cash flow stream as the first product; therefore, the value of the prototype plan is $2 million.

In Step 5, the option value is calculated using the Black–Scholes formula. We cannot go into sufficient depth on the subject of this formula in this book; however, we do have three of the required numbers: (1) the value of the underlying asset is $2 million, (2) the exercise price is $150,000, and (3) the duration is six months. Therefore, we know that once the investors pay for the feasibility study, they have six months before they have to decide to pay $150,000 for the prototype development plan. Two other numbers are required for the Black–Scholes formula: the risk-free rate and the volatility factor. Treasury bills are a common proxy for the risk-free rate because the rate they pay to the investor is fixed and guaranteed. For purposes of this example, we'll assume 5 percent as the risk-free rate. Volatility is the amount of unpredictable change in business conditions over time. Volatility is a more difficult number to achieve, but historical monthly volatilities of listed stocks can be found at the Chicago Board of Option Exchange (CBOE) website (www.cboe.com), where a bundle of similar companies can be compared. For purposes of this example, let's assume that the volatility factor for Newtech is 40 percent. These critical numbers can be entered into an option calculator to arrive at a value of $1,853,703.

In the final step, total value is calculated by the following:

$$\text{TV} = \text{EV(Step 1)} + [\text{Option Value (Step 4)} - \text{Option cost (Step 3)}]$$

$$\$2 \text{ million} + [\$1,853,703 - \$50,000] = \$3,803,703$$

In general, when the option is worth more than it costs, as is definitely true in this case, the investors would go ahead and purchase. Of course, investors would discount this total value number based on any risks that might be unique to this business or any market risks they perceive that might affect the probability of a positive outcome.

Real options are very appropriate for today's staged funding where the investor bets on a milestone; if that milestone is achieved, the investor has the right to bet on the next milestone at a fixed price—the exercise or strike price. The investor will invest if the present value of the expected revenues from the technology exceeds the cost to develop and produce it.

VENTURE CAPITAL METHODS

The VC methods of valuing a technology or a company are often determined by the requirements of the VC portfolio of companies. Depending on the business and the risk involved, VCs may seek to multiply their investment three times in 5 years (compounded annual ROI of 71 percent) or 10 times in 5 years (58 percent). These rates tend to drop as the company matures; so where the VC firm may seek a return greater than 40 percent for a start-up company, it may only need 25 to 30 percent for a company that is close to launching an IPO, because the risk of the investment has been substantially reduced and the time to liquidity is relatively shorter. In the following sections, some commonly used VC valuation techniques are examined.

THE HOCKEY STICK APPROACH: THE BASICS

With the hockey stick approach, the VC firm determines at the outset what return on investment they require during the holding period; the VC then applies a P/E ratio or multiple to earnings at the end of the defined period to calculate the terminal value of the company. The term *hockey stick* comes from the fact that when graphed, this method usually produces a curve that represents no earnings in the early stages and then rapid growth.

Suppose a technology entrepreneur needed an investment of $1.5 million over 3 years. The investor expects an IRR of 60 percent. The company's after-tax earnings in the third year are forecasted to be $3 million, and the investor has determined that the appropriate P/E ratio based on comparables in the public market is 10. The investor must own enough of the company to achieve a 60 percent return on investment when his or her stock is sold at the end of 3 years. To accomplish that, the investor's stock must be worth the following:

$$\text{Required value of investment} = (1 + \text{ IRR}) \text{ years} \times (\text{investment})$$
$$= (1 + .60)^3 \times (\$1.5 \text{ million})$$
$$= \$6,144,000$$

In the third year, the company will be valued at (terminal value):

$$\text{Terminal Value} = \text{P/E} \times \text{Terminal Net Income}$$
$$= 10 \times \$3 \text{ million}$$
$$= \$30,000,000$$

To achieve the required return on investment, the investor would need to own 20 percent of the company.

$$\text{Equity stake required} = \frac{\text{Future value of the investment}}{\text{Terminal value}}$$
$$= \frac{\$6,144,000}{\$30,000,000} = 20\%$$

Note that the 20 percent ownership stake represents 20 percent of the total stocked owned after new shares are issued. Sometimes to avoid dilution, the company will need to issue new shares. For example, suppose the company has one million shares outstanding. To determine the number of new shares that must be issued in the example:

$$\text{New shares required} = \frac{\%\text{ownership}}{1 - (\%\text{ownership})} \times \text{old shares}$$

$$\frac{.20}{.80} \times 1{,}000{,}000 = 250{,}000 \text{ new shares}$$

Thus, the company must issue an additional 250,000 shares. With this information, the post-money valuation of the company can be calculated.

$$\text{Post-money valuation} = \frac{\text{Investment}}{\%\text{Investor ownership}}$$

$$= \frac{\$1.5 \text{ million}}{.20}$$

$$= \$7.5 \text{ million}$$

Note that $1.5 million of this post-money valuation consists of the investment capital. That means that the pre-money valuation ($7.5 million less the investment) is $6 million. What has been presented here is a common way that VCs look at a potential investment, but there are others, and often they are used in concert.

MARKET COMPARISON AND COMPARABLE TRANSACTION METHODS

With the market comparison method, public companies are studied and their multiples in recent transactions are compared to the company being valued. In the comparable transaction method, by contrast, recent transactions of similar businesses are considered and their actual multiples are used to devise the appropriate multiple of earnings for the business being valued. In general, comparative income flows and other measures of earning power are considered. So, for example, if an examination determines that similar companies are selling for multiples of between 6 and 8 times earnings, this range of multiples would serve as the boundaries for the ultimate valuation and they might be adjusted depending on the level of perceived risk the investor attaches to the business. The effectiveness of market comparison methods is a function of the accuracy of the sample company figures and their compatibility with the firm in question. It is also important to recognize that market values are affected by unique characteristics of the business or nonrecurring events, either of which could move the valuation up or down. One of the big weaknesses of these methods is that they do not take into consideration the characteristics of the buyer and the seller and the influence of that dynamic on the multiples employed.

THE ISSUE OF DILUTION

The valuation examples previously given do not take into account what happens when a subsequent round of funding occurs that provides for new shares to new investors. With each successive round of investment, the original investors lose some percentage of their original holdings.[15] The amount that they are left with is referred to as *retention*. The percent of their original investment that they hold following the new round is found by:

$$\text{Retention \%} = 1 - (\text{total of future final \% ownerships})$$

What this means is that the first round investors will always experience more dilution than later rounds. For example, if a second round investor purchases 30 percent of the company, the original investor will now own 1–30 percent or 70 percent of his or her original ownership stake. First-round investors who know that the company will go for subsequent rounds can incorporate the potential dilution into their calculation of how many shares they must purchase to retain the level of ownership they desire.

VALUING A LICENSE AGREEMENT

The licensing of technology proves that value can be created even without an operating business. Licensing produces a market where technologies can be freely bought and sold, and is, therefore, another benchmark for the valuation of technology.[16] The value of a license agreement is the result of a negotiation between the licensor and the licensee and is a function of the rights being granted to the licensee. It has nothing to do with past costs of development of the technology; these costs are irrelevant. If more than one party is interested in the license and the license is exclusive, there may be a bid-up of the value. Because license agreements are essentially partnerships between the licensor and the licensee, there is every incentive to ensure that the agreement is a win-win for both parties so that the value is maximized for both.

Licensing scenarios generally fall into two broad categories: those involving proven technologies and and those involving unproven or partially proven technologies.[17] With proven technologies, setting the correct royalty rate and the total value of the license agreement is the result of striking a fine balance between technology gains and market forces. Industry examples and precedents on which to base the decision are usually available. With unproven technologies, however, the royalty rate is generally less because the licensee is assuming a great deal of risk in developing and proving the technology in the marketplace. In effect, the licensee is becoming a product developer and reducing some of the risk for the licensor. The licensee will have to invest some of his or her own capital and then attempt to recover the cost of acquiring the money, along with a reasonable premium for the risk taken, from the return on his or her investment.

Most industries have established royalty rates from which licensors don't deviate if they hope to acquire licensees. The rates can vary from 2 to 3 percent in some industries to 15 percent in others. In addition, the one-quarter rule of thumb suggests that pretax profits from the invention be divided in the following manner: 25 percent to the inventor, 25 percent to the developer, 25 percent to the manufacturer, and 25 percent to the distributor. If the invention represents only a small part of the value of the total product, however, the royalty rate may be discounted to reflect this. By applying the royalty rate to the size of the market and capitalizing it, a rough estimate of the value of the technology can be achieved. But how is a discount rate chosen? The licensee will probably want a rate that is equal to the actual cost of capital if the risk is not more than a person would normally take in the day-to-day business. However, if the risk is substantially greater, the discount rate would be equivalently higher. The cost of any alternative means to achieving goals, such as the cost of inventing around the patent or the cost of delay in product development should also be considered. Other factors that affect the royalty rate and the value of the license to the licensee include:

- The nature and scope of intellectual property protection.
- The nature and size of the market.
- The stage of development of the technology.
- The significance of the technology.
- The scope of applications for the technology.
- The patentability of the technology.
- The lag time for substantial adoption (the Adoption-Diffusion model).
- The existence and nature of competing technologies.
- The amount of investment required to develop and commercialize the technology.

Licensing is discussed in more detail in Chapter 6.

Valuation of a technology or a technology company is in many respects more art than science. Although a number of financial models are available, the art lies in factoring in the right numbers so that the valuation is realistic.

Summary

When investors consider the valuation of a technology company, they look at a number of factors, including the size of the market and its readiness to adopt the technology, the sustainable competitive advantage, and the skills and track record of the management team. Growth, new applications of a technology, a balanced portfolio of technologies, and license agreements drive value. Poor management, high financial leverage, the magnitude of nonoperating assets, and the opportunity cost of not exploiting the technology are discounted from the value of a technology. There are a variety of financial models for assessing value, including cost-based valuations, the pro forma DCF model, real options, and several VC methods in addition to the valuation of license agreements.

Discussion Questions

1. What are some of the challenges that investors face when employing quantitative methods such as DCF analysis and real options theory?
2. How do the drivers of value relate to the business model?
3. What is the value of the real options approach to valuation?
4. How does the valuation process for licenses agreements differ for proven and unproven technologies?

CASE STUDY

Value is in the Eyes of the Beholder

Entrepreneurs have rarely been accused of being too conservative in the valuation of their companies. Quite the contrary. Like homeowners who fervently believe that their home should command a much higher price than the surrounding homes, entrepreneurs tend to look at similar company valuations and say, "we should exceed that because . . . ." Anees Ahmed, cofounder of Mistral Software, is a case in point. His company, based in Bangalore, India, was started in 1997 to provide embedded systems for cell phones, the tiny computer inside the phone that makes all the functions work. Mistral was started with $12,000, 16 employees, and a big vision to become an international company. Its first round of funding—$2.75 million—was secured in 2001 with a valuation of $14,000, and that funding helped to take the company to profitability and to the $8.4 million mark in sales by 2005.

By 2006, Mistral employed 260 people in three offices in India and three in the United States. That year Ahmed and his partners decided it was time to go for another round of funding that would enable them to grow the business and perhaps do some acquisitions. He believed strongly that with global customers such as Texas Instruments and projections of $24 million in revenues in 2008, that company had to be worth $25–$35 million.

Mistral had some positives on its side for a higher valuation. The company was growing at a faster rate than others in the industry, and the founders were investing a lot in R&D. Furthermore, the management team was capable and could carry on without a hiccough if Ahmed got hit by a bus. The biggest competition would be a larger company that might try to compete by cutting prices or spending more on marketing. Some professional business appraisers put the value of Mistral at $30 million on the high side. But others didn't paint such a rosy picture. They found it difficult to value any assets the company held by traditional financial means, particularly the potential licenses that could come from the software that Mistral was developing. Figuring that an investor would want a 35 percent return after three years, the financial appraisers calculated that the investor would need to invest $14 million, the net present value of the company at that date.

(continued)

(*continued*)

For Ahmed, neither number was high enough, so he began looking for potential investors who might be willing to place a high value on his technical team and the intellectual property they were developing. In July, 2007, Ahmed and his partners decided to aggregate Mistral Software Pvt. Ltd. into their other company, Mistral Solutions Pvt. Ltd—a systems integration and value-added services company—and retain that name. The goal was to create new value by providing a complete solution of hardware and software leading to a higher valuation for the brand.

Finally, in February 2008, Mistral Solutions announced that it had raised a $6.5 million second round of funding from Nexus India Ventures and JAFCO Asia. These companies tend to invest early and play a role in the development of the company. After 11 years, Ahmed has yet to see his company's valuation where he thinks it should be.

Sources: Mistral Solutions, www.mistralsolutions.com, accessed May 17, 2008 (February 6, 2008). "Mistral Raises USD 6.5 Million Funding from Leading Private Investors," *Computing News,* http://home.nestor.minsk.by/computers/press/2008/02/0612.html (July 31, 2007). "Mistral Software Becomes Mistral Solutions," *EDA Geek,* edageek.com; Wellner, A.S. (January, 2006). "Mistral Software," *Inc. Magazine,* www.inc.com.

Endnotes

1. Dissel, M., Farrukh, C., Probert, D., & Phaal, R. (2005). "Evaluating Early Stage Technology Valuation Methods: What Is Available and What Really Matters," *ASEE* 0-7803-9139-X/05, p. 302.
2. Lev, B. (2001). *Intangibles: Management, Measurement, and Reporting* (Washington DC: Brookings Institution Press).
3. Boer, F.B. (September–October 1998). "Traps, Pitfalls and Snares in the Valuation of Technology," *Research Technology Management* 41(5): 45.
4. Armstrong, J.S. (2001). "Standards and Practices for Forecasting," *Principles of Forecasting: A Handbook for Researchers and Practitioners* (Norwell, MA: Kluwer Academic Publishers).
5. Kappel, T.A. (2001). "Perspectives on Roadmaps: How Organizations Talk About the Future," *Journal of Product Innovation Management* 18(1): 39–50. Kostoff, R.N., &. Schaller, R.R. (2001). "Science and Technology Roadmaps," *IEEE Transactions of Engineering Management* 38(2): 132–143.
6. Bose, S., & Oh, K.B. (2004). "Measuring Strategic Value-Drivers for Managing Intellectual Capital," *The Learning Organization* 11(4/5): 347.
7. Day, G.S. (1999). *Market Driven Strategy* (New York: Free Press).
8. Razgaitis, R. (1999). *Early-Stage Technologies: Valuation and Pricing* (Brisbane: John Wiley).
9. Thanks to Scott Adelson, Houlihan Lokey Howard & Zukin, Los Angeles, CA.
10. Park Y., & Park, G. (2004). "A New Method for Technology Valuation in Monetary Value: Procedure and Application," *Technovation* 24: 387–394; Tenenbaum, D. (2002). "Valuing Intellectual Property Assets," *The Computer and Internet Lawyer* 18(2): 1–7; Mun, J. (2002). *Real Options Analysis* (Hoboken, NJ: Wiley).
11. Boer, F.P. (1999). *The Valuation of Technology: Business and Financial Issues in R&D* (New York: John Wiley & Sons).

12. Amram, M., & Kulatilaka, N. (1999). *Real Options; Managing Strategic Investment in an Uncertain World* (Boston: Harvard Business School Press, 1999); Trigeorgis, L. (1998). *Real Options; Managerial Flexibility and Strategy in Resource Allocation* (Cambridge, MA: The MIT Press).

13. Boer, F.P. (January 17, 2000). "Valuation of Technology Using "Real Options," www.boer.org, accessed September 21, 2008.

14. Boer, F.P. (2002). *The Real Options Solution* (New York: John Wiley & Sons).

15. Sahlman, W.A. (February 5, 2004). "The Basic Venture Capital Formula," *Harvard Business School,* JBS Case No.L 288-006.

16. Megantz, R.C. (1996). *How To License Technology* (New York: John Wiley & Sons), pp. 55–69.

17. Boer, *op. cit.*, 264.

INDEX